COMMUNICATING IN RELATIONSHIPS

A Guide for Couples
and Professionals

Frank D. Fincham
Leyan O.L. Fernandes
Keith Humphreys

Research Press
2612 North Mattis Avenue
Champaign, Illinois 61821

Advisory Editor, Frederick H. Kanfer

Cover design by Jim Hampton
Composition by Wadley Graphix Corporation
Printed by Malloy Lithographing, Inc.

ISBN 0–87822–342–8
Library of Congress Catalog No. 93–84517

Contents

Figures and Tables

Exercises

Author Note

This book was written while the first author was supported by grant #MH–44078 from the National Institute of Mental Health and by grants from the W. T. Grant Foundation and the Guggenheim Foundation.

We wish to thank Fred Kanfer for prompting us to write this book. As colleague and mentor, he has provided invaluable encouragement and guidance. We are also grateful to Steve Beach for his valuable comments on the appendixes.

The order of authors' names does not reflect differences in contributions. All three authors contributed equally to this book.

Preface

Visiting a foreign country can be difficult, particularly if you don't have a command of the language or knowledge of the landmarks. That's where tour guides come in: They can help the traveler overcome language barriers and explore new territories. *Communicating in Relationships* is a tour guide to improved relationships. Based on state-of-the-art knowledge from research and clinical practice, it speaks to couples and professionals in plain language and helps readers explore the aspects of relationships that are of most concern to them.

We designed this book for people in a variety of situations. You will find it helpful if you are beginning, currently in, or thinking about ending a close relationship—or if you work with others who are trying to improve their relationships (e.g., you are a therapist, a member of the clergy, a professional counselor in training). The book is also meant for people in different types of relationships (e.g., romantic relationships, marriage, multicultural relationships, gay or lesbian relationships, parent-child relationships); it explains how personal and cultural factors can affect relationships. Although the main focus is communication, you will find special sections on gender differences, cultural differences, dual-career relationships, sexuality, spirituality, parenting, gay or lesbian relationships, and breakup and divorce.

We invite all readers to look into each part of the book. If you are a layperson you need not read the sections for the professional to enhance your relationship, but we have tried to write these sections so that they will be accessible to everyone.

CHAPTER

1 *Introduction*

We have all heard the story of Cinderella, but we don't all have fairy godmothers to wave away the troubles in our relationships. Cinderella and her Prince Charming lived happily ever after—but what kind of life did they really have? They lived isolated from others in their castle. No friends were ever mentioned in their story. And whatever happened to Cinderella's relationships with her stepmother and stepsisters? Real-life relationships are more difficult, to be sure, but they can be much more rewarding.

FOR COUPLES

Why This Book?

A national survey showed that relationship difficulties are the most common problem for which people seek professional help. Moreover, lack of good communication is the most common problem reported by people seeking help for their relationships and by professionals who work with couples.

Miscommunications occur in every relationship. Although no one can completely prevent miscommunications, you can minimize their frequency and their impact on your relationships. This book applies up-to-date knowledge from research and clinical practice to help you enhance your current and future relationships through improved communication. It draws on information from various sources to give you the greatest possible benefit. The book consists of readings interspersed with exercises that give you a hands-on approach to learning.

Who Can Use This Book?

This book is meant as a resource for many kinds of couples. Although we frequently refer to couples as "husband and wife," "partners," or "him and her," we do this simply for convenience. You do not have to be married or involved in a heterosexual relationship to benefit from the book. You can use it whether you are currently having difficulty in a relationship or just want to make a good relationship better. Exercise 1.1 will give you some idea of how much help you can expect from the book.

1

Exercise 1.1   Is This Book For Me?

Read the statements and see if they describe your relationship. If any of these statements apply to you or your partner, this book may not be enough to help you reach your goals, and we suggest that you consult a professional about your relationship.

1. In the past 12 months, my partner has or I have had four or more intimate relationships that have failed.

2. In the past 2 months, my partner has or I have had difficulty sleeping (e.g., early morning awakening, difficulty falling asleep), had a lack of energy to do things that are usually enjoyable, had difficulty concentrating for periods of 3 days or more, and felt blue.

3. In the past 2 months, my partner has or I have experienced periods of increased energy, needed 3 hours less sleep than usual, and found it difficult to sit still.

4. My partner has or I have experienced panic attacks or anxiety attacks with a sudden feeling of fright or with physical symptoms like shortness of breath, dizziness, or heart palpitations.

5. My partner has threatened or hurt me with a weapon (e.g., gun, knife) or an object that could be used as a weapon (e.g., wrench, bottle, frying pan, belt).

6. My partner has physically hurt me by choking me, punching me, throwing me, kicking me, or doing something else that caused me to bruise or bleed.

7. My partner has or I have had difficulty controlling impulses to physically hurt oneself or other people.

8. My partner is or I am currently thinking about suicide, or one of us has attempted to commit suicide.

9. My partner is or I am taking medications for emotional problems, or one of us has taken such medications.

10. My partner has or I have heard voices or seen fantastic images that others cannot see.

11. My partner has or I have been arrested two or more times on charges related to substance abuse (e.g., driving under the influence of alcohol, possession of cocaine, drunk and disorderly conduct), or one of us has needed medical assistance for substance abuse.

12. In the past 12 months, friends, coworkers, family members, or my partner has expressed concerns over my partner's or my use of alcohol, cocaine, heroin, or any other drug.

How Do I Use This Book?

Close relationships require attention and work. In using this book to improve your relationship, you'll need to set aside specific times to read the text and practice the exercises. You'll benefit more by using this book with your relationship partner, but you can use the exercises with a variety of people. Find a quiet place to read with little or no interruption and plan on practicing the exercises soon after reading each chapter. Some of the exercises are designed to be completed together; others are structured so that you complete them independently. If you are sharing a book, you will need to avoid looking at each other's answers until the exercise calls for joint discussion.

To maximize your chances of improving your relationship, both you and your partner will need to put some effort into the exercises. Keep trying your best, even if you think you are doing more work than your partner.

What Am I in For?

We begin by helping you become aware of and explore your expectations about your relationship. We then explain how miscommunications occur and help you assess where you stand on a number of the factors that are important for clear communication. We look at gender differences as a major factor in communication. The heart of the book, chapters 6 through 8, takes you through a series of 18 steps for learning communication skills. We describe the skills and outline procedures for integrating them into your relationship.

After you have mastered the communication skills, we'll explore how you can use them to enhance other relationships—for instance, with friends, family, and children. We'll also explain why good relationships require care and how "tune-ups" can save you major work later.

But what if your relationship still seems hopeless? Chapter 11 examines issues related to breakup or divorce. We explore the legal and psychological aspects of the end of a relationship as well as its impact on friends, relatives, and children.

The final chapter, chapter 12, is meant primarily for people who work with couples. It explains the rationale for the structure of the book. At the end of the chapter is an annotated bibliography for couples and counselors, which all readers may wish to consult. The two appendixes give technical information about the theoretical and empirical bases of the communication training approach and the properties of the measures used in this book.

Exercise 1.2 will get you started in the process of change.

Exercise 1.2   Looking Into Your Past

Most couples have fond memories from their relationships. They may take pleasure in remembering the first time they met, the qualities that attracted them to each other, the things that they did together, and so on. Write down some fond memories from your relationship. Each partner should list on a sheet of paper at least three to five memories. Then tell each other what you've written.

FOR PEOPLE WHO WORK WITH COUPLES

Why This Book?

Communication has long been recognized as a crucial part of close relationships, and early books on communication (e.g., Gottman, Notarius, Gonso, & Markman, 1976) can still be found in many classrooms and consulting offices. Unfortunately, books on communication for couples have not kept up with the enormous changes in psychology and society in the past two decades. This book therefore integrates a number of important issues. Discussions of these issues follow.

Emotional and Cognitive Influences on Communication

Classic texts on marital therapy (e.g., Jacobson & Margolin, 1979) treat communication simply as a set of behavioral skills that would improve almost any relationship as long as the couple learned and used them. In the past 15 years, therapists and researchers have become increasingly aware that the matter is not that simple. Since the "cognitive revolution" in psychology, more and more evidence has accrued that spouses do not solely attend to what the partner does, but instead actively interpret the partner's behavior and make attributions about the partner's motives. Interpretation and attribution will amplify or minimize the effectiveness of the partner's behavioral communication skills, whether those skills are strong or weak. It does not matter how many times a wife says, "I love you" if her husband is convinced that she is nice to him only because she wants his money or because a marital counselor told her to say those words. Further, it is only recently that the role of emotion in communication has received intensive study. For example, some spouses cannot communicate deep compassion for their partners because it is not part of their experience. Simply teaching such a spouse to utter verbal expressions of caring will not alter this sad fact. Unlike most previous books on communication, this book recognizes the role of cognition and affect in close relationships and will help you and your clients improve all aspects of relationship communication, including behavior, affect, and cognition.

The Strengths of Clients

The days of the all-powerful, all-knowing, mysterious analyst are mostly behind us, and the era of self-help is here. It is now generally acknowledged that clients have strengths as well as problems and can contribute significantly to the therapy process. Greater client involvement in therapy in and out of session improves outcomes and increases clients' motivation (Kanfer & Schefft, 1988). Because we want to help you tap into your clients' potential to participate responsively and actively in therapy, we speak to couples in jargon-free language and provide exercises they can do on their own.

The Talents of a Wide Range of Helpers

The helping professions have become increasingly aware that counselors do not need doctoral degrees to be effective in helping clients: Master's level psychologists, social workers, and paraprofessionals help thousands of couples each year. This book is for all these helpers as well as for members of the clergy, who see more couples each year than all mental health professionals combined. Although this is not a book on pastoral counseling, it gives some attention to the role of religion and spirituality in relationships and thus could serve as a resource for ministers or pastoral counselors.

Gender and Cultural Differences

The changing role of women in our society has dramatically altered intimate relationships and the institution of marriage. Psychotherapists and psycholinguists have responded to rising concern about gender issues in relationships by trying to understand the different ways in which men and women experience relationships and communicate with their partners. We discuss gender differences in communication to help couples and counselors better see how men and women behave in and interpret relationships. Within our treatment of gender, we also discuss issues that commonly arise in gay and lesbian relationships. To a lesser extent, we also address the cross-cultural issues in communication that arise as our society becomes increasingly diverse and cross-cultural relationships become more common.

A Holistic View of the Family

The work of family systems theorists has made therapists aware that relationships exist in the context of larger family systems. Recognizing this context and the increasing strain on families in this country, we go beyond previous works on communication by addressing communication not only between spouses but also between parents and children. Thus, although our book is directed toward couples, it is also appropriate for families and family therapists.

The Instability of Marriage

We cannot ignore the high divorce rate in our society. While we hope that our book will contribute to the prevention of some divorces, we recognize that divorce or breakup is sometimes a couple's best option. We have therefore included a section on divorce so that couples and counselors can be well informed about the psychological and legal consequences of divorce should it become necessary.

Is This Book for Me?

This book is for anyone who works with couples: psychologists, social workers, marital therapists, family therapists, psychiatrists, sex therapists, clergy, pastoral counselors, and paraprofessional counselors. It can also serve as a resource for students or instructors in couples therapy practicums or internships, clinical or counseling psychology programs, social work, human development, or other related fields. Finally, couples can use it as an adjunct to therapy or in an effort to improve their relationships on their own.

How Do I Use This Book?

There are many ways to use this book. We recommend using it in whichever of the following ways best suits your situation.

As a Reference

Therapists, instructors, or students can use this book as a source of information about relationships and communication. The appendixes may prove particularly useful.

Appendix 1 summarizes the empirical bases of the approach used in this book and surveys treatment outcome research as well as basic research concerning communication in couples. Appendix 2 provides psychometric information on measures used in the book.

As a Supplement to Counseling

The book includes concrete, stand-alone exercises that couples can complete as an adjunct to counseling. Thus, you can use the exercises to expand on themes and/or improve the skills you develop in your sessions. Alternatively, you may wish to make the book central to your therapy, while serving as a consultant to couples as they read the book and do the exercises. Research has shown that clients who do readings and exercises between therapy sessions are more motivated to work in session (Kanfer & Schefft, 1988).

As an Aid to Couples on Waiting Lists

Because this book is written for both professionals and nonprofessionals, it is a potential resource for couples who are on waiting lists for counseling. When people have an understanding of counseling and the change process before attending the first session, they enter therapy with some insight and are primed to work on their relationship. This preparation can greatly enhance the outcome of therapy.

As Bibliotherapy

The book can serve as a stand-alone intervention for couples. Some couples who are encountered at assessment agencies (e.g., employee assistance programs) or in non-therapy settings (e.g., self-help groups, church groups, encounter groups, marital enrichment programs, premarital religious counseling, crisis intervention centers) may not need counseling but could benefit from bibliotherapy. As an ounce of prevention is worth a pound of cure, you may save younger couples considerable pain by giving them this book when you see them for brief, premarital consultation in a religious or psychological setting.

Regardless of how you foresee using this book at present, we believe that you will find a variety of additional applications for it as you read the sections directed at couples.

CHAPTER

2 *Getting Started*

Starting a relationship is a lot like embarking on a sailing journey with someone. You could sail alone, but you'd rather share the fun (and the work) with another person. Unfortunately, it occasionally rains during the voyage, even if you aren't expecting it. At times the rain washes off the decks, but at other times the boat may begin to take on water. When things are going well, the sailors can usually work together to make sure the hatches are battened down, the pumps are running, and the bow is pointed in the right direction. When things are not going well, you can end up taking on water at a time when cooperation seems hardest. Yet if you do not work together, your boat may sink.

It is sometimes hard to bounce back and be cooperative when you have been hurt or disappointed by your partner. Why should you work with someone who has hurt you or made you sad and angry? Why should you have to exert effort when you believe your partner is at fault? If you, like most couples, have at some point experienced problems in your relationship, you have probably asked these questions before.

Few things are as painful as being hurt by someone close to you. When difficulties arise, it is natural for both people to feel disappointed, sad, and angry. You may also feel powerless, especially if you believe that you have been trying hard to make things go well and your partner has not. The chances are that your partner feels the same way: It is not unusual for *both* partners to feel that they have been pulling more than their share of the weight. These are common, understandable reactions to a painful situation. You do not need to deny such feelings to work on your relationship.

Though you might not feel like cooperating with your partner, it is only through cooperation that things can change. Change may not be easy for you, and it is often scary and risky. It means making yourself vulnerable and showing that you care. Partners who feel nothing for each other rarely get hurt, but they also rarely gain anything from their relationship because they are not invested in it. If you and your partner are both hurting, it is a sign that you are both still invested in the relationship; this is a strength that you can draw on to heal and improve the relationship.

Partners have as much potential to help each other as to hurt each other. The first step is to see that you both want to save the boat and would like to be happy in the relationship. The only way you can both get what you want is to work together. What makes it so hard to accept this fact?

THOUGHTS THAT STOP COOPERATION

It is common for people who are in relationships to have occasional thoughts that hinder or totally prevent cooperation. For example, one partner may think, "It's hopeless" or "I'll never be able to have a good relationship." Such thoughts are like dark glasses that make it hard to see the other person and the relationship in a positive light. When you are wearing dark glasses and your partner tries hard to change but fails, you see only the failure, not the effort. It is important to let yourself see the good and the bad and view your partner as a collaborator, not a competitor.

One way to control thoughts that stop cooperation is to challenge them. Often, when you question such thoughts, you quickly see that things are not as bad as you think. For example, if you find yourself thinking, "My partner does not care about our relationship," question that belief by asking yourself, "If my partner does not care about our relationship, why is he or she still in it?" You might answer that question by thinking, "Maybe it's not that my partner doesn't care. Maybe I just can't see the caring very well because I've been angry lately." As you reflect, you may become aware of signs of your partner's caring that you previously overlooked. Because we tend to look for information to confirm our beliefs, it is important to make a sincere effort to see if there is evidence that contradicts your beliefs. Ultimately, you may conclude that your partner in fact does not care about the relationship. Whatever your conclusion, you will have more confidence in it if you first question the belief.

Exercise 2.1 will help you examine your thoughts.

10?

① 2

② 2

③ 2

⊛

9.8 ① both

② both

③ ?

④ ?

⑤ ?

2.1

① he does care, I just get stressed. ⑥ no

he loves me.   yes

doesn't know   no

② yes

yes

③ no

the same

no

④ his voice

yes

⑤ no

many

Exercise 2.1   Thoughts That Can Stop Cooperation

Following are some common thoughts that stop couples from cooperating. After each thought are questions you can ask yourself to keep these thoughts from darkening your view of the relationship. Each partner should answer the questions independently.

1. My partner does not care about our relationship.

   Questions: If your partner does not care about the relationship, why is he or she still in it?

   Why did your partner get into it in the first place?

   Why is he or she reading this book or going to see a counselor?

2. Men and women will never get along.

   Questions: Can the differences between men and women actually make a relationship exciting?

   Are there happy marriages that last a lifetime?

3. It's all my partner's fault—there is nothing I can do.

   Questions: Can one person be totally responsible for what happens between two people?

   If I were my partner, how would I see things?

   Would I feel motivated to change if someone told me that everything was my fault?

4. There has never been anything good in our relationship.

   Questions: What first attracted me to my partner?

   Are there things about my partner that I like?

5. We are headed for disaster, so there is no point in trying.

   Questions: Can I really know for sure what the future holds?

   Have other couples resolved problems in their relationships, either on their own or with help from books or counselors?

6. Everything is fine in my opinion, so I do not need to change.

   Questions: Can I have a good relationship with my partner if my partner is unhappy?

   If I care about my partner, should I try to make him or her happier?

   Would I stay in a relationship where I was not getting what I wanted but my partner was?

After you have answered the questions in the list, try to identify other thoughts that may be blocking cooperation in your relationship. Write down each thought and try to think of questions that counter it.

Arguing with yourself may seem strange or difficult at first, but in the long run it will help you view your relationship more accurately. You will have more chances to practice this technique later on in the book. In the meantime, you can repeat this procedure when you notice yourself entertaining negative, hopeless thoughts. Many people find it useful to keep handy their answers to questions that challenge negative thoughts and refer to them when the thoughts recur. If this seems like too much effort right now—if you are still wondering whether you should invest any more energy in your relationship—read the next section before abandoning the exercise altogether.

WHY SHOULD I TRY TO WORK ON THIS RELATIONSHIP?

Why should you read this book and do the exercises? What's in it for you? These are fair questions.

One answer is that, by being in an intimate relationship, you have already done a lot of work. You have invested time and energy in that relationship. If you had invested a great deal of money in a car, you wouldn't junk it just because it needed repairs. You would protect your investment by assessing carefully what repairs were needed and whether they were worth the cost. Try to look at your relationship in this light: You owe it to yourself to consider carefully whether the relationship is worth enhancing or preserving. Are you in a position to make a final judgment right now? Or would giving the relationship your best effort offer you a better chance to really see if it is worth it? Deciding to work on your relationship does not necessarily mean that you consider the problems your fault, nor does it prevent you from changing your mind later. It just means that you care about your relationship and would like it to be as good as it can be. Perhaps that won't be good enough for you—but you can never know without trying.

But what if you and your partner cannot work things out? Will you have wasted your time? Again, these are legitimate questions, but whatever happens in your present relationship, we believe that this book can benefit you. It will help you in other current relationships and in future relationships. It will also help you better understand how men and women communicate and experience relationships.

If you are male, you probably have been confused at some point about the way women act in relationships. Why does a woman want to talk about the relationship when everything seems fine to you? Why does she complain about things and then do nothing to change them? You have probably experienced a situation in which your partner complained about a problem and you offered an obvious, simple solution, only to have your partner ignore it or—worse still—get angry at you when you were trying to help!

If you are female, you have almost surely had trouble understanding the way men behave in relationships. Why don't they talk about how they really feel? Why won't they do things that are important to a woman without being asked? When you simply want to be supported and listened to, why do men instead tell you what to do, leaving you feeling frustrated and unheard?

The less you understand such gender differences, the more problems they will cause. This book will give you a better appreciation of how the opposite sex tends to communicate and view relationships. Understanding and accepting the differences between men and women can reduce conflicts, make both partners feel better understood, and give each one a new perspective.

A further benefit of this book is that you will learn to understand how your feelings, thoughts, and behaviors affect your communication with others. Communication skills are widely used by counselors to improve relationships. Partners can use them to talk about almost anything, including household duties, parenting, sex, feelings, plans, spirituality, relationship problems, and relationship strengths. Communication skills have the potential to enhance not only your intimate relationship but other aspects of your life as well. You can use those skills to get along better with your children, parents, and coworkers. There is increasing recognition in the workplace that communication skills help people be more effective managers and better colleagues. Whether or not you improve your present relationship to your satisfaction, you can take these communication skills with you wherever you go.

If you are a parent, using this book can improve your parenting in two ways. First, better communication between you and your partner will let you parent together more effectively. Children respond better to their parents when they see their mother and father united. Second, a section in chapter 9 devoted to communication with children will help you use your communication skills in interactions with your children.

If you are in a nontraditional relationship—for example, with someone of another race or culture or of the same sex—the book will also give you a better understanding of the difficulties of nontraditional relationships. Knowing what has helped other couples in such relationships can help you enrich your own.

More than anything else, what any reader has to gain is a relationship with another person that is emotionally, sexually, and spiritually fulfilling. Very few people wish to go through life completely alone. This book will help you learn how sharing the journey can be easier and more enjoyable. No relationship is perfect, but if you and your partner care about each other and are willing to work together on your partnership, you can build a connection that will strengthen both of you and enrich both of your lives. If this is something you want to do, how do you get started?

AN AGREEMENT

At the start of a new project, it always helps to know that there is good faith on the part of all participants. One way to ensure this is to have both partners agree to a set of rules. We have written an agreement that covers the ground rules that a couple must honor if they are to work successfully on their relationship. Each of you should read over this agreement and sign it (see Figure 2.1). Then post it where you can both see it; if you do not live together, keep one copy in each partner's home.

If, after reading the agreement, one of you feels unwilling or unable to sign it, the chances of the relationship improving are slim. Still, admitting that you will not or cannot comply with the conditions is better than signing and then not following through. If you can't sign in good conscience, you may wish to consult a professional counselor if you have not done so already. If that does not help, read chapter 11, on breakup and divorce.

These are the points of the relationship agreement:

I am invested in and care about this relationship: If you are not invested in the relationship, your partner has a right to know that. If both you and your partner care about each other and are invested in this relationship, you have the foundation for improving it.

I admit that part of the responsibility for our relationship is mine: In order for your relationship to change, both you and your partner need to accept responsibility for it. By consenting to this condition, you are promising not to blame your partner

Figure 2.1   Relationship Agreement

1. I am invested in and care about this relationship.

2. I admit that part of the responsibility for our relationship is mine.

3. I will make an effort to improve the relationship.

4. I am willing to compromise on some things.

5. I will not abuse my partner.

6. I will not carry on an affair.

7. I will focus on our relationship as it is now and not bring up problems from the past.

8. I will take the time needed to work together on our relationship and to do the exercises in this book.

9. I will suspend judgment of our relationship for at least 3 months until I've made a sincere effort to change it.

Signed _____   Date _____

Signed _____   Date _____

for what has gone wrong or may go wrong in the future. One advantage of assuming responsibility for the relationship is that it demonstrates that you are not helpless: You have some power to determine how your relationship will develop. Also, your partner will have more motivation to change if he or she is not labeled as "the problem."

I will make an effort to improve the relationship: By agreeing to this condition, you are saying that your effort does not depend on your partner's effort. Rather than play "Who's going to try first?" you will give it your best effort in good faith from day one.

I am willing to compromise on some things: All relationships require some compromise on both sides. This might involve taking turns getting things you want, or it might involve both partners compromising on the same issue. By agreeing to this condition of the contract, you recognize the importance of compromise. If you are willing to meet your partner halfway, you are likely to get the same consideration in return.

I will not abuse my partner: In order for change to occur, each of you needs to feel safe enough to let down your guard. Although it may be difficult at first, both partners must agree to refrain from any abuse, including calling each other names, shouting and swearing at each other, damaging each other's property, or hitting and shoving each other. If you think this will be a problem, you should consider getting a counselor's help in complying with this condition of the contract.

I will not carry on an affair: If one or both of you is intimately involved with another person, you are unlikely to have any success building a positive relationship with each other. Third parties siphon off energy and cause understandable resentment and jealousy. If you are serious about working on this relationship, it is important to break off any other sexual relationships.

I will focus on our relationship as it is now and not bring up problems from the past: This is a difficult condition for many people to consent to because they feel they can never forget past hurts. Unfortunately, the past cannot be changed by your partner or anyone else, so bringing up old hurts usually only aggravates the situation. In starting with a clean slate, you are saying not that past events are forgiven or unimportant but that you are willing to work toward a better future. You will probably find that focusing on the present and the future feels more hopeful and lightens the burden of resentment.

I will take the time needed to work together on our relationship and to do the exercises in this book: What is made over months or years is not undone in a day. Changing a relationship takes work, commitment, and time. In agreeing to this condition, you are promising to try the exercises in good faith. You are also agreeing to answer the questions in the book honestly.

I will suspend judgment of our relationship for at least 3 months until I've made a sincere effort to change it: Change takes time and goes more easily if the specter of judgment is not hanging overhead. Letting go of judgments will free you to try new things without recrimination. After 3 months or more, you can reassess the situation and see if it has improved. Although things may improve within the first few weeks, you will need to continue your efforts if the change is to be lasting. Until then, you are agreeing to give it your best shot.

Once you have signed the agreement, we suggest that you try Exercise 2.2. It will help you start working on the relationship and may lead to some surprises.

Exercise 2.2   Looking for Something?

Partner 1

There is nothing like looking if you want to find something. This exercise will help you notice some of the good things in your relationship. Each day for the next week, write down two things your partner does that you like. Also, try to be aware of the feelings you have when your partner does the things you like. They do not have to be big things—little steps are fine. Though you do not have to tell your partner what you write down, people often want to tell their partners about the small actions that make them feel good.

Examples

FIRST TWO DAYS OF HAROLD'S LIST

Things Luwanda did that I liked		**My feelings**
Monday:	Congratulated me on promotion at work	Proud
	Let me read the paper without interruption	Relaxed
Tuesday:	Cooked breakfast for me when I was running late	Relieved, supported
	Washed my back in the shower	Turned on

FIRST TWO DAYS OF LUWANDA'S LIST

Things Harold did that I liked		**My feelings**
Monday:	Let me know he would be late for dinner	Respected, important
Tuesday:	Bathed the kids and put them to bed	Relaxed, cared about
	Kissed me and told me he loved me	Loved

Your List

What your partner did that you liked		**How you felt**
Monday	1. _____	_____
	2. _____	_____
Tuesday	1. _____	_____
	2. _____	_____
Wednesday	1. _____	_____
	2. _____	_____
Thursday	1. _____	_____
	2. _____	_____
Friday	1. _____	_____
	2. _____	_____
Saturday	1. _____	_____
	2. _____	_____
Sunday	1. _____	_____
	2. _____	_____

Partner 2

There is nothing like looking if you want to find something. This exercise will help you notice some of the good things in your relationship. Each day for the next week, write down two things your partner does that you like. Also, try to be aware of the feelings you have when your partner does the things you like. They do not have to be big things—little steps are fine. Though you do not have to tell your partner what you write down, people often want to tell their partners about the small actions that make them feel good.

Examples

FIRST TWO DAYS OF HAROLD'S LIST

Things Luwanda did that I liked		**My feelings**
Monday:	Congratulated me on promotion at work	Proud
	Let me read the paper without interruption	Relaxed
Tuesday:	Cooked breakfast for me when I was running late	Relieved, supported
	Washed my back in the shower	Turned on

FIRST TWO DAYS OF LUWANDA'S LIST

Things Harold did that I liked		**My feelings**
Monday:	Let me know he would be late for dinner	Respected, important
Tuesday:	Bathed the kids and put them to bed	Relaxed, cared about
	Kissed me and told me he loved me	Loved

Your List

What your partner did that you liked		**How you felt**
Monday	1. _____	_____
	2. _____	_____
Tuesday	1. _____	_____
	2. _____	_____
Wednesday	1. _____	_____
	2. _____	_____
Thursday	1. _____	_____
	2. _____	_____
Friday	1. _____	_____
	2. _____	_____
Saturday	1. _____	_____
	2. _____	_____
Sunday	1. _____	_____
	2. _____	_____

3 *Expectations in Traditional and Nontraditional Relationships*

Now that you have signed an agreement with your partner, it is time to examine what you want from this relationship. Because most complaints in relationships can be traced to unmet or violated expectations, you owe it to both yourself and your partner to know exactly what you expect. This is not quite as simple as it sounds. There are at least three different levels at which you need to examine expectations.

First, you need to identify and become fully aware of your expectations. You are quite likely to have expectations about your partner or your relationship that influence the way you feel, think, and act without your being conscious of them. Such implicit expectations can wreak havoc in a relationship unless they are made explicit. Even when both partners are skilled in communication, expectations can be problematic as long as they remain unstated. What happens in that case is that the couple communicates without addressing the real issue, the underlying expectations.

The second step in examining expectations is to ask whether they are realistic. It is easy to develop unrealistic expectations for a relationship. Most relationships go through a phase where the partner is idealized as the perfect mate, capable of fulfilling one's every need, a perception made possible only because unmet needs are overlooked or ignored. In addition, popular culture often portrays intimate relationships in an idealistic manner that reinforces unrealistic expectations.

The third step in dealing with your expectations is to ask whether your partner knows about them and has agreed to do his or her part to meet them. It is critical for each partner to understand what the other expects. After all, if either of you is unaware of the other's expectations, it is difficult—and sometimes impossible—to be responsive to them.

Because expectations are so crucial in a relationship, we begin by focusing on them. In this chapter we look at expectations briefly because they receive attention in other sections of the book (e.g., chapter 4). Here we concentrate on helping you become aware of your expectations and see how different expectations are formed by different backgrounds. People's expectations in their relationships depend on cultural background, self-identity (how people think of themselves, especially concerning the way they fit into their surrounding environment), and the status of the relationship as traditional or nontraditional in the eyes of the surrounding culture. When partners are not aware of the nature and source of their expectations for the relationship, they are likely to have difficulty in communication. Because expectations are usually less clear in relationships viewed as nontraditional, we give special attention to expectations and self-identity in multicultural and gay or lesbian relationships.

You need only read the sections of this chapter that are relevant to your relationship. However, all readers should complete Exercise 3.1, which applies to all relationships.

TRADITIONAL RELATIONSHIPS

Expectations

How do people learn to have relationships? When do they know they are in love? How do they know what to expect? How do they know where things stand? For heterosexual couples, the answer to all of these questions is "By watching other people in relationships like ours." Heterosexual men and women find role models on television; in movies, books, poems, or songs; and in public life. Social standards and rituals, such as engagement and marriage, also serve as guideposts in a relationship. With so much information available to heterosexual couples, you might expect few disagreements over the expectations men and women have for their relationships. Unfortunately, this is not the case. As we shall see in chapter 5, men and women differ in the way they expect their partners to communicate. However, gender alone does not account for differences in expectations.

Each individual brings a unique blend of qualities to a relationship, and this uniqueness often leads to differences in expectations. Overall expectations for the relationship can differ, and expectations regarding specific behaviors can vary with different settings, audiences, and times. Have you ever noticed how different your behavior may be when you attend a sporting event and when you are at work? These behaviors reflect differences in expectations from one setting to another. Thus, for a good relationship, partners must continually clarify expectations.

The importance of making expectations explicit in relationships is also heightened by our changing society. Role models for heterosexual relationships keep changing. It is no longer true that all wives and mothers stay at home and take care of the children. The dual-career couple is now as much a part of our world as is the single parent or the custodial father. Still, not everyone identifies with the role of a liberated woman or a parenting man. For some of us these roles are fine; however, others may prefer more traditional roles. There are no right or wrong role choices; however, clarifying expectations about roles is extremely important. Failure to do so can produce conflict in our relationships. Exercise 3.1 will help you clarify your expectations.

Exercise 3.1   Expectations About Relationships

Partner 1

Everyone has expectations about relationships in general, and these expectations serve as guideposts. You and your partner should independently indicate whether you agree or disagree with each of the 10 statements in the list. These questions pertain to your view of the way relationships should be in general, not the state of your relationship right now. Then share your answers and talk them over. The purpose is not to argue but to get a sense of where each partner stands.

	Agree	Disagree
1. My partner will never do anything to hurt me.	☐	☐
2. My partner will sense what I need without my telling him or her.	☐	☐
3. My partner will never be sexually attracted to anyone else.	☐	☐
4. If my partner truly loves me, he or she will always try to please me.	☐	☐
5. Love means never being angry or disappointed with each other.	☐	☐
6. The thought of ending our relationship will never cross either of our minds.	☐	☐
7. Our sexual relationship will always be exciting.	☐	☐
8. My partner will always be honest, open, and direct with me.	☐	☐
9. My partner will always respect, understand, and accept me no matter what I say or do.	☐	☐
10. My relationship with my partner will meet all my needs.	☐	☐

Partner 2

Everyone has expectations about relationships in general, and these expectations serve as guideposts. You and your partner should independently indicate whether you agree or disagree with each of the 10 statements in the list. These questions pertain to your view of the way relationships should be in general, not the state of your relationship right now. Then share your answers and talk them over. The purpose is not to argue but to get a sense of where each partner stands.

	Agree	Disagree
1. My partner will never do anything to hurt me.	☐	☐
2. My partner will sense what I need without my telling him or her.	☐	☐
3. My partner will never be sexually attracted to anyone else.	☐	☐
4. If my partner truly loves me, he or she will always try to please me.	☐	☐
5. Love means never being angry or disappointed with each other.	☐	☐
6. The thought of ending our relationship will never cross either of our minds.	☐	☐
7. Our sexual relationship will always be exciting.	☐	☐
8. My partner will always be honest, open, and direct with me.	☐	☐
9. My partner will always respect, understand, and accept me no matter what I say or do.	☐	☐
10. My relationship with my partner will meet all my needs.	☐	☐

If you agreed with any of the statements in the exercise, you are certainly not alone. Many couples believe in these rules, and our culture reinforces them through television, romance novels, and movies. Unfortunately, none of them is true. In fact, counselors call them the "deadly expectations" (Bornstein & Bornstein, 1986). If you agreed with more than two or three of the statements, your standards for a relationship may be unusually high. The disadvantage of having high standards is that you may consider your relationship worse than it really is, relative to other people's relationships. However, if you can recognize your high expectations, you have an advantage: You can increase your satisfaction by lowering your expectations, and you may feel relief that your relationship does not have to be perfect. For example, every couple fights from time to time. If you believe that other couples never fight, you will be distressed by something that is a normal part of a relationship.

Self-Identity

Although our focus is on the relationship, it is important not to lose sight of your own identity. Before you came into your relationship you were an individual, and you still are! Losing sight of yourself can be a serious mistake. It is healthy to examine your own wants and needs and sometimes to put yourself before your relationship. Couples who are able to balance their individual needs with those of the relationship often report the greatest satisfaction from relationships. Take a few minutes now to write down the things that you consider important to you as an individual.

NONTRADITIONAL RELATIONSHIPS

The remainder of this chapter highlights concerns that often emerge in nontraditional relationships. Issues that arise in multicultural and gay or lesbian relationships are often ignored in books on relationship communication. Although one of the greatest difficulties for nontraditional couples is societal prejudice, it is not in our power or yours to change this fact. What we can do, however, is help you develop and maintain a good relationship in a frequently judgmental and unsupportive society.

Multicultural Relationships

Multicultural relationships are becoming increasingly common in our society. Interracial marriages account for 2% of all marriages in the United States. The number of births to black-and-white couples more than quintupled (from 9,600 to 51,000) from 1968 to 1988. More than half of all Asian Americans born in the United States intermarry, as do 40% of Latinos (National Center for Health Statistics, 1991). For many couples, cultural diversity can make for a unique and exciting experience. However, more often than not, cultural factors can also be a source of continuing strain in the relationship. For this reason, the multicultural relationship deserves some special attention. Whether you are involved with someone from a different culture or race, are the offspring of multicultural or multiracial parents, or are simply interested in multicultural relationships, you may find this section helpful.

Expectations

Our society offers few role models for the multicultural couple, so the guideposts for a successful multicultural relationship may not always be evident. Therefore, it is extremely important for you and your partner to be explicit about your expectations for your relationship. To complicate matters further, culture may not always be easy to define. Does a member of a particular race automatically identify with a particular culture? Do cultural values differ among people of the same race? How do mixed-race or adopted people select their cultural values? How does assimilation affect cultural values? These are difficult questions to answer. The answers depend upon the person, the culture, and the environment, and the answers may vary according to time, situation, and context. We raise these questions to highlight the importance of clarifying your own cultural values so that you can try to prevent misunderstandings in your relationship.

To have a successful multicultural relationship, partners are not obligated to have the same cultural values. In fact, it is often the cultural differences that pull people together when they first become involved in a multicultural relationship. However, the cultural differences that may have attracted you to your partner in the first place can lead to frustration in the long run if you lack good communication skills to discuss them. Among the most common sources of frustration for multicultural couples are differences in values concerning relationships, traditions, religious beliefs, and parenting. These differences can become barriers between partners.

Other barriers arise from differing expectations regarding communication styles. When two people from different cultures communicate, there is more room for misunderstanding than if a single culture is involved. This is because different cultures place different values on communicative actions, and different actions have different meanings for different cultures. For example, eye contact during a conversation may in one culture be a sign of attention to the speaker. However, this same gesture could be interpreted as rude in another culture. It will be extremely important for you to understand how your expectations regarding communication style might affect your communication with your partner. Exercise 3.2 is designed to highlight differences in communication style.

Exercise 3.2   Understanding Nonverbal Communication

*With your partner, read the questions about nonverbal communication behaviors.
Discuss your answers and see whether they reveal similar or different expectations.*

1. How far away do you stand from another person when talking?

2. What does standing close to someone mean?

3. What does standing far away mean?

4. Do you shake hands when greeting someone? If so, how?

5. Is eye contact appropriate for all conversations? If not, when is it appropriate?

6. What posture do you assume in communicating? Are some postures better than others?

7. Is it OK to display facial expressions? If not, when is it inappropriate?

8. What does smiling mean?

9. What does lifting the chin or shaking the head mean?

10. How loud do you usually speak? What do pauses, silences, hestiations, inflections, and your rate of speaking indicate?

Another area of potential misunderstanding for multicultural couples involves high- versus low-context communications (Sue & Sue, 1990; see also Hall, 1976). In high-context communications, less emphasis is placed on the explicit content of the message; communication relies more on nonverbal behaviors and group understanding. For instance, in some Asian cultures an invitation to dinner is considered seriously only after several invitations are made. For the hosts to issue only one invitation would mean that they were not sincere. Here, the content of the message takes a back seat to the way in which the message is delivered. In contrast, low-context communications rely more on verbal content and less on nonverbal behaviors. An example is a communication with a judge: It doesn't matter how he or she says you're going to jail; what counts in this context is that the content is explicitly stated once. To what degree do you think you and your partner engage in high- and low-context communications?

Communication styles are one manifestation of cultural values. Exercise 3.3 will help you clarify your overall cultural values.

Exercise 3.3   Expectations in Multicultural Relationships

Partner 1

You and your partner should complete the exercise independently, then discuss the similarities and differences in your answers. In the discussion, observe your own communication style.

	Strongly agree	Agree	Disagree	Strongly disagree
1. I consider myself to have strong cultural values.	☐	☐	☐	☐
2. I have never examined my own cultural values.	☐	☐	☐	☐
3. My partner and I have never discussed our different cultures.	☐	☐	☐	☐
4. My relationship takes precedence over my cultural values.	☐	☐	☐	☐
5. My partner is accepting of my culture.	☐	☐	☐	☐
6. My partner and I agree on the importance of family.	☐	☐	☐	☐
7. My partner's family makes me feel accepted.	☐	☐	☐	☐
8. My partner and I agree on the way to raise children.	☐	☐	☐	☐
9. My partner and I agree on the way to discipline children.	☐	☐	☐	☐
10. My partner and I share the same religious beliefs.	☐	☐	☐	☐
11. My partner and I celebrate the same holidays.	☐	☐	☐	☐
12. My partner and I participate in each other's cultural traditions.	☐	☐	☐	☐
13. My partner and I feel comfortable about our relationship in public places.	☐	☐	☐	☐
14. I feel comfortable expressing physical affection for my partner in public.	☐	☐	☐	☐
15. I expect sexual fidelity in our relationship.	☐	☐	☐	☐
16. Divorce is unacceptable in my culture.	☐	☐	☐	☐

Partner 2

You and your partner should complete the exercise independently, then discuss the similarities and differences in your answers. In the discussion, observe your own communication style.

	Strongly agree	Agree	Disagree	Strongly disagree
1. I consider myself to have strong cultural values.	☐	☐	☐	☐
2. I have never examined my own cultural values.	☐	☐	☐	☐
3. My partner and I have never discussed our different cultures.	☐	☐	☐	☐
4. My relationship takes precedence over my cultural values.	☐	☐	☐	☐
5. My partner is accepting of my culture.	☐	☐	☐	☐
6. My partner and I agree on the importance of family.	☐	☐	☐	☐
7. My partner's family makes me feel accepted.	☐	☐	☐	☐
8. My partner and I agree on the way to raise children.	☐	☐	☐	☐
9. My partner and I agree on the way to discipline children.	☐	☐	☐	☐
10. My partner and I share the same religious beliefs.	☐	☐	☐	☐
11. My partner and I celebrate the same holidays.	☐	☐	☐	☐
12. My partner and I participate in each other's cultural traditions.	☐	☐	☐	☐
13. My partner and I feel comfortable about our relationship in public places.	☐	☐	☐	☐
14. I feel comfortable expressing physical affection for my partner in public.	☐	☐	☐	☐
15. I expect sexual fidelity in our relationship.	☐	☐	☐	☐
16. Divorce is unacceptable in my culture.	☐	☐	☐	☐

Self-Identity

The last exercise may prompt you and your partner (if you have not already done so) to begin developing cultural identities for yourselves, as well as an identity as a multicultural couple. Having a cultural identity will not only help you communicate better with your partner, it will also help you to define your roles in your relationship, clarify your beliefs, and cope effectively with labeling or discrimination. Bear in mind, however, that cultural and couple identities change with time and place. So, for example, a Hispanic American born and raised in the United States could have a different cultural identity when he is in Iowa than when he is in Mexico. Therefore, if you are in doubt about how your partner views something, take time to clarify those views.

As you continue to work through this book, stop and ask yourself how your responses to the exercises reflect your cultural values and cultural identity. Also ask how they relate to your expectations for communication style and for your relationship. You may want to return to this section after you've completed some of the steps in learning to communicate more effectively.

Gay and Lesbian Relationships

Although same-sex relationships have been viewed as sinful and immoral through most of American history, this attitude has softened slightly in recent years. The American Psychiatric Association removed homosexuality from the list of mental disorders in 1973, and openly gay politicians have been elected to public office. Despite this increasing tolerance, negative attitudes about gays and lesbians are still well entrenched in American culture and continue to make same-sex intimate relationships difficult. Because of these obstacles, it takes some courage and extra work to build a good gay or lesbian relationship. If you are gay or lesbian, you may find that the following sections help you reap rewards in your relationship.

Expectations

Ray and Tim have been living together for 2 months. The following scenario illustrates one kind of difficulty that can arise when a couple lacks clearly defined expectations.

Ray: My parents are coming into town this weekend, and—uh— I wonder if maybe we could set up the spare room to look like your room.

Tim: What?!

Ray: Well, don't take this the wrong way, but I told my parents we were roommates.

Tim: Roommates? I thought you told them the truth about us.

Ray: I really meant to, but I can't. They don't understand . . .

Tim: That's not my problem—my parents know we're together, and so do my friends.

Ray: Look, my parents are older than yours, and I've told you how religious they are. I can't tell them the truth.

Tim: Won't tell them, you mean. If you weren't ashamed of me,
       you'd tell them.

Ray: What are you making such a big deal for? I'm just asking for
       a favor for one weekend.

Tim: You're asking me to put on a show because you and your redneck
       parents are living in the 50s!

Society offers few guideposts for gay and lesbian couples. Models for good homosexual relationships tend to be hidden from public view. This can leave you feeling confused about what to do to achieve a successful relationship. Because of the lack of socially defined expectations for same-sex relationships, it is particularly important for gay and lesbian couples to be very clear about their personal wishes, expectations, and standards. Ray and Tim have different expectations for dealing with a parental visit because there is no set rule for the way gay couples should handle that situation. Ray's suggestion would seem ridiculous if Tim were his wife instead of his lover. In the absence of such a societal standard, a fight is almost inevitable. Expectations are critical to satisfaction in all relationships, but they are especially critical in same-sex relationships because there are no "default" expectations provided by society. For example, it is very common in gay and lesbian relationships for partners to have different expectations about being "out," observing emotional and sexual fidelity, and making a political statement by means of the relationship.

The lack of socially sanctioned relationship markers can also obscure where the partners stand in a relationship. You may find yourself getting rapidly involved with someone without talking about what you want, how serious you are, and where the relationship is headed. Heterosexual couples are to a degree pressured to talk about these issues because of the social customs of pinning, engagement, and marriage. Without this pressure, it is easy to forget about reviewing what you want with your partner. It will be easier if you initiate the discussion when things are going well rather than wait for a conflict to show you where the disagreements lie.

There is also a positive feature in the lack of rules: It frees you to be quite creative in your relationship. The rules that help heterosexual couples can also sometimes confine them because rules about what is "normal" often ignore individual differences. You and your partner can develop the rules that work best for you. The key to a successful gay or lesbian relationship lies in consciously taking the time to develop your rules together, to make your expectations explicit. This will not only let your partner know where you stand, it will also help you clarify in your own mind what you want. Exercise 3.1 in the section for traditional couples can give you a start in talking about expectations in general. Exercise 3.4 will help you examine your expectations about issues specific to gay and lesbian relationships.

Exercise 3.4   Expectations in Gay and Lesbian Relationships

Partner 1

You and your partner should independently read the statements and indicate whether you agree or disagree with each one. Then share your answers and talk them over. The purpose is not to argue but to get a sense of where each partner stands.

	Strongly agree	Agree	Disagree	Strongly disagree
1. It is important to me that my family know that I am in a gay/lesbian relationship.	☐	☐	☐	☐
2. It is important to me that my partner's family know that he or she is involved with me.	☐	☐	☐	☐
3. I do not want people I work with to know about my relationship.	☐	☐	☐	☐
4. I want to go to parties and other social events as a couple.	☐	☐	☐	☐
5. I expect sexual fidelity in a relationship.	☐	☐	☐	☐
6. I would like to be a parent with my partner.	☐	☐	☐	☐
7. I want my partner and myself to think of our relationship as a political statement.	☐	☐	☐	☐
8. I see myself and my partner being together for years to come.	☐	☐	☐	☐
9. I would like to perform a commitment ritual.	☐	☐	☐	☐
10. I want to settle down and build a home with my partner.	☐	☐	☐	☐
11. I feel comfortable expressing physical affection for my partner in public.	☐	☐	☐	☐
12. It is important to me that my partner and I discuss safe sex.	☐	☐	☐	☐

Partner 2

You and your partner should independently read the statements and indicate whether you agree or disagree with each one. Then share your answers and talk them over. The purpose is not to argue but to get a sense of where each partner stands.

	Strongly agree	Agree	Disagree	Strongly disagree
1. It is important to me that my family know that I am in a gay/lesbian relationship.	☐	☐	☐	☐
2. It is important to me that my partner's family know that he or she is involved with me.	☐	☐	☐	☐
3. I do not want people I work with to know about my relationship.	☐	☐	☐	☐
4. I want to go to parties and other social events as a couple.	☐	☐	☐	☐
5. I expect sexual fidelity in a relationship.	☐	☐	☐	☐
6. I would like to be a parent with my partner.	☐	☐	☐	☐
7. I want my partner and myself to think of our relationship as a political statement.	☐	☐	☐	☐
8. I see myself and my partner being together for years to come.	☐	☐	☐	☐
9. I would like to perform a commitment ritual.	☐	☐	☐	☐
10. I want to settle down and build a home with my partner.	☐	☐	☐	☐
11. I feel comfortable expressing physical affection for my partner in public.	☐	☐	☐	☐
12. It is important to me that my partner and I discuss safe sex.	☐	☐	☐	☐

Self-Identity

Because of homophobia in our society, it is not uncommon for people in gay or lesbian relationships to have developed negative attitudes about their sexual orientation. If you are gay or lesbian, you may have absorbed some of the attitudes of the dominant culture and come to see yourself as sinful, psychologically unhealthy, or somehow less valuable than heterosexuals. You may be conscious of these beliefs, or they may operate outside your awareness. Such beliefs can lead to two types of relationship problems: attributing all of your relationship problems to your sexual orientation and feeling a need to compete with heterosexual standards.

All people, whatever their sexual orientation, have relationship difficulties from time to time. Loving, healthy people sometimes have strong disagreements. Heterosexuals have an advantage: They have been told all their lives that heterosexuality is normal, so they never blame their relationship problems on their sexual orientation. In contrast, gays and lesbians are so inundated with negative messages about their sexual orientation that, when relationship problems develop, they often feel that it must be the underlying cause. Whether or not this seems to apply to you, you should take some time to examine your beliefs and—even if you are not conscious of such negative ideas— to observe yourself and see if some of your actions reflect such beliefs. You may need to "stop the action" and make a conscious effort to change what you say to yourself and what you do. You might start by reminding yourself that heterosexual couples often fight, experience unhappiness, or break up, just as gay and lesbian couples sometimes do. Select some positive statements (e.g., "There is nothing about my sexual orientation that makes a good relationship impossible") to replace your negative beliefs, and repeat them to yourself at least once a day. Even if this practice feels a bit artificial, keep in mind that we tend to believe familiar messages and evaluate them positively.

A second problem that can arise from internalized negative attitudes is the feeling that you must compete with the socially approved heterosexual model of relationships. This can put pressure on the couple to have a "perfect" relationship—which is, of course, impossible for any couple. Ultimately, if you and your partner are satisfied, your relationship is a good one. Whether it bears any resemblance to a straight relationship is beside the point. As long as you compare yourself to straight models, you are putting yourself in a one-down position. The way to freedom from heterosexual standards is not to compete with them but to forget about them and do what works for you and your partner.

The problems mentioned so far are common to both gay and lesbian relationships. In the next two sections we focus on each of these relationships in turn.

Issues Common in Gay Relationships

Fidelity

The most common conflict in gay relationships concerns sexual fidelity. Many men, gay as well as straight, do not see sex outside of a love relationship as a threat to that relationship. They seem to make a distinction between emotional fidelity and sexual fidelity. In gay relationships, problems arise when one partner feels that sex outside the relationship is acceptable while the other does not. Simply demanding fidelity from a partner does not usually promote peace; resentment and breakup are more likely results. The best solution is for you and your partner to communicate honestly about your expectations, using the communication and problem-solving skills outlined in this book, and to work toward an agreement. Try not to blame your partner for what he wants; the relationship problem might just be a poor match between men who want different things. If you agree that sex outside the relationship is acceptable, you should periodically review this agreement. In any romantic relationship, sex with a third person can lead to sharing and intimacy that can cause conflict in the primary relationship.

AIDS and Safer Sex

Sexually transmitted diseases are a concern in all relationships, but the high incidence of Acquired Immune Deficiency Syndrome (AIDS) among gays makes safer sex an issue of particular concern for most gay men. The way you handle this issue depends heavily on the length of time you have been with your partner, the degree of trust between you, and each partner's standards for sexual fidelity. At the start of a new relationship, a serious discussion of sexual histories can be both awkward and a turnoff. Nevertheless, if you talk in advance you will probably find that you can relax more during sex and enjoy it without worry. If your partner is not open about his sexual history, you can still protect yourself by keeping latex condoms and a water-soluble lubricant (preferably one containing nonoxynol-9) at hand and by refusing to engage in the sexual activities most likely to transmit the AIDS virus (e.g., unprotected anal intercourse or fisting, ejaculating into the mouth, sharing sex toys). Whether you are starting a relationship or are in an established one, the communication skills outlined in this book should help you share information with each other in a respectful and sensitive fashion.

For Further Information

These are only a sampling of common problems in gay relationships. If you would like to read further about communication and relationships, see Rik Isensee's book *Love Between Men*, which focuses exclusively on gay relationships.

Issues Common in Lesbian Relationships

Lack of Legitimation and Social Support

In many communities, lesbians are "invisible people." Many people do not want to acknowledge the presence of lesbians in the community, much less legitimate and support their relationships. If you are in a city that is large enough to sustain a lesbian community, you are more likely to find people who can support you in your relationship. If this is not the case (and sometimes even if it is), you and your partner may understandably find yourselves feeling that it is "you and me against the world." Whether or not this is an accurate assessment, it certainly can lead partners to overdepend on each other. Although it is good to be close to your partner, looking to one person for everything is unrealistic and puts undue pressure on a relationship. There are two ways to relieve this pressure. The most drastic solution is to move to a community that is more accepting (in Minneapolis, for example, gay and lesbian couples can register their partnership at city hall and have the ceremony announced in the newspaper). A less radical alternative is to reach out to others for friendship and support, using the skills you will develop through this book. Reaching out may not meet all your needs, but it will take some pressure off of your relationship.

Pressure to Make the Relationship
a Political Statement

Lesbians are in many ways caught in a double bind. Outside of a lesbian community, they enjoy little legitimation. However, immersion in a lesbian community can also create difficulties for a couple. For many lesbians, the relationship is a political statement about traditional male-female relationships, which they see as patriarchal and destructive to women. Thus, they want the lesbian relationship to make a political statement by being perfectly egalitarian, free of jealousy, and in general better than what they perceive as the heterosexual model. If these are your politics, the ideal standard may seem desirable, but it is impossible for any relationship to meet any ideal standard all the time. All couples make mistakes in their relationships. Unrealistically high standards only complicate the task of dealing with these mistakes.

If you do not see your relationship as a political statement, you may feel as pressured by politically oriented members of the lesbian community as by mainstream society. You may also find that politicized lesbians do not want to hear about certain relationship problems (e.g., loss of sexual interest, jealousy) because they associate such worries with patriarchal relationships (see Nichols, 1987). Ultimately, you are the judge of how satisfying your relationship is and what it means to you. If you and your partner agree on this political issue, the opinions of the rest of world will become less important.

CHAPTER

4 *How Do Couples Communicate?*

You have signed an agreement with your partner and have become aware of the need to identify, examine, and communicate your expectations. It is now time to consider how communication works. Many couples can agree that they have trouble talking to each other but can describe their communication difficulties only in very general terms (e.g., "He doesn't listen to me"; "She nags too much"). Although such general complaints may describe your experience, they often do not paint a complete picture of communication in the relationship and are not enough to bring about changes in communication. To improve your communication, you must describe what is happening between you and your partner in more concrete and specific terms. Until you do this, you won't know exactly what needs to be changed.

BEGINNING TO UNDERSTAND COMMUNICATION

Getting more concrete and specific about communication sounds simple, but most couples find it quite difficult to do. One way to make the task easier is to understand what communication is and how it works. In this chapter, we will try to help you do that.

What is communication? Imagine that you are the speaker and your partner is the listener. At its simplest level, communication means that you send a message and your partner receives the message. That is, you send a message with a particular INTENT, and the message has an IMPACT on your partner (see part 1 of Figure 4.1). This simple process can easily result in miscommunication: The message you intend may not be the same as the message your partner receives. To understand the many ways in which miscommunication can occur, we need to examine communication in more detail.

Your goal is to develop accurate communication, in which the intent of your message matches its impact on your partner. Part 2 of Figure 4.1 shows that accurate communication requires at least two important processes. First, you must ENCODE your message accurately—you must turn your intent (e.g., to compliment your partner) into words and say the words in a way that is consistent with your intent. This is not as easy as it seems; there are many points where the message can go astray. For example, you may choose the wrong words (e.g., say, "You did a much better paint job than I expected"), use a tone of voice that contradicts the message (e.g., sound sarcastic), or use nonverbal behavior that undermines your message (e.g., avoid eye contact while talking).

The second important process involves the listener, who must accurately DECODE the speaker's message. This means that your partner must infer the correct intent from

Figure 4.1   Intent and Impact in Messages

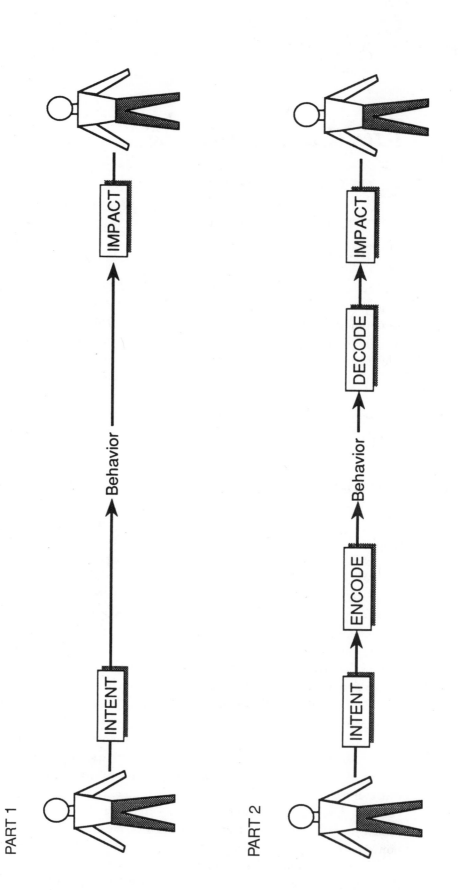

your words and the way you speak them. This task requires your partner to have some knowledge of the relationship between behaviors and the intents that they reflect. A person can make the same statement with different intents, and identifying the speaker's intent may depend on the listener's sensitivity to very subtle cues (e.g., the inflection of the speaker's voice). You can minimize miscommunication due to listening or decoding errors by ensuring that communication behaviors are obvious enough to make your intent really clear. In other words, one way to maximize the likelihood of accurate communication is to send messages in which the intent is so obvious that there is little or no room for misinterpretation.

Four Paths to Miscommunication

Together, the processes of encoding and decoding point to four basic ways in which communication can go wrong.

First, the speaker's intent and the message may not correspond—for instance, when the speaker smirks while making a complimentary comment. Such encoding errors seldom occur intentionally (unless the speaker is trying to be misleading). They can result from a variety of factors, including poor verbal skills, unawareness of one's own feelings and habitual thoughts, inattention to nonverbal aspects of communication, and so on.

Second, the listener may infer the wrong intent from the message even though the speaker encodes it properly. For example, the listener may interpret a sincere expression of sympathy to be patronizing. Such decoding errors can occur for some of the same reasons as those just mentioned: the listener's lack of awareness of his or her feelings and habitual thoughts, inattentiveness to the speaker's nonverbal behavior, and so on.

A third kind of miscommunication can occur when both the speaker and listener make errors. In such cases, one or both persons may feel unheard and may end up being quite frustrated.

A fourth important type of miscommunication occurs when both the speaker and the listener perform their tasks adequately and neither makes an error. How, then, can miscommunication happen? The answer lies in the rules relating behavior and intent. The speaker may use one set of rules to translate intent into behavior, and the listener may use a different set of rules to infer intent from the behavior. Both people may perform their tasks adequately, but miscommunication occurs nonetheless because they are using different sets of rules. This form of miscommunication is most obvious when people come from different cultures in which the same behavior may mean different things. For example, on a tour of Australia, a United States president held up two fingers in a gesture that insulted Australians. The president was making what would be considered a peace sign in United States culture, but from the Australian cultural perspective his gesture could be seen as hostile. Neither the president nor his Australian audience erred in perceiving the relation between behavior and intent, yet miscommunication occurred because they were using different rules.

Miscommunication due to the use of different rules also occurs in relationships where people know each other intimately. Of course, much of what people learn in any culture is shared (thus, most North Americans would have seen the president's gesture as a peace sign), yet every person is unique and has a different communication background. Without shared learning, a culture might lack the cooperation needed to survive. However, shared learning itself can lead to problems in communication: Because so much is held in common, the unique individual characteristics that may affect communication can easily be neglected. Underlying many communication difficulties is the assumption that partners are using exactly the same rules of communication when in fact they are not.

A DEEPER UNDERSTANDING OF COMMUNICATION

Against this background we can now elaborate on our picture of communication in relationships by including the context of communication. All communication takes place in a context, which consists of what each person brings to the situation (i.e., background and personality) and what each person is experiencing at the time of the communication. Each partner's context is fully known only to him or her and is therefore private. Figure 4.2 schematizes the private and public aspects of communication.

The private aspect consists of each partner's internal world (e.g., memories, desires, intentions, mood). Of particular importance are the person's thoughts, feelings, and communication background. Thoughts and feelings can be momentary (e.g., a fleeting thought, a temporary mood) or enduring (e.g., expectations for relationships, a stable mood). Communication background is shaped throughout life and influences all relationships. This background is determined by communications in the family of origin, culture, gender, sexual orientation, general style of relating to other people, experiences in previous intimate relationships, notions about relationships, and personality. Much of your communication background was in place before you entered your current relationship, yet it still influences that relationship. It is critical to recognize that each partner has direct access only to his or her own internal world.

The public aspect of communication consists of behavior that both partners can observe. When a couple communicates, speaker and listener engage in various behaviors such as smiling, asking questions, hugging, yelling, and crying. Through these behaviors each person lets the other know what is happening in his or her private, internal world. Because behavior alone is in the shared, external world of the couple, it is the only medium through which they can communicate. Thoughts and feelings do not transmit from one person to another without being translated into behavior. Thus, changing behavior is critical to changing communication.

In Figure 4.2, the arrows between the private and public aspects of communication are double-headed because the internal world of each partner both influences and is influenced by behavior. What you think and feel affects your behavior and the way you react to your partner's behavior. Your partner's or your own behavior can in turn change the way you think or feel. Thus, the private world of each partner and the external world of the relationship are constantly interacting and changing each other.

Each element shown in the diagram (thoughts, feelings, communication background, and behavior) is critical to effective communication. In the next sections, we discuss how each one can enhance or detract from communication.

Communication Background

Whether differences in communication backgrounds enhance or detract from a relationship depends on the partners' awareness of them. When we are unaware of another person's communication background, we often wrongly assume that the person's background is the same as our own—and therefore that the person's behavior means to him or her what it means to us. As in the case of the United States president's gesture to his Australian audience, this erroneous assumption leads to miscommunication.

Figure 4.2 Communication in Context

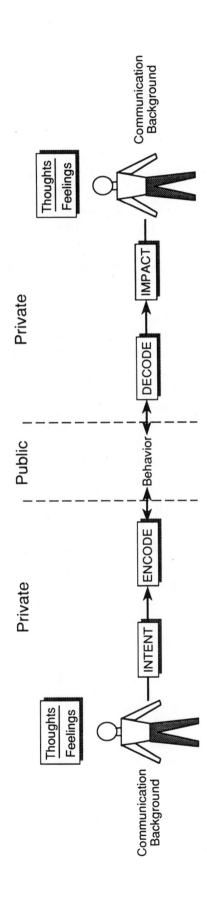

In intimate relationships, one of the most common differences in communication background relates to gender. Many couples are unaware, for example, that men and women learn different ways to communicate about problems. Most men learn that when someone tells you about a problem, you are supposed to help solve it by offering practical solutions. In contrast, part of the communication background of most women is the assumption that sharing problems is a way to make connections with others and feel supported, even if the problem is insoluble. Unawareness of this difference often leads to frustration for a couple: The woman complains about problems, and the man tells her how to solve them. Not surprisingly, the woman feels that her partner is not listening but rather is trying to "fix her," and the man feels that the woman merely wants to complain because she never tries to enact his solutions. However, a couple who knows about the differences between men's and women's communication backgrounds can usually forestall such miscommunications because each partner has a better understanding of what the other is really communicating. Once you and your partner are aware of the differences in your communication backgrounds, these differences will become less and less a source of strain and increasingly a source of variety and interest.

In addition to miscommunication resulting from ignorance of our partners' communication backgrounds, relationship difficulties can also arise when we are not aware of our own communication backgrounds. For example, some people may not realize that they have always viewed a good relationship as a state of unending bliss, and they may react strongly to any expressions of discontent from their partners, misinterpreting these expressions as signs of a failing relationship. The partners, who may see relationships more realistically, may be surprised and confused by the reaction they receive when they bring up difficulties.

Your communication background is like a pair of glasses through which you see everything that happens in your relationship. If you know what kinds of lenses you and your partner are wearing, you can more easily distinguish reality from your personal interpretation or distortion of it. Thus, increasing your awareness of the lenses through which you and others see things is crucial to improving communication.

Several chapters in this book are designed to expand your awareness of the communication backgrounds you and your partner bring to your relationship. Chapter 5, "His and Her Relationship," deals with the different ways in which men and women learn to communicate and view relationships. Chapter 3, on nontraditional relationships, described the communication backgrounds that partners may bring to multicultural, gay, and lesbian relationships.

Thoughts

What you have on your mind when your partner says or does something will strongly influence the way you understand—or misunderstand—your partner's behavior. The following scenario is an illustration. After dinner Roscoe gets up from his chair, tells Beth, "I'm going next door to talk with Alex," and leaves the house. What does this communication mean? If Beth had just been thinking, "I wish Roscoe would develop more outside friendships," she would probably evaluate the message positively. If Beth's mind had been on a letter she had been meaning to write to her mother, she might think of the communication as unimportant or neutral. In contrast, if she had been racking her brain and wondering, "Why do we spend so little time talking these days?" the message might seem negative or even hurtful.

Like our communication backgrounds, our thoughts can cause miscommunication if we are unaware of them. If Beth in our example is thinking that the couple doesn't talk enough, she may assume that Roscoe is attempting to be hurtful and may respond defensively by saying, "Well, I have other people I can talk to also, so don't expect me to be here when you get back!" Assuming that Roscoe was not intending to be hurtful, this response may seem baffling or unwarranted.

When couples are aware of the way their thoughts influence their communications, they can tell each other how they interpret the communications. As we noted earlier, thoughts are not part of the public aspect of communication; they must be translated into behavior so others can identify and understand them. Consider how different the communication would have been if Beth had said, "I was just thinking that we haven't spent much time talking lately—are you leaving because you're bored with me?" Roscoe would then be aware of his partner's thoughts and could clarify the intended message—perhaps by saying, "I'm not bored with you, but Alex borrowed a book from me and I want to get it back. I'd like it if we could go for a walk together when I get back and catch up on things." When we make our thoughts, inferences, and attributions explicit, we sometimes discover that we have misinterpreted the intent of a message.

It is not always clear how our thoughts influence communication because some thoughts are so automatic that we are often unconscious of them. Such automatic thoughts can wreak havoc on communication. The only way to become aware of them is to pay attention to what is going through your mind when a miscommunication occurs. Because this is difficult to do at the time, it usually means reliving the situation in your imagination and watching what passes through your mind. In any event, it may take some work to become aware of the thoughts that impede communication.

Being aware of and communicating your thoughts is one way to enhance communication. On occasion it is also necessary to change your thoughts. We have already discussed thoughts that stop cooperation (chapter 2) and expectations that can lead to relationship difficulties (chapter 3). Other kinds of thoughts can influence communication as well. Some beliefs—for instance, "Partners cannot change once the relationship is established" or "I must always perform well in bed or else my partner will not love me"—interfere with communication even if both partners are aware of them. Moreover, such thoughts are maladaptive in themselves—they are not conducive to healthy relationships. The chapters that follow will teach you what thoughts are maladaptive and how to change them. You will also learn how to become aware of thoughts that affect your relationship and how to communicate them.

Feelings

Emotions are, of course, an important part of every intimate relationship, even if the partners do not tend to discuss their feelings. The way you interpret your partner's communication is shaped by your current mood. Suppose, for example, your partner asks whether you've paid this month's bills. If you are in a relaxed mood, the question may seem to be a perfectly innocent one. On the other hand, if you are feeling angry or pressured, it may seem like badgering. Being aware of the mood you are in will make you better able to communicate effectively with your partner.

Intense emotions such as rage and jealousy have great potential to distort communication. Intense emotions hamper our ability to examine situations carefully, and they can lead us to make poor judgments or say and do things we later regret.

Nevertheless, though intense emotions are an inevitable part of life, people who are sensitive to their effects can prevent difficulty simply by postponing important decision making or problem solving until the feelings have passed. This book will help you to learn to become aware of your emotions and recognize the signs that they are beginning to affect you.

Of course, emotions have positive effects as well. The ability to communicate emotions will enhance your relationship: You can let your partner know how to make you feel good. The connection between behavior and emotions is reciprocal, but because your feelings are in your personal world, you must communicate them to make their links to behavior obvious. For example, you might say, "I feel cared about when you give me a hug" or "I feel hurt when you turn away from me as I talk." An age-old myth says that when people care about each another, they easily sense each other's wishes and feelings. This myth has little basis in reality. To have the best possible relationship, you must learn how to make feelings explicit. The material in chapters 6 through 8 will help you do this.

Behaviors

Even if you have good intentions and full awareness of your internal world, you may still have difficulty communicating with your partner. For instance, you may be aware that you feel affection for your partner and think the relationship is going well, but unless you express this affection and contentment in a behavior that your partner appreciates and understands, your intention may not be realized. From your point of view, taking your partner out to dinner may be a clear expression of your feelings, but your partner may interpret it to mean many things—perhaps that you do not enjoy the food at home or are simply too tired to prepare a meal. It is not safe to assume that both partners use the same behaviors to express the same thoughts and feelings. Often, couples need to agree on a "common language" so that they can understand each other's messages and clarify the meanings of various behaviors in their relationship.

The right behaviors can translate good intentions into good communication. Through the step-by-step approach in chapters 6 through 8, you will learn communication skills that will give you and your partner a common language.

ASSESSING YOUR PRESENT RELATIONSHIP

Before you can bring about change in your relationship, you need to assess where things stand between you and your partner right now. This is important for at least three reasons. First, it is difficult to change what happens between you and your partner unless you are aware of what is happening. Second, the very act of paying attention to what is occurring in your communications may lead to changes. Finally, change begins to occur only after you recognize and admit to the way things are. The remainder of this chapter is devoted to helping you and your partner assess the present state of your relationship.

Exercise 4.1 consists of seven questionnaires. Each one relates to a part of the communication process just described. Please take time to complete the questionnaires before you read ahead in the text because the text contains information that could influence your responses to the questions. Each partner should complete the questionnaires independently.

These questionnaires were developed for married couples. We chose them because, of the measures available, they have the most research support. Readers who are in same-sex relationships or who are not married will need to substitute the word *partner* for *spouse* and *relationship* for *marriage* in some of the questionnaires. (We look forward to a time when researchers devote more attention to assessing the relationships of gay, lesbian, and unmarried persons.)

In the last part of the chapter we will discuss the questionnaires and explain how to interpret the scores. If you are a professional who works with couples, you may also be interested in Appendix 2, which gives psychometric information on these measures.

Exercise 4.1   Assessing Your Relationship

QUESTIONNAIRE 1: THE MARITAL ADJUSTMENT TEST

Partner 1

1. Check the dot on the scale below which best describes the degree of happiness, everything considered, of your present marriage. The middle point, "Happy," represents the degree of happiness which most people get from marriage, and the scale gradually ranges on one side to those few who are very unhappy in marriage, and on the other, to those few who experience extreme joy or felicity in marriage.

    •   •   •   •   •   •   •

Very unhappy	Happy	Perfectly happy

State the approximate extent of agreement or disagreement between you and your mate on the following items. Please respond to each item.

	Always agree	Almost always agree	Occasionally disagree	Frequently disagree	Almost always disagree	Always disagree
2. Handling family finances	☐	☐	☐	☐	☐	☐
3. Matters of recreation	☐	☐	☐	☐	☐	☐
4. Demonstrations of affection	☐	☐	☐	☐	☐	☐
5. Friends	☐	☐	☐	☐	☐	☐
6. Sex relations	☐	☐	☐	☐	☐	☐
7. Conventionality (right, good, or proper conduct)	☐	☐	☐	☐	☐	☐
8. Philosophy of life	☐	☐	☐	☐	☐	☐
9. Ways of dealing with in-laws	☐	☐	☐	☐	☐	☐

Note. From "Short Marital-Adjustment and Prediction Tests: Their Reliability and Validity" by H. J. Locke and K. M. Wallace, 1959, *Marriage and Family Living, 21*, p. 252. Copyrighted 1959 by the National Council on Family Relations, 3989 Central Avenue N.E., Suite 550, Minneapolis, MN 55421. Reprinted by permission.

10. When disagreements arise, they usually result in:

    Husband giving in ☐   Wife giving in ☐   Agreement by mutual give and take ☐

11. Do you and your mate engage in outside interests together?

    All of them ☐   Some of them ☐   Very few of them ☐   None of them ☐

12. In leisure time do you generally prefer:

    To be "on the go" ☐   To stay at home ☐

    Does your mate generally prefer:

    To be "on the go" ☐   To stay at home ☐

13. Do you ever wish you had not married?

    Frequently ☐   Occasionally ☐   Rarely ☐   Never ☐

14. If you had your life to live over, do you think you would:

    Marry the same person ☐   Marry a different person ☐   Not marry at all ☐

15. Do you confide in your mate?

    Almost never ☐   Rarely ☐   In most things ☐   In everything ☐

For scoring instructions, see the next page.

SCORING INSTRUCTIONS: Score all items and add to compute your total score. Total scores should range from 2 to 158.

SCORING KEY

1. Check the dot on the scale below which best describes the degree of happiness, everything considered, of your present marriage. The middle point, "Happy," represents the degree of happiness which most people get from marriage, and the scale gradually ranges on one side to those few who are very unhappy in marriage, and on the other, to those few who experience extreme joy or felicity in marriage.

0	2	7	15	20	25	35
•	•	•	•	•	•	•

| Very unhappy | | Happy | | Perfectly happy | | |

State the approximate extent of agreement or disagreement between you and your mate on the following items. Please respond to each item.

	Always agree	**Almost always agree**	**Occasionally disagree**	**Frequently disagree**	**Almost always disagree**	**Always disagree**
2. Handling family finances	5	4	3	2	1	0
3. Matters of recreation	5	4	3	2	1	0
4. Demonstrations of affection	8	6	4	2	1	0
5. Friends	5	4	3	2	1	0
6. Sex relations	15	12	9	4	1	0
7. Conventionality (right, good, or proper conduct)	5	4	3	2	1	0
8. Philosophy of life	5	4	3	2	1	0
9. Ways of dealing with in-laws	5	4	3	2	1	0

10. When disagreements arise, they usually result in:

    Husband giving in _0_   Wife giving in _2_   Agreement by mutual give and take _10_

11. Do you and your mate engage in outside interests together?

    All of them _10_   Some of them _8_   Very few of them _3_   None of them _0_

12. In leisure time do you generally prefer:

    To be "on the go" ☐   To stay at home ☐

    Does your mate generally prefer:

    To be "on the go" ☐   To stay at home ☐

    Both "stay at home" = 10
    Both "on the go" = 3
    Disagreement = 2

13. Do you ever wish you had not married?

    Frequently _0_   Occasionally _3_   Rarely _8_   Never _15_

14. If you had your life to live over, do you think you would:

    Marry the same person _15_   Marry a different person _0_   Not marry at all _1_

15. Do you confide in your mate?

    Almost never _0_   Rarely _2_   In most things _10_   In everything _10_

MARITAL ADJUSTMENT TEST TOTAL SCORE _____

Partner 2

1. Check the dot on the scale below which best describes the degree of happiness, everything considered, of your present marriage. The middle point, "Happy," represents the degree of happiness which most people get from marriage, and the scale gradually ranges on one side to those few who are very unhappy in marriage, and on the other, to those few who experience extreme joy or felicity in marriage.

•   •   •   •   •   •   •

| Very
unhappy | Happy | Perfectly
happy |

State the approximate extent of agreement or disagreement between you and your mate on the following items. Please respond to each item.

	Always agree	Almost always agree	Occasionally disagree	Frequently disagree	Almost always disagree	Always disagree
2. Handling family finances	☐	☐	☐	☐	☐	☐
3. Matters of recreation	☐	☐	☐	☐	☐	☐
4. Demonstrations of affection	☐	☐	☐	☐	☐	☐
5. Friends	☐	☐	☐	☐	☐	☐
6. Sex relations	☐	☐	☐	☐	☐	☐
7. Conventionality (right, good, or proper conduct)	☐	☐	☐	☐	☐	☐
8. Philosophy of life	☐	☐	☐	☐	☐	☐
9. Ways of dealing with in-laws	☐	☐	☐	☐	☐	☐

10. When disagreements arise, they usually result in:

    Husband giving in ☐   Wife giving in ☐   Agreement by mutual give and take ☐

11. Do you and your mate engage in outside interests together?

    All of them ☐   Some of them ☐   Very few of them ☐   None of them ☐

12. In leisure time do you generally prefer:

    To be "on the go" ☐   To stay at home ☐

    Does your mate generally prefer:

    To be "on the go" ☐   To stay at home ☐

13. Do you ever wish you had not married?

    Frequently ☐   Occasionally ☐   Rarely ☐   Never ☐

14. If you had your life to live over, do you think you would:

    Marry the same person ☐   Marry a different person ☐   Not marry at all ☐

15. Do you confide in your mate?

    Almost never ☐   Rarely ☐   In most things ☐   In everything ☐

For scoring instructions, see the next page.

SCORING INSTRUCTIONS: Score all items and add to compute your total score.
Total scores should range from 2 to 158.

SCORING KEY

1. Check the dot on the scale below which best describes the degree of happiness, everything considered, of your present marriage. The middle point, "Happy," represents the degree of happiness which most people get from marriage, and the scale gradually ranges on one side to those few who are very unhappy in marriage, and on the other, to those few who experience extreme joy or felicity in marriage.

0	2	7	15	20	25	35
•	•	•	•	•	•	•

Very unhappy   Happy   Perfectly happy

State the approximate extent of agreement or disagreement between you and your mate on the following items. Please respond to each item.

	Always agree	Almost always agree	Occasionally disagree	Frequently disagree	Almost always disagree	Always disagree
2. Handling family finances	5	4	3	2	1	0
3. Matters of recreation	5	4	3	2	1	0
4. Demonstrations of affection	8	6	4	2	1	0
5. Friends	5	4	3	2	1	0
6. Sex relations	15	12	9	4	1	0
7. Conventionality (right, good, or proper conduct)	5	4	3	2	1	0
8. Philosophy of life	5	4	3	2	1	0
9. Ways of dealing with in-laws	5	4	3	2	1	0

10. When disagreements arise, they usually result in:

    Husband giving in _0_   Wife giving in _2_   Agreement by mutual give and take _10_

11. Do you and your mate engage in outside interests together?

    All of them _10_   Some of them _8_   Very few of them _3_   None of them _0_

12. In leisure time do you generally prefer:

    To be "on the go" ☐   To stay at home ☐

    Does your mate generally prefer:

    To be "on the go" ☐   To stay at home ☐

    Both "stay at home" = 10
    Both "on the go" = 3
    Disagreement = 2

13. Do you ever wish you had not married?

    Frequently _0_   Occasionally _3_   Rarely _8_   Never _15_

14. If you had your life to live over, do you think you would:

    Marry the same person _15_   Marry a different person _0_   Not marry at all _1_

15. Do you confide in your mate?

    Almost never _0_   Rarely _2_   In most things _10_   In everything _10_

MARITAL ADJUSTMENT TEST TOTAL SCORE _____

QUESTIONNAIRE 2: COMMUNICATION PATTERNS QUESTIONNAIRE

Partner 1

Please indicate the extent to which you agree or disagree with the following statements concerning the disagreements and conflicts that arise between you and your partner. We are interested in how you and your partner typically deal with problems in your relationship. Please rate each item on a scale of 1 (= very unlikely) to 9 (= very likely).

WHEN SOME PROBLEM IN THE RELATIONSHIP ARISES:

	Very unlikely								**Very likely**
1. Both members avoid discussing the problem.	1	2	3	4	5	6	7	8	9
*2. Both members try to discuss the problem.	1	2	3	4	5	6	7	8	9
3. My partner tries to start a discussion while I try to avoid a discussion.	1	2	3	4	5	6	7	8	9
4. I try to start a discussion while my partner tries to avoid a discussion.	1	2	3	4	5	6	7	8	9

DURING A DISCUSSION OF A RELATIONSHIP PROBLEM:

	Very unlikely								**Very likely**
1. Both members blame, accuse, and criticize each other.	1	2	3	4	5	6	7	8	9
*2. Both members express their feelings with each other.	1	2	3	4	5	6	7	8	9
3. Both members threaten each other with negative consequences.	1	2	3	4	5	6	7	8	9
*4. Both members suggest possible solutions and compromises.	1	2	3	4	5	6	7	8	9
5. My partner nags and demands while I withdraw, become silent, or refuse to discuss the matter further.	1	2	3	4	5	6	7	8	9
6. I nag and demand while my partner withdraws, becomes silent, or refuses to discuss the matter further.	1	2	3	4	5	6	7	8	9

Note. From *Communication Patterns Questionnaire* by A. Christensen and M. Sullaway, 1984, Los Angeles: Unpublished manuscript, University of California. Copyright 1984 by the authors. Adapted by permission.

		Very unlikely								Very likely
7. My partner criticizes while I defend myself.		1	2	3	4	5	6	7	8	9
8. I criticize while my partner defends himself/herself.		1	2	3	4	5	6	7	8	9
9. My partner threatens negative consequences and I give in or back down.		1	2	3	4	5	6	7	8	9
10. I threaten negative consequences and my partner gives in or backs down.		1	2	3	4	5	6	7	8	9
11. My partner calls me names, swears at me or attacks my character.		1	2	3	4	5	6	7	8	9
12. I call my partner names, swear at him/her, or attack his/her character.		1	2	3	4	5	6	7	8	9

AFTER A DISCUSSION OF A RELATIONSHIP PROBLEM:

		Very unlikely								Very likely
*1. Both feel each other has understood his/her position.		1	2	3	4	5	6	7	8	9
2. Both withdraw from each other after the discussion.		1	2	3	4	5	6	7	8	9
*3. Both feel that the problem has been solved.		1	2	3	4	5	6	7	8	9
4. After the discussion, both try to be especially nice to the other.		1	2	3	4	5	6	7	8	9
5. My partner tries to be especially nice, acts as if things are back to normal, while I act distant.		1	2	3	4	5	6	7	8	9
6. I try to be especially nice, act as if things are back to normal, while my partner acts distant.		1	2	3	4	5	6	7	8	9

SCORING INSTRUCTIONS: For our purposes, add your ratings on those items with an asterisk (*) before the item number. This is your Mutual Constructive Communication Score.

MUTUAL CONSTRUCTIVE COMMUNICATION SCORE _____

Partner 2

Please indicate the extent to which you agree or disagree with the following statements concerning the disagreements and conflicts that arise between you and your partner. We are interested in how you and your partner typically deal with problems in your relationship. Please rate each item on a scale of 1 (= very unlikely) to 9 (= very likely).

WHEN SOME PROBLEM IN THE RELATIONSHIP ARISES:

	Very unlikely								**Very likely**
1. Both members avoid discussing the problem.	1	2	3	4	5	6	7	8	9
*2. Both members try to discuss the problem.	1	2	3	4	5	6	7	8	9
3. My partner tries to start a discussion while I try to avoid a discussion.	1	2	3	4	5	6	7	8	9
4. I try to start a discussion while my partner tries to avoid a discussion.	1	2	3	4	5	6	7	8	9

DURING A DISCUSSION OF A RELATIONSHIP PROBLEM:

	Very unlikely								**Very likely**
1. Both members blame, accuse, and criticize each other.	1	2	3	4	5	6	7	8	9
*2. Both members express their feelings with each other.	1	2	3	4	5	6	7	8	9
3. Both members threaten each other with negative consequences.	1	2	3	4	5	6	7	8	9
*4. Both members suggest possible solutions and compromises.	1	2	3	4	5	6	7	8	9
5. My partner nags and demands while I withdraw, become silent, or refuse to discuss the matter further.	1	2	3	4	5	6	7	8	9
6. I nag and demand while my partner withdraws, becomes silent, or refuses to discuss the matter further.	1	2	3	4	5	6	7	8	9

		Very **unlikely**								**Very** **likely**
7.	My partner criticizes while I defend myself.	1	2	3	4	5	6	7	8	9
8.	I criticize while my partner defends himself/herself.	1	2	3	4	5	6	7	8	9
9.	My partner threatens negative consequences and I give in or back down.	1	2	3	4	5	6	7	8	9
10.	I threaten negative consequences and my partner gives in or backs down.	1	2	3	4	5	6	7	8	9
11.	My partner calls me names, swears at me or attacks my character.	1	2	3	4	5	6	7	8	9
12.	I call my partner names, swear at him/her, or attack his/her character.	1	2	3	4	5	6	7	8	9

AFTER A DISCUSSION OF A RELATIONSHIP PROBLEM:

		Very **unlikely**								**Very** **likely**
*1.	Both feel each other has understood his/her position.	1	2	3	4	5	6	7	8	9
2.	Both withdraw from each other after the discussion.	1	2	3	4	5	6	7	8	9
*3.	Both feel that the problem has been solved.	1	2	3	4	5	6	7	8	9
4.	After the discussion, both try to be especially nice to the other.	1	2	3	4	5	6	7	8	9
5.	My partner tries to be especially nice, acts as if things are back to normal, while I act distant.	1	2	3	4	5	6	7	8	9
6.	I try to be especially nice, act as if things are back to normal, while my partner acts distant.	1	2	3	4	5	6	7	8	9

SCORING INSTRUCTIONS: For our purposes, add your ratings on those items with an asterisk (*) before the item number. This is your Mutual Constructive Communication Score.

MUTUAL CONSTRUCTIVE COMMUNICATION SCORE _____

QUESTIONNAIRE 3: INVENTORY OF RELATIONSHIP PROBLEMS

Partner 1

All couples experience some difficulties in marriage, even if they are only very minor ones. Listed below are a number of issues that might be difficulties in your marriage. For each issue, check one column to indicate how much it is a source of difficulty or disagreement for you and your partner.

	Not a problem	Minor problem	Somewhat of a problem	Major problem
a. Children	☐	☐	☐	☐
b. Religion	☐	☐	☐	☐
c. In-laws, parents, relatives	☐	☐	☐	☐
d. Recreation and leisure time	☐	☐	☐	☐
e. Communication	☐	☐	☐	☐
f. Household management	☐	☐	☐	☐
g. Showing affection	☐	☐	☐	☐
h. Making decisions	☐	☐	☐	☐
i. Friends	☐	☐	☐	☐
j. Unrealistic expectations	☐	☐	☐	☐
k. Money	☐	☐	☐	☐
l. Sex	☐	☐	☐	☐
m. Jealousy	☐	☐	☐	☐
n. Solving problems	☐	☐	☐	☐
o. Trust	☐	☐	☐	☐
p. Independence	☐	☐	☐	☐
q. Drugs and alcohol	☐	☐	☐	☐
r. Career decisions	☐	☐	☐	☐
s. Amount of time spent together	☐	☐	☐	☐

Please add any other difficulties:

	Not a problem	Minor problem	Somewhat of a problem	Major problem
t. _____	☐	☐	☐	☐
u. _____	☐	☐	☐	☐

SCORING INSTRUCTIONS: The primary purpose of this questionnaire is to identify topics that are areas of difficulty in your relationship. This is particularly important for the communication exercises in chapters 6 through 8. Any item that you checked as being somewhat of a problem or a major problem should be considered a "hot" topic. We suggest that you avoid these topics until you are instructed to work on them in chapter 8.

Partner 2

All couples experience some difficulties in marriage, even if they are only very minor ones. Listed below are a number of issues that might be difficulties in your marriage. For each issue, check one column to indicate how much it is a source of difficulty or disagreement for you and your partner.

	Not a problem	Minor problem	Somewhat of a problem	Major problem
a. Children	☐	☐	☐	☐
b. Religion	☐	☐	☐	☐
c. In-laws, parents, relatives	☐	☐	☐	☐
d. Recreation and leisure time	☐	☐	☐	☐
e. Communication	☐	☐	☐	☐
f. Household management	☐	☐	☐	☐
g. Showing affection	☐	☐	☐	☐
h. Making decisions	☐	☐	☐	☐
i. Friends	☐	☐	☐	☐
j. Unrealistic expectations	☐	☐	☐	☐
k. Money	☐	☐	☐	☐
l. Sex	☐	☐	☐	☐
m. Jealousy	☐	☐	☐	☐
n. Solving problems	☐	☐	☐	☐
o. Trust	☐	☐	☐	☐
p. Independence	☐	☐	☐	☐
q. Drugs and alcohol	☐	☐	☐	☐
r. Career decisions	☐	☐	☐	☐
s. Amount of time spent together	☐	☐	☐	☐

Please add any other difficulties:

t. _____	☐	☐	☐	☐
u. _____	☐	☐	☐	☐

SCORING INSTRUCTIONS: The primary purpose of this questionnaire is to identify topics that are areas of difficulty in your relationship. This is particularly important for the communication exercises in chapters 6 through 8. Any item that you checked as being somewhat of a problem or a major problem should be considered a "hot" topic. We suggest that you avoid these topics until you are instructed to work on them in chapter 8.

QUESTIONNAIRE 4: RELATIONSHIP BELIEF INVENTORY

Partner 1

The statements below describe ways in which a person might feel about a relationship with another person. Please mark the space next to each statement according to how strongly you believe that it is true or false for you. Please mark every one. Write in 5, 4, 3, 2, 1, or 0 to stand for the following answers.

5   I *strongly* believe that the statement is *true*.
4   I believe that the statement is *true*.
3   I believe that the statement is *probably true*, or more true than false.
2   I believe that the statement is *probably false*, or more false than true.
1   I believe that the statement is *false*.
0   I *strongly* believe that the statement is *false*.

_____   1.   If your partner expresses disagreement with your ideas, s/he probably does not think highly of you.
_____   2.   I do not expect my partner to sense all my moods.
_____   3.   Damages done early in a relationship probably cannot be reversed.
_____   4.   I get upset if I think I have not completely satisfied my partner sexually.
_____   5.   Men and women have the same basic emotional needs.
_____   6.   I cannot accept it when my partner disagrees with me.
_____   7.   If I have to tell my partner that something is important to me, it does not mean that s/he is insensitive to me.
_____   8.   My partner does not seem capable of behaving other than s/he does now.
_____   9.   If I'm not in the mood for sex when my partner is, I don't get upset about it.
_____   10. Misunderstandings between partners generally are due to inborn differences in psychological makeups of men and women.
_____   11. I take it as a personal insult when my partner disagrees with an important idea of mine.
_____   12. I get very upset if my partner does not recognize how I am feeling and I have to tell him/her.
_____   13. A partner can learn to become more responsive to his/her partner's needs.
_____   14. A good sexual partner can get himself/herself aroused for sex whenever necessary.
_____   15. Men and women probably will never understand the opposite sex very well.
_____   16. I like it when my partner presents views different from mine.
_____   17. People who have a close relationship can sense each other's needs as if they could read each other's minds.
_____   18. Just because my partner has acted in ways that upset me does not mean that s/he will do so in the future.
_____   19. If I cannot perform well sexually whenever my partner is in the mood, I would consider that I have a problem.
_____   20. Men and women need the same basic things out of a relationship.
_____   21. I get very upset when my partner and I cannot see things the same way.
_____   22. It is important to me for my partner to anticipate my needs by sensing changes in my moods.

Note. Information about the Relationship Belief Inventory appears in "Cognition and Relationship Maladjustment: Development of a Measure of Dysfunctional Relationship Beliefs" by R. J. Eidelson and N. Epstein, 1982, *Journal of Consulting and Clinical Psychology, 50*, 715–720. Reprinted by permission of the authors.

_____ 23. A partner who hurts you badly once probably will hurt you again.

_____ 24. I can feel OK about my lovemaking even if my partner does not achieve orgasm.

_____ 25. Biological differences between men and women are not major sources of couples' problems.

_____ 26. I cannot tolerate it when my partner argues with me.

_____ 27. A partner should know what you are thinking or feeling without you having to tell.

_____ 28. If my partner wants to change, I believe that s/he can do it.

_____ 29. If my sexual partner does not get satisfied completely, it does not mean that I have failed.

_____ 30. One of the major causes of marital problems is men and women have different emotional needs.

_____ 31. When my partner and I disagree, I feel like our relationship is falling apart.

_____ 32. People who love each other know exactly what each other's thoughts are without a word ever being said.

_____ 33. If you don't like the way a relationship is going, you can make it better.

_____ 34. Some difficulties in my sexual performance do not mean personal failure to me.

_____ 35. You can't really understand someone of the opposite sex.

_____ 36. I do not doubt my partner's feelings for me when we argue.

_____ 37. If you have to ask your partner for something, it shows that s/he was not "tuned into" your needs.

_____ 38. I do not expect my partner to be able to change.

_____ 39. When I do not seem to be performing well sexually, I get upset.

_____ 40. Men and women will always be mysteries to each other.

SCORING INSTRUCTIONS: Add scores for each group of items (subscale) to determine a subscale score. Subscale scores vary from 0 to 40. To obtain a total score, add the scores for each subscale.

Some items are positive, and others are negative. When you add subscale scores, assign positive items the same score as your actual response. Thus, a response of "5" is scored as "5," a response of "4" is scored as "4," and so on. However, when scoring negatively keyed items, the scoring must be reversed. Thus, a response of "5" is scored as "0," a response of "4" is scored as "1," and so on, as shown in the chart.

Response		Scoring of negatively keyed items
5	=	0
4	=	1
3	=	2
2	=	3
1	=	4
0	=	5

Subscale	Positive Items (a)	Negative Items (b)
Disagreement is destructive (D)	1, 6, 11, 21, 26, 31	16, 36
Mindreading is expected (M)	12, 17, 22, 27, 32, 37	2, 7
Partners cannot change (C)	3, 8, 23, 38	13, 18, 28, 33
Sexual perfectionism (S)	4, 14, 19, 39	9, 24, 29, 34
The sexes are different (MF)	10, 15, 30, 35, 40	5, 20, 25

RELATIONSHIP BELIEF INVENTORY SUBSCALE SCORES

Disagreement is destructive (D)	_____
Mindreading is expected (M)	_____
Partners cannot change (C)	_____
Sexual perfectionism (S)	_____
The sexes are different (MF)	_____

RELATIONSHIP BELIEF INVENTORY TOTAL SCORE _____

Partner 2

The statements below describe ways in which a person might feel about a relationship with another person. Please mark the space next to each statement according to how strongly you believe that it is true or false for you. Please mark every one. Write in 5, 4, 3, 2, 1, or 0 to stand for the following answers.

5   I *strongly* believe that the statement is *true.*
4   I believe that the statement is *true.*
3   I believe that the statement is *probably true,* or more true than false.
2   I believe that the statement is *probably false,* or more false than true.
1   I believe that the statement is *false.*
0   I *strongly* believe that the statement is *false.*

_____ 1. If your partner expresses disagreement with your ideas, s/he probably does not think highly of you.
_____ 2. I do not expect my partner to sense all my moods.
_____ 3. Damages done early in a relationship probably cannot be reversed.
_____ 4. I get upset if I think I have not completely satisfied my partner sexually.
_____ 5. Men and women have the same basic emotional needs.
_____ 6. I cannot accept it when my partner disagrees with me.
_____ 7. If I have to tell my partner that something is important to me, it does not mean that s/he is insensitive to me.
_____ 8. My partner does not seem capable of behaving other than s/he does now.
_____ 9. If I'm not in the mood for sex when my partner is, I don't get upset about it.
_____ 10. Misunderstandings between partners generally are due to inborn differences in psychological makeups of men and women.
_____ 11. I take it as a personal insult when my partner disagrees with an important idea of mine.
_____ 12. I get very upset if my partner does not recognize how I am feeling and I have to tell him/her.
_____ 13. A partner can learn to become more responsive to his/her partner's needs.
_____ 14. A good sexual partner can get himself/herself aroused for sex whenever necessary.
_____ 15. Men and women probably will never understand the opposite sex very well.
_____ 16. I like it when my partner presents views different from mine.
_____ 17. People who have a close relationship can sense each other's needs as if they could read each other's minds.
_____ 18. Just because my partner has acted in ways that upset me does not mean that s/he will do so in the future.
_____ 19. If I cannot perform well sexually whenever my partner is in the mood, I would consider that I have a problem.
_____ 20. Men and women need the same basic things out of a relationship.
_____ 21. I get very upset when my partner and I cannot see things the same way.
_____ 22. It is important to me for my partner to anticipate my needs by sensing changes in my moods.

_____ 23. A partner who hurts you badly once probably will hurt you again.

_____ 24. I can feel OK about my lovemaking even if my partner does not achieve orgasm.

_____ 25. Biological differences between men and women are not major sources of couples' problems.

_____ 26. I cannot tolerate it when my partner argues with me.

_____ 27. A partner should know what you are thinking or feeling without you having to tell.

_____ 28. If my partner wants to change, I believe that s/he can do it.

_____ 29. If my sexual partner does not get satisfied completely, it does not mean that I have failed.

_____ 30. One of the major causes of marital problems is men and women have different emotional needs.

_____ 31. When my partner and I disagree, I feel like our relationship is falling apart.

_____ 32. People who love each other know exactly what each other's thoughts are without a word ever being said.

_____ 33. If you don't like the way a relationship is going, you can make it better.

_____ 34. Some difficulties in my sexual performance do not mean personal failure to me.

_____ 35. You can't really understand someone of the opposite sex.

_____ 36. I do not doubt my partner's feelings for me when we argue.

_____ 37. If you have to ask your partner for something, it shows that s/he was not "tuned into" your needs.

_____ 38. I do not expect my partner to be able to change.

_____ 39. When I do not seem to be performing well sexually, I get upset.

_____ 40. Men and women will always be mysteries to each other.

SCORING INSTRUCTIONS: Add scores for each group of items (subscale) to determine a subscale score. Subscale scores vary from 0 to 40. To obtain a total score, add the scores for each subscale.

Some items are positive, and others are negative. When you add subscale scores, assign positive items the same score as your actual response. Thus, a response of "5" is scored as "5," a response of "4" is scored as "4," and so on. However, when scoring negatively keyed items, the scoring must be reversed. Thus, a response of "5" is scored as "0," a response of "4" is scored as "1," and so on, as shown in the chart.

Response		**Scoring of negatively keyed items**
5	=	0
4	=	1
3	=	2
2	=	3
1	=	4
0	=	5

Subscale	**Positive Items (a)**	**Negative Items (b)**
Disagreement is destructive (D)	1, 6, 11, 21, 26, 31	16, 36
Mindreading is expected (M)	12, 17, 22, 27, 32, 37	2, 7
Partners cannot change (C)	3, 8, 23, 38	13, 18, 28, 33
Sexual perfectionism (S)	4, 14, 19, 39	9, 24, 29, 34
The sexes are different (MF)	10, 15, 30, 35, 40	5, 20, 25

RELATIONSHIP BELIEF INVENTORY SUBSCALE SCORES

Disagreement is destructive (D)	_____
Mindreading is expected (M)	_____
Partners cannot change (C)	_____
Sexual perfectionism (S)	_____
The sexes are different (MF)	_____

RELATIONSHIP BELIEF INVENTORY TOTAL SCORE _____

QUESTIONNAIRE 5: THE RELATIONSHIP ATTRIBUTION MEASURE

Partner 1

This questionnaire describes several things that your partner might do. Imagine your partner performing each behavior and then read the statements that follow it. Please circle the number that indicates how much you agree or disagree with each statement, using the rating scale below:

1	2	3	4	5	6
Disagree strongly	**Disagree**	**Disagree somewhat**	**Agree somewhat**	**Agree**	**Agree strongly**

YOUR PARTNER CRITICIZES SOMETHING YOU SAY:

1 2 3 4 5 6   My partner's behavior was due to something about him/her (e.g., the type of person he/she is, the mood he/she was in).

1 2 3 4 5 6   The reason my partner criticized me is *not* likely to change.

1 2 3 4 5 6   The reason my partner criticized me is something that affects other areas of our relationship.

1 2 3 4 5 6   My partner criticized me on purpose rather than unintentionally.

1 2 3 4 5 6   My partner's behavior was motivated by selfish rather than *un*selfish concerns.

1 2 3 4 5 6   My partner deserves to be blamed for criticizing me.

YOUR PARTNER BEGINS TO SPEND LESS TIME WITH YOU:

1 2 3 4 5 6   The reason my partner began to spend less time with me is *not* likely to change.

1 2 3 4 5 6   My partner's behavior was due to something about him/her (e.g., the type of person he/she is, the mood he/she was in).

1 2 3 4 5 6   The reason my partner began spending less time with me is something that affects other areas of our relationship.

1 2 3 4 5 6   My partner's behavior was motivated by selfish rather than *un*selfish concerns.

1 2 3 4 5 6   My partner deserves to be blamed for what he/she did.

1 2 3 4 5 6   My partner spent less time with me on purpose rather than unintentionally.

Note. From "Assessing Attributions in Marriage: The Relationship Attribution Measure" by F. D. Fincham and T. N. Bradbury, 1992, *Journal of Personality and Social Psychology, 62,* p. 468. Copyright 1992 by the American Psychological Association. Adapted by permission.

YOUR PARTNER DOES NOT PAY ATTENTION TO WHAT YOU ARE SAYING:

1 2 3 4 5 6   The reason my partner did not pay attention is something that affects other areas of our relationship.

1 2 3 4 5 6   My partner's behavior was due to something about him/her (e.g., the type of person he/she is, the mood he/she was in).

1 2 3 4 5 6   The reason my partner did not pay attention is *not* likely to change.

1 2 3 4 5 6   My partner's behavior was motivated by selfish rather than *un*selfish concerns.

1 2 3 4 5 6   My partner did not pay attention on purpose rather than unintentionally.

1 2 3 4 5 6   My partner deserves to be blamed for what he/she did.

YOUR PARTNER IS COOL AND DISTANT:

1 2 3 4 5 6   The reason my partner was distant is *not* likely to change.

1 2 3 4 5 6   The reason my partner was distant is something that affects other areas of our relationship.

1 2 3 4 5 6   My partner's behavior was due to something about him/her (e.g., the type of person he/she is, the mood he/she was in).

1 2 3 4 5 6   My partner was distant on purpose rather than unintentionally.

1 2 3 4 5 6   My partner deserves to be blamed for what he/she did.

1 2 3 4 5 6   My partner's behavior was motivated by selfish rather than *un*selfish concerns.

SCORING INSTRUCTIONS: Obtain a total score by adding the scores for all items.

RELATIONSHIP ATTRIBUTION MEASURE TOTAL SCORE _____

Partner 2

This questionnaire describes several things that your partner might do. Imagine your partner performing each behavior and then read the statements that follow it. Please circle the number that indicates how much you agree or disagree with each statement, using the rating scale below:

1	2	3	4	5	6
Disagree strongly	**Disagree**	**Disagree somewhat**	**Agree somewhat**	**Agree**	**Agree strongly**

YOUR PARTNER CRITICIZES SOMETHING YOU SAY:

1 2 3 4 5 6   My partner's behavior was due to something about him/her (e.g., the type of person he/she is, the mood he/she was in).

1 2 3 4 5 6   The reason my partner criticized me is *not* likely to change.

1 2 3 4 5 6   The reason my partner criticized me is something that affects other areas of our relationship.

1 2 3 4 5 6   My partner criticized me on purpose rather than unintentionally.

1 2 3 4 5 6   My partner's behavior was motivated by selfish rather than *un*selfish concerns.

1 2 3 4 5 6   My partner deserves to be blamed for criticizing me.

YOUR PARTNER BEGINS TO SPEND LESS TIME WITH YOU:

1 2 3 4 5 6   The reason my partner began to spend less time with me is *not* likely to change.

1 2 3 4 5 6   My partner's behavior was due to something about him/her (e.g., the type of person he/she is, the mood he/she was in).

1 2 3 4 5 6   The reason my partner began spending less time with me is something that affects other areas of our relationship.

1 2 3 4 5 6   My partner's behavior was motivated by selfish rather than *un*selfish concerns.

1 2 3 4 5 6   My partner deserves to be blamed for what he/she did.

1 2 3 4 5 6   My partner spent less time with me on purpose rather than unintentionally.

YOUR PARTNER DOES NOT PAY ATTENTION TO WHAT YOU ARE SAYING:

1 2 3 4 5 6   The reason my partner did not pay attention is something that affects other areas of our relationship.

1 2 3 4 5 6   My partner's behavior was due to something about him/her (e.g., the type of person he/she is, the mood he/she was in).

1 2 3 4 5 6   The reason my partner did not pay attention is *not* likely to change.

1 2 3 4 5 6   My partner's behavior was motivated by selfish rather than *un*selfish concerns.

1 2 3 4 5 6   My partner did not pay attention on purpose rather than unintentionally.

1 2 3 4 5 6   My partner deserves to be blamed for what he/she did.

YOUR PARTNER IS COOL AND DISTANT:

1 2 3 4 5 6   The reason my partner was distant is *not* likely to change.

1 2 3 4 5 6   The reason my partner was distant is something that affects other areas of our relationship.

1 2 3 4 5 6   My partner's behavior was due to something about him/her (e.g., the type of person he/she is, the mood he/she was in).

1 2 3 4 5 6   My partner was distant on purpose rather than unintentionally.

1 2 3 4 5 6   My partner deserves to be blamed for what he/she did.

1 2 3 4 5 6   My partner's behavior was motivated by selfish rather than *un*selfish concerns.

SCORING INSTRUCTIONS: Obtain a total score by adding the scores for all items.

RELATIONSHIP ATTRIBUTION MEASURE TOTAL SCORE _____

QUESTIONNAIRE 6: THE POSITIVE AND NEGATIVE AFFECT SCHEDULE

Partner 1

This scale consists of a number of words that describe different feelings and emotions. Read each item and then mark the appropriate answer in the space next to that word. Indicate to what extent you generally feel this way, that is, how you feel on the average. Use the following scale to record your answers.

1 **Very slightly**	2 **A little**	3 **Moderately**	4 **Quite a bit**	5 **Extremely**

_____ interested		_____ irritable
_____ distressed		_____ alert
_____ excited		_____ ashamed
_____ upset		_____ inspired
_____ strong		_____ nervous
_____ guilty		_____ determined
_____ scared		_____ attentive
_____ hostile		_____ jittery
_____ enthusiastic		_____ active
_____ proud		_____ afraid

SCORING INSTRUCTIONS: Add your scores on the following items to determine your score on the Positive Affect Scale and the Negative Affect Scale.

_____ interested	_____ distressed
_____ excited	_____ upset
_____ strong	_____ guilty
_____ enthusiastic	_____ scared
_____ proud	_____ hostile
_____ alert	_____ irritable
_____ inspired	_____ ashamed
_____ determined	_____ nervous
_____ attentive	_____ jittery
_____ active	_____ afraid
_____ = POSITIVE AFFECT SCALE SCORE	_____ = NEGATIVE AFFECT SCALE SCORE

Note. From "Development and Validation of Brief Measures of Positive and Negative Affect" by D. Watson, L. A. Clark, and A. Tellegen, 1988, *Journal of Personality and Social Psychology, 54,* p. 1070. Copyright 1988 by the American Psychological Association. Reprinted by permission.

Partner 2

This scale consists of a number of words that describe different feelings and emotions. Read each item and then mark the appropriate answer in the space next to that word. Indicate to what extent you generally feel this way, that is, how you feel on the average. Use the following scale to record your answers.

1 **Very slightly**	2 **A little**	3 **Moderately**	4 **Quite a bit**	5 **Extremely**

_____ interested		_____ irritable
_____ distressed		_____ alert
_____ excited		_____ ashamed
_____ upset		_____ inspired
_____ strong		_____ nervous
_____ guilty		_____ determined
_____ scared		_____ attentive
_____ hostile		_____ jittery
_____ enthusiastic		_____ active
_____ proud		_____ afraid

SCORING INSTRUCTIONS: Add your scores on the following items to determine your score on the Positive Affect Scale and the Negative Affect Scale.

_____ interested	_____ distressed
_____ excited	_____ upset
_____ strong	_____ guilty
_____ enthusiastic	_____ scared
_____ proud	_____ hostile
_____ alert	_____ irritable
_____ inspired	_____ ashamed
_____ determined	_____ nervous
_____ attentive	_____ jittery
_____ active	_____ afraid
_____ = POSITIVE AFFECT SCALE SCORE	_____ = NEGATIVE AFFECT SCALE SCORE

QUESTIONNAIRE 7: MODIFIED POSITIVE FEELINGS QUESTIONNAIRE

Partner 1: Assessment of Feeling

Below is a list of questions about various feelings between people in a relationship. Answer each one of them in terms of how you generally feel about your partner, taking into account the last few months. The rating you choose should reflect how you actually feel, not how you think you should feel or would like to feel.

Please answer each question by choosing the best number to show how you have generally been feeling in the past few months. Choose only one number for each question.

1	2	3	4	5	6	7
Extremely negative	**Quite negative**	**Slightly negative**	**Neutral**	**Slightly positive**	**Quite positive**	**Extremely positive**

1. How do you feel about your partner as a friend to you? 1 2 3 4 5 6 7
2. How do you feel about the future of your relationship? 1 2 3 4 5 6 7
3. How do you feel about having a relationship with your partner? 1 2 3 4 5 6 7
4. How do you feel about your partner's ability to put you in a good mood so that you can laugh and smile? 1 2 3 4 5 6 7
5. How do you feel about your partner's ability to handle stress? 1 2 3 4 5 6 7
6. How do you feel about the degree to which your partner understands you? 1 2 3 4 5 6 7
7. How do you feel about your partner's honesty? 1 2 3 4 5 6 7
8. How do you feel about the degree to which you can trust your partner? 1 2 3 4 5 6 7

The following nine items are in the form of statements rather than questions. However, please complete them in the same manner, remembering to base your responses on how you generally feel about your partner, taking into account the last few months.

1. Touching my partner makes me feel 1 2 3 4 5 6 7
2. Being alone with my partner makes me feel 1 2 3 4 5 6 7
3. Having sexual relations with my partner makes me feel 1 2 3 4 5 6 7
4. Talking and communicating with my partner makes me feel 1 2 3 4 5 6 7
5. My partner's encouragement of my individual growth makes me feel 1 2 3 4 5 6 7
6. My partner's physical appearance makes me feel 1 2 3 4 5 6 7
7. Seeking comfort from my partner makes me feel 1 2 3 4 5 6 7
8. Kissing my partner makes me feel 1 2 3 4 5 6 7
9. Sitting or lying close to my partner makes me feel 1 2 3 4 5 6 7

SCORING INSTRUCTIONS: Obtain a total score by adding the scores for all items.

POSITIVE FEELINGS QUESTIONNAIRE TOTAL SCORE _____

Note. Information about the Positive Feelings Questionnaire appears in "Assessment of Positive Feelings Toward Spouse" by K. D. O'Leary, F. D. Fincham, and H. Turkewitz, 1983, *Journal of Consulting and Clinical Psychology, 51,* 949–951. Adapted by permission of the authors.

Partner 2: Assessment of Feeling

Below is a list of questions about various feelings between people in a relationship. Answer each one of them in terms of how you generally *feel about your partner, taking into account the last few months. The rating you choose should reflect how you* actually *feel, not how you think you should feel or would like to feel.*

Please answer each question by choosing the best number to show how you have generally been feeling in the past few months. Choose only one number *for each question.*

1	2	3	4	5	6	7
Extremely negative	**Quite negative**	**Slightly negative**	**Neutral**	**Slightly positive**	**Quite positive**	**Extremely positive**

1. How do you feel about your partner as a friend to you?   1 2 3 4 5 6 7
2. How do you feel about the future of your relationship?   1 2 3 4 5 6 7
3. How do you feel about having a relationship with your partner?   1 2 3 4 5 6 7
4. How do you feel about your partner's ability to put you in a good mood so that you can laugh and smile?   1 2 3 4 5 6 7
5. How do you feel about your partner's ability to handle stress?   1 2 3 4 5 6 7
6. How do you feel about the degree to which your partner understands you?   1 2 3 4 5 6 7
7. How do you feel about your partner's honesty?   1 2 3 4 5 6 7
8. How do you feel about the degree to which you can trust your partner?   1 2 3 4 5 6 7

The following nine items are in the form of statements rather than questions. However, please complete them in the same manner, remembering to base your responses on how you generally *feel about your partner, taking into account the last few months.*

1. Touching my partner makes me feel   1 2 3 4 5 6 7
2. Being alone with my partner makes me feel   1 2 3 4 5 6 7
3. Having sexual relations with my partner makes me feel   1 2 3 4 5 6 7
4. Talking and communicating with my partner makes me feel   1 2 3 4 5 6 7
5. My partner's encouragement of my individual growth makes me feel   1 2 3 4 5 6 7
6. My partner's physical appearance makes me feel   1 2 3 4 5 6 7
7. Seeking comfort from my partner makes me feel   1 2 3 4 5 6 7
8. Kissing my partner makes me feel   1 2 3 4 5 6 7
9. Sitting or lying close to my partner makes me feel   1 2 3 4 5 6 7

SCORING INSTRUCTIONS: Obtain a total score by adding the scores for all items.

POSITIVE FEELINGS QUESTIONNAIRE TOTAL SCORE _____

Relationship Satisfaction

An important factor in any contemporary relationship is the satisfaction felt by each partner. The degree of satisfaction you feel in the relationship can influence the way you encode and decode messages, and it is a critical part of the context in which your communication takes place. For example, a dissatisfied husband will tend to notice negative events in the relationship and to interpret his wife's communications (e.g., "Can I get you a drink?") in a negative manner (e.g., "She is only being nice to me because she wants me to do something"), whereas a husband who is satisfied is likely to think, "She really cares about me." Relationship satisfaction, then, can be seen as part of the communication background that influences interaction between partners.

The Marital Adjustment Test (Questionnaire 1) is a widely-used measure of marital satisfaction. There is a great deal of research showing that couples who seek marital counseling obtain lower scores on this test than those who do not seek counseling. Scores can range from 2 to 158. A score of 100 on this test is usually used to distinguish satisfied spouses (scores greater than 100) from dissatisfied ones (scores less than 100). There is always a margin of error in such tests, and scores just below 100 do not necessarily indicate dissatisfaction. However, if you scored below 90, you should seriously look at ways to improve your satisfaction in your relationship. If things have not changed for you after you've worked through this book, we strongly recommend that you seek professional help.

What if you scored well above 100 on this test? For extremely high scorers—people above 130—there probably is not much room to increase your relationship satisfaction. However, this does not mean that you should stop reading now. Because it takes two to make a satisfactory relationship, we recommend that you consider both your score and your partner's. If both of you scored above 130, you and your partner are in a mutually satisfying relationship, and the benefits you will obtain from this book are likely to be limited. You may still choose to work through it because you recognize the value of preventive maintenance: A good relationship can change for the worse if it is taken for granted.

Communication Style

Typically in close relationships, partners develop consistent patterns of relating to each other. These patterns, and the behaviors they consist of, influence the way both partners think and feel about the relationship. For example, if a husband avoids discussing a problem with his wife and this in turn makes her withdraw, these behaviors can lead to negative thoughts about the relationship or feelings of resentment or anger. But suppose the husband avoids discussing problems because he fears that his wife will blame him, or the wife withdraws because she feels that the problem is her fault. In this case, the husband's avoidance and the wife's withdrawal represent behaviors that can easily be encoded or decoded erroneously. Through the assessment of communication style, you can pinpoint behaviors and patterns that cause difficulty in your relationship.

The Communication Patterns Questionnaire (Questionnaire 2) is designed to assess problematic communication patterns during three phases of relationship conflict: when a relationship problem arises, during the discussion of a problem, and after such a discussion. What interests us here is your Mutual Constructive Communication (MCC) score from that questionnaire. Spouses with relatively high levels of marital adjustment typically have MCC scores above 35; a score below 25 usually reflects a relatively low level of marital adjustment. If your MCC score is 25 or less, we suggest that you become quite comfortable using the skills in chapters 6 and 7 (on basic and intermediate steps in communication) and then pay particular attention to chapter 8 (advanced steps). At the end of chapter 8, you can reexamine your responses to the Communication Patterns Questionnaire to monitor your progress.

Areas of Difficulty

Once you have identified concrete and specific communication behaviors that are of concern in your relationship, it is important to recognize that these behaviors are unlikely to occur all the time. Rather, they are probably linked to specific situations or areas of difficulty. The Inventory of Relationship Problems (Questionnaire 3) is designed to help you identify those areas.

Knowing to what extent particular areas or topics are a source of difficulty in your relationship is important in itself. As you will see when you get to the communication skills chapters, it is best to work on those skills using topics that are not a source of great conflict between you.

Thoughts

Three types of thoughts that are important in close relationships are relationship expectations or standards, beliefs about relationships, and explanations for partner behavior. Chapter 3 dealt with relationship expectations in some detail. In this section we focus on relationship beliefs and explanations.

Beliefs

The beliefs you bring to a relationship can cause difficulties if they are unrealistic. Most people have at least some unrealistic beliefs about relationships because our society reinforces such beliefs. Film and television often portray relationships that are remote from the reality of everyday life. Adult versions of the Cinderella story may make for good entertainment, but the models they provide can cause problems when people expect to attain this ideal in their lives.

The Relationship Belief Inventory (Questionnaire 4) assesses five types of unrealistic beliefs that have been shown to be important in relationships: (1) mindreading is expected (e.g., "People who have a close relationship can sense each other's needs as if they could read each other's minds"), (2) disagreement is destructive (e.g., "I cannot accept it when my partner disagrees with me"), (3) partners cannot change (e.g., "Damage done early in a relationship probably cannot be reversed"), (4) sexual relations must be perfect (e.g., "I get upset if I think I have not completely satisfied my partner sexually"), and (5) the sexes are different (e.g., "Men and women probably will never understand the opposite sex very well").

Scores vary from 0 to 40 on each subscale; the total score is the sum of the scores for all subscales. The higher the score, the more likely these beliefs are to engender dissatisfaction in the relationship. The authors of the scale found that scores for spouses in marital counseling (average score = 74.5) differed reliably from scores for spouses not in counseling (average score = 64.6; Eidelson & Epstein, 1982). In a more recent study using couples who spanned the full range of marital satisfaction (Fincham &

Bradbury, 1989), husbands obtained an average score of 77 and wives averaged 71. Allowing for measurement error, we suggest that you consider your score in the average range if it is below 94 (husbands) or 89 (wives).

Attributions

When our beliefs about a relationship are violated (e.g., "Partners should always agree"), we often ask why this occurred (e.g., "Why did he disagree with me?"). Our explanation can influence the way we feel about our partner: A benign or positive explanation (e.g., "He was trying to help me improve my understanding of the politician's policy") can positively influence feelings toward the partner, whereas a negative explanation can lead to negative feelings and create distress ("He wanted to exert power over me"). A person can raise or lower the level of satisfaction derived from the relationship by using either type of explanation consistently.

The Relationship Attribution Measure (Questionnaire 5) assesses attributions or explanations for partner behaviors. These attributions concern the cause or motivation behind the event as well as assignment of blame or fault. Attributions are important in relationships, especially when the event in question is a negative one. Benign attributions for negative events give the partner the benefit of the doubt, whereas nonbenign attributions place responsibility squarely on the partner and often involve some personality trait (e.g., "He is selfish"). A lower score on this measure reflects a tendency to assign benign attributions; a higher score results from nonbenign or negative attributions.

The average attribution ratings made by maritally distressed couples are 100 for husbands and 108 for wives; for happily married couples they are 79 for husbands and 85 for wives. As always, it is important to remember measurement error and not to take the figures too literally. However, if your score is high (above 115 for wives or above 107 for husbands), you should pay careful attention to the way you explain your partner's behavior. If you do not already feel dissatisfaction with the relationship, the way you currently see your partner's actions will ultimately contribute to unhappiness. If you are already dissatisfied with the relationship, the attributions you make are probably helping to keep you dissatisfied.

Feelings

In this section we consider general mood as well as feelings within the relationship because both can influence communication.

General Mood

People vary in their experience of emotions. Some people seem to spend most of their lives in an optimistic mood, whereas others tend to be perpetually glum, always seeing the negative side of things. There is considerable room between these two extremes. Because your general mood can influence communication between you and your partner, we included the Positive and Negative Affect Schedule (Questionnaire 6) among the measures you completed. As you may recall, this measure applies to you as an individual and does not refer specifically to your relationship.

Considerable research has shown that two independent dimensions characterize mood. Positive moods and negative moods are not opposites of each other; they are related to different things. For example, negative mood is related to reports of stress and health complaints, whereas positive mood is related to degree of social activity and frequency of pleasant events.

Using a large sample of student respondents, the authors of the Positive and Negative Affect Schedule (Watson, Clark, & Tellegen, 1988) found that the average response for the Positive Scale was 35 and the average for the Negative Scale was 18.1 (no differences were found between males and females). Given the nature of the sample and the possibility of measurement error, we suggest that you consider your score average unless it falls within the top or bottom 5% of responses—that is, above 45.5 or below 24.5 for the Positive Scale and above 27.8 or below 8.4 for the Negative Scale.

Feelings in the Relationship

The way you generally feel as an individual is likely to be related to the feelings you have for your partner. However, though the two are related, they are not necessarily the same. Consequently, we included the Modified Positive Feelings Questionnaire (Questionnaire 7) for you to complete. The average score of spouses is near 100 (husbands = 100; wives = 104; O'Leary, Fincham, & Turkewitz, 1983). Because of measurement error, we recommend that you use a broader average range (husbands = 88–112; wives = 94–114) to situate your score. If your score falls below this average, there is much room to improve your feelings, and we encourage you to continue with this book. High scorers may also want to continue: It is easy to take one's feelings for granted and neglect them, only to find later that they have changed considerably.

In this chapter we have described how communication works and alerted you to several ways in which miscommunication can occur. We then asked you to assess where things stand in your relationship. The path we have followed has led us to become more concrete and specific about communication. Although improved communication depends on changes in behavior that can be observed by both partners, bringing about such changes requires us to consider much more than observable behavior. Behavior during communication is influenced by a number of factors, particularly each partner's communication background. Before proceeding to the communication exercises in chapters 6 through 8, we need to examine a final factor that influences communication in all relationships, gender.

5 *His and Her Relationship*

Chapter 4 helped you realize how the communication backgrounds both partners bring to the relationship affect communication. Everyone's communication background is unique, and if partners are not aware of the differences, miscommunication is likely. Although it is hard to generalize, gender differences in communication background are probably among the most common sources of miscommunication in intimate, hetero-sexual relationships. Awareness of the impact of gender can also enrich communication in same-sex relationships. This chapter will alert you to gender differences in communication background so that these differences can enhance rather than inhibit communication in your relationship. After describing these gender differences, we outline ways to cope with them.

GENDER DIFFERENCES IN COMMUNICATION BACKGROUND

Waldo and Sarah Meyer are having breakfast together. Their conversation illustrates gender differences in communication background and shows how men and women tend to follow different conversational rules.

Waldo: Could you hand me the paper?

Sarah: Sure. What are you going to do at work today?

Waldo: Same old thing.

Sarah: Oh. I was thinking I'd go get some tulip bulbs for the garden this morning. The Pattersons planted some last year, and they look beautiful. Have you seen their garden?

Waldo: No.

Sarah: What color tulips do you think would look the best?

Waldo: Whatever you want is fine.

Sarah: Since our fence is white, I thought some bright-colored tulips would stand out more. Do you think red would be good?

Waldo: Sure. Whatever you want is fine.

Sarah: Are you listening to me?

Waldo: Yes.

Sarah: So why don't you tell me what color tulips you'd like?

Waldo: I just said whatever you want is fine.

Sarah: When we first got married we used to talk about everything.

Waldo: Look, it's 7:00 in the morning. I'm tired like I am every morning. I have 30 minutes to eat breakfast, gulp down some coffee, read the paper, and get to my crummy job.

Sarah: It's too bad that you don't have enough energy in the morning to carry on a conversation.

Waldo: Well, welcome to real life.

Waldo keeps reading his paper; Sarah gets up angrily and leaves the table.

When people grow up in different countries with different languages and customs, we expect them to have some trouble understanding each other. Yet when women and men have trouble understanding each other, we are sometimes surprised. Perhaps we overestimate the similarity between the life experiences of men and women. Differences in life experiences begin early; you can see them on any playground. Although there are exceptions, on most playgrounds you will see boys playing with boys and girls playing with girls. You will also notice that groups of boys behave very differently from groups of girls. When boys play, they are more likely than girls to be physically active and competitive, to give information and express opinions, to play in large groups, to tell jokes and heckle one another, to be assertive with one another, and to interrupt one another. Girls are more likely to talk in smaller groups, to shy away from competitive activities, to take turns speaking, and to try to influence one another more indirectly than boys do.

The critical point is that boys and girls have different communication backgrounds because they learn different ways to communicate with one another and to view relationships. Among adults, when these learned styles come together in intimate relationships, the result is at times maddening, at times fascinating, and at times enriching and delightful. In general, the less you know about the different ways men and women talk and think about relationships, the more you will find gender differences frustrating rather than enriching.

Waldo and Sarah, after their breakfast table conversation, both end up feeling frustrated and angry. Waldo feels that Sarah is blaming him for being tired when she knows he must go to work to support the family. He also feels that she won't stop badgering him about trivial issues, even though he is pressed for time. Finally, he feels that his wife is blaming him for not living up to a set of fairy-tale expectations. Meanwhile, Sarah feels hurt and shut out. She doesn't understand why her husband will not share his opinions and feelings. She is also angry that, when she shows interest in his life by asking about his work, he fails to reciprocate by showing interest in her day. Finally, when she expresses sympathy for his tiredness, she is shocked that her husband reacts as if she has put him down.

Waldo would probably be surprised to know that his wife does not really care much about the color of the tulips either. Sarah would probably be surprised to discover that Waldo feels that she does not try to support and understand him. The misunderstanding arises from the different ways in which men and women communicate. Waldo and Sarah are simply not aware of the gender differences that have shaped their communication backgrounds. Let's replay the conversation slowly and see where things break down.

Sarah asks Waldo, "What are you going to do at work today?" Sarah's question reflects two rules of female communication:

1. Asking a question is a good way to show someone that you are interested in him or her.

2. Talking about problems can be a relief, and sharing complaints is a way to be close and supportive (Sarah knows that Waldo is dissatisfied with his job).

Despite Sarah's good intentions, her questions irritate Waldo. He has told Sarah many times what he does at work, and he does not see much point in rehashing it. Waldo has also told Sarah that he hates his job and thinks she should know better than to ask him to talk about something that makes him feel bad. In interpreting Sarah's question, Waldo is using two principles of male communication:

1. Ask a question only when you want information.

2. Don't dwell on the negative. Complaining never helped anyone.

When Waldo says "Same old thing" in response to Sarah's question, she feels that he does not want to be close to her or have her support. Waldo is unaware of this: He sees his wife as unsupportive and is relieved that his answer stops his wife's line of questioning.

At this stage Sarah is slightly disturbed, but she tries again by turning the conversation to the subject of tulips. She gives some background information about the Pattersons' garden and the Meyer's own fence and asks a number of questions to which Waldo gives brief, curt answers. Sarah's exasperation with his responses shows when she asks, "Are you listening to me?" She then asks her husband why he won't say what he thinks about the tulips, but to her dismay he again refuses to state an opinion. Three additional rules of female communication guide Sarah's conversation here:

3. Background details help someone understand a situation.

4. Discussing a problem shows that you think the person is important, even if the problem isn't.

5. People feel comfortable expressing opinions only when you ask them what they think.

Men usually do not follow those three rules. Rather, three different rules guide the male approach:

3. Get to the point—details are boring and often irrelevant.

4. There is no point in discussing a trivial problem; just make a decision and be done with it.

5. Say what you want directly. If you don't, that's your problem.

Waldo is of course following these male rules. Thus, he is rather bored to hear about the Pattersons' garden and the color of the fence, and his lack of interest shows in his short answers. In fact, he is bored with the whole issue of tulip color, which he sees as trivial. He wishes his wife would just say, "I'm going to plant red tulips in the garden today—is that all right with you?" so that he could just say yes and forget about it. Sarah knows that tulip color is a trivial issue; what she is seeking is simply some indication that Waldo is interested in her, that they are close to each other, and that each is a part of the other's life. When Waldo dismisses the issue of the tulips, Sarah feels personally dismissed as unimportant.

The gender difference regarding directness in expressing one's views (Rule 5) also causes the couple difficulties. Waldo does not like being asked twice for his opinion: If he had a preference he would say so, and he does not like being accused of holding back. Sarah asks again because she wants Waldo to be comfortable voicing his opinion; she sees the second question as giving him permission to share his views. She is also irritated that he has not helped her explore her opinions but just says, "Whatever you want is fine." Waldo needs no help stating his opinions, so he does not understand that his wife needs some evidence of interest from him to explore her own. Sarah can, of course, decide on her own what color tulips to plant; what she is looking for is the sense that her opinions matter to her husband.

The interaction concludes when Sarah says, "When we first got married we used to talk about everything" and "It's too bad that you don't have enough energy in the morning to carry on a conversation." Waldo responds to the first remark by saying that he has many things to do in the morning and does not have time to talk. To Sarah's second remark he responds, "Well, welcome to real life." Sarah is shocked. She has been trying to express sympathy for her husband and create an opportunity to connect and commiserate about the fact that they do not have as much time to talk as they once did. To her, Waldo's remarks are defensive and patronizing. She resents hearing a lecture about his morning routine that tells her nothing she does not already know. Sarah is following two further rules of female communication:

6. Acknowledging that someone is in a bad situation is a way to express sympathy and be supportive.

7. Complaining that a relationship falls short of a romantic ideal is a way to let both partners share their disappointments and get closer.

Waldo is not female, of course, so these are not the rules under which he operates. When Sarah says, "In the beginning we used to talk about everything," he feels as though she is blaming him for a perfectly natural development in all relationships. Life is not a fairy tale, and he feels his wife is holding him to that standard. Waldo also feels criticized by her remark about his lack of energy. He is doing the best that he can to work hard and support his wife—and she is criticizing him for being tired when anyone in his shoes would be. His last remark is a way for him to say, "There are no Prince Charmings, so why don't you get off my back?" Waldo is using the following rules of male communication:

6. Pointing out that someone is in a bad situation is a form of putdown through pity.

7. Being unrealistic about relationships is a mistake, as is complaining about and blaming others for things that can't be changed.

To summarize, men and women often misunderstand each other because they follow different rules in their communication. A necessary first step to avoid misunderstandings is to be aware of the rules used by each gender. These rules are summarized in Table 5.1.

Table 5.1   Male and Female Rules of Communication

Female rules of communication	Male rules of communication
1. Asking a question is a good way to show someone that you are interested in him or her.	1. Ask a question only when you want information.
2. Talking about problems can be a relief, and sharing complaints is a way to be close and supportive.	2. Don't dwell on the negative. Complaining never helped anyone.
3. Background details help someone understand a situation.	3. Get to the point—details are boring and often irrelevant.
4. Discussing a problem shows that you think the person is important, even if the problem isn't.	4. There is no point in discussing a trivial problem; just make a decision and be done with it.
5. People feel comfortable expressing opinions only when you ask them what they think.	5. Say what you want directly. If you don't, that's your problem.
6. Acknowledging that someone is in a bad situation is a way to express sympathy and be supportive.	6. Pointing out that someone is in a bad situation is a form of putdown through pity.
7. Complaining that a relationship falls short of a romantic ideal is a way to let both partners share their disappointments and get closer.	7. Being unrealistic about relationships is a mistake, as is complaining about and blaming others for things that can't be changed.

OTHER IMPORTANT GENDER DIFFERENCES

In addition to the gender differences in communication background illustrated in Waldo and Sarah's conversation, there are several other gender differences in communication.

Silence

To put it simply, men tend to assume that everything is fine when there is no talking, whereas women tend to assume that, if no one is talking, something is wrong. To men, it sometimes feels that the more the couple talks about the relationship, the worse things get. They don't understand why women can't let well enough alone instead of talking everything to death. In contrast, women feel that the only way to resolve issues is to talk about them. To be silent is to ignore problems, and as a result things will only get worse.

Sharing Feelings Verbally Versus Showing Them

Typically, for a woman, the preferred way to feel loved is to hear her partner say how much he loves her and how wonderful their relationship is. For a man, it is often better to demonstrate caring through action. Thus, working a detested job to support his partner can be a man's way of saying, "I love you," although he may never say it directly and she may not know that it is true.

A WORD OF CAUTION

Keep in mind that these are generalizations; they do not apply to every individual. Some women have a more masculine style of communication, and some men have a more feminine style. Some people can use both styles at different times and in different situations.

Why must we put up with these differences? Why can't women simply be like men? Why can't men just communicate as women do? Granted, it would be simpler if we all communicated the same way. It would also be simpler if we ate the same food every day, dressed the same way every day, and never made new friends. What we give up in simplicity we gain in variety. Men and women find each other interesting partly *because* they are different—they can give each other something new.

The person who insists that the opposite sex must change may face a bleak future. Like other aspects of a person's communication background, the impact of gender is hard to change. In the short run, attempts to change one's partner might be successful, but the success would probably come at a high cost. Over time, resentment would build and either heighten conflict or lead the resentful partner to break off the relationship, much to the surprise of the other. In the worst case, attempting to change the opposite sex can precipitate immediate and severe conflict.

In our view, both male and female styles can be assets in a relationship. In fact, people in satisfying relationships often find that they communicate more effectively when they can incorporate some of the opposite gender's communication style into their own. In this book we attempt to balance male and female communication styles because we know that both partners have things to offer and that neither one would want to change the relationship solely on the opposite gender's terms.

LIVING WITH THE DIFFERENCES

Keeping gender differences (or any other difference in communication background) from being a problem entails two steps. The first step is to be aware of the differences. One way to heighten your awareness is to read this chapter carefully and complete Exercise 5.1, at the end of this chapter, with someone who has the opposite communication style. The second step is to apply what you know by being honest and open with your partner about several things: how you interpret what your partner says, how he or she can communicate in a way you understand, how you acknowledge that you understand your partner's communication, and what your assumptions are about the relationship.

Let's return to Waldo and Sarah and see how things might have gone differently if they had understood the gender differences we have discussed. Let's see how Waldo might have handled his wife's question "What are you going to do at work today?" Instead of "Same old thing" he could have said:

Waldo:　I guess you're trying to be supportive [acknowledges what his wife is trying to do], but talking about work makes me feel bad [gives information].

Sarah:　Are you saying you don't like talking to me [checks out interpretation]?

Waldo:　No, I'm saying I'd rather talk about something else.

Sarah:　OK. Whatever you want to talk about is fine. You're right— I just want to be supportive of you because I know you're putting up with this job just to support us financially.

Now complete Exercise 5.1 to help you begin exploring gender differences in your own communication.

Exercise 5.1   Communication and Gender

Do this exercise with a partner who has the opposite style of communication. Following are a number of conversation clips. After each one are questions about what each person is really saying and feeling. Write the answers to the questions independently on a sheet of paper, then share your answers with your partner. The purpose of sharing is not to decide who is right but to improve your understanding of the opposite gender's communication background. Following each group of questions is an additional question about alternatives; you should answer this question together.

Conversation 1

Karen and her husband Armand are in the car together.

Karen: I'm worried that the county budget cuts will mean that I'll lose my teaching job.

Armand: Actually, I saw a poll yesterday that said that over 70% of the community is going to vote for an increase in school funding.

Karen: Still, I'd hate to have to look for a new job.

Armand: Well, that isn't going to happen, so there's no point in getting stressed out about it.

Answer independently:

1. What is Karen really saying to Armand?
2. How does she want Armand to respond?
3. What is Armand really saying to Karen?
4. What is Armand trying to do?
5. How are Armand and Karen feeling at the end of the conversation?

Answer together:

6. How might Karen and Armand handle this situation better?

Conversation 2

Jim and Elena have just finished dinner in a restaurant.

Elena: Do you want to order dessert?

Jim: No, I'm really stuffed.
[They go to the parking lot and get in the car.]

Jim: Is something wrong?

Elena: I wish we'd ordered dessert.

Jim: Well, why didn't you say something?!

Answer independently:

1. How did Jim feel in the restaurant?
2. How does Jim feel in the car?
3. How did Elena feel in the restaurant?
4. How does Elena feel in the car?
5. Why didn't Elena order dessert?

Answer together:

6. How might Jim and Elena handle this situation better?

Conversation 3

Ben and Laura are at home on a Thursday evening.

> Ben: I'm going to go with Jack Wilson to see the Tigers game tomorrow and then stay in Detroit at his friend's place. I'll be back Saturday afternoon.

> Laura: Why didn't you tell me about this?

> Ben: I just did.

> Laura: Why didn't you tell me before you made the plans?

> Ben: Right, just what I need! The next time Jack asks me to do something I'll tell him I have to get my wife's permission first.

Answer independently:

1. How does Ben feel?
2. How does Laura feel?
3. What is Laura asking for?
4. How does Ben interpret what Laura says?

Answer together:

5. How might Ben and Laura handle this situation better?

6 Learning to Communicate Effectively: Basic Steps

Chapters 4 and 5 were designed to help you understand your communication background. An awareness of what you bring to a relationship is important for improving communication within the relationship. However, that awareness alone is not sufficient to bring about change. As we noted in chapter 4, you must change behavior to change communication. This chapter and the two that follow outline specific ways you can change your behavior to improve communication with your partner. These chapters present sequences of communication steps that we have labeled basic, intermediate, and advanced. These steps build on one another in a logical way. As you learn about and—most important—practice each step, communication should gradually become more satisfying and helpful to both partners.

This chapter will cover six basic steps, which are outlined in Table 6.1. At the end of the chapter is an exercise you can use to review these steps.

Table 6.1 Basic Steps for Getting Started on Communication

1. Form realistic expectations.

2. Set the scene.

3. Keep things friendly.

4. Maintain a positive outlook.

5. Avoid roadblocks.

6. Note your progress.

STEP 1: FORMING REALISTIC EXPECTATIONS

If things are going badly in your relationship, you may be tempted to race through these chapters in search of a quick fix. However, exaggerated expectations can work against even the most caring and motivated of couples. Expecting too much too fast often prevents couples from seeing the real progress they are making. Remind yourself frequently that change takes time and steady effort. Your relationship did not reach its present state overnight, and it will change only gradually. Try to suspend judgment until you have reached the end of chapter 8.

It *is* reasonable to expect that if both you and your partner are working on your relationship each day and practicing the skills outlined in these chapters, you will start moving in the right direction. It is quite common for one partner to be more realistic than the other about the pace of possible change. If it is easier for you than for your partner to acknowledge that change will be slow rather than dramatic and immediate, you can help your partner by pointing out improvements he or she has made and ways the relationship has improved.

As you recall from the communication model presented in chapter 4, your perception of your partner's behavior is always filtered through your own feelings, thoughts, and expectations. Thus, if you are expecting the relationship to improve dramatically in a short time, you may overlook or take for granted the everyday, positive things that happen between the two of you (e.g., a reassuring smile, an offer to make a cup of coffee). Similarly, when you feel irritable or despondent, you may focus on the negative aspects of your relationship. You can counter such thoughts just as you counter thoughts that stop cooperation (discussed in chapter 2). In both cases, you must be aware of your thoughts and have available arguments against distressing thoughts and expectations. When negative thoughts surface, remind yourself of the positive features of your relationship.

We suggest keeping a relationship improvement diary, beginning now. Carry a small notepad with you at all times, and record any positive event or behavior, no matter how insignificant it seems. Note feelings, thoughts, and actions, whether your own or your partner's. You'll be surprised how many signs of improvement occur each day if you care to notice them. When you feel discouraged about the relationship, look at your list. This will probably make you feel better and boost your faith in the relationship. Following is a list of some small signs that a relationship is improving. If you watch for these and other signs, you may be surprised at how many you can notice.

Feelings

Feeling more relaxed at mealtime with your partner

Feeling sexually attracted to your partner

Feeling more hopeful about the relationship

Feeling happier or more at ease than you did several weeks ago

Thoughts

Having a warm memory of your partner come to mind

Thinking good things about your partner or the relationship while you are alone

Seeing your partner trying to make things better for both of you

Expecting to have pleasant interactions with your partner

Actions

Smiling at your partner more; having your partner smile at you

Being able to hold a conversation with your partner

Making more eye contact with your partner

Touching or hugging each other

Feeling more energetic around home

Going to sleep more easily

STEP 2: SETTING THE SCENE

When you signed the contract at the end of chapter 2, you agreed to take some time each day to work on your relationship. To put this into action, it is helpful to establish a routine.

Time and Place

Pick a time and a place that are comfortable for you and your partner. The place should be one where you can talk undisturbed. The time should be one when both of you are free and can concentrate on your relationship (e.g., not 10 minutes before one of you must rush off to work). It is best to set aside the same time each day so that both of you can anticipate it. That way, if something is bothering you, you'll know you will get a chance to talk it over with your partner.

Some couples like to talk at the kitchen table after the children are in bed. Others talk on the living room couch (with the television off, of course) after they have had dinner and washed the dishes. Bed is generally not a good place for the arranged conversations. If you are preoccupied with communication, you may find over time that you have trouble falling asleep. You should plan at least 15 minutes each day to talk face to face (phone conversation is not a good idea unless one of you is obligated to be away from home). Before you read further, agree with your partner on the time and place you will designate for your conversations.

Getting Started

Ideally, each partner should simply show up at the agreed place at the appointed time. However, as people tend to forget or lose track of time, one of you should take responsibility each day to get things started if both of you are not at your prearranged place on time (within 2 minutes). You and your partner should take responsibility for issuing the reminder on alternate days. You should both rely on the same household clock for your starting time. If you start a few minutes late, you should end later as well so that you talk for at least 15 minutes. Take time now to decide which days each of you will be responsible for and which clock you will use.

Time-Out Rule

The last step in setting up a routine for practicing communication is to establish a time-out rule. Sometimes partners become so angry or upset with each other that they cannot talk constructively. At such times, it is easy to say hurtful things that you will later regret. For this reason, it is important to have a time-out rule so that each of you can cool off if necessary.

The rule specifies what time-out signal to use, where to go, and how long to stay away. A signal can be a T made with the hands or just a statement like "I'm really upset and I need a time-out." Each of you should choose a place in the house where you can go to cool off alone. Also, you should agree in advance how long a time-out will last. Most couples need only a few minutes, but allow as much time as you think you may need. When you take a time-out, stop the clock and continue the discussion afterward. In other words, if you take a 5-minute time-out, add 5 minutes to your usual discussion time to compensate for the missed minutes. Time-out should not become a way to avoid discussion. We recommend that, in your planning, each of you allow at least 10 minutes longer than the scheduled discussion period. (This time may vary depending on the extent to which a couple uses time-out.)

When to Use Time-Out

If time-out is to work, you must know when to use it. Some good times to call time-out are when one of you is about to:

1. Call the other person names
2. Yell at the other person
3. Act out (e.g., throw something) or shove the other person
4. Get so angry or emotionally upset that you can no longer listen to the other person

Of course, it is much better to declare a time-out before these things happen, but if they do occur, call time-out immediately. As you become aware of the signals that you are becoming angry (e.g., feeling your face flush, talking faster, raising your voice) or upset (e.g., feeling tears well up in your eyes), you will find it easier to know when to call time-out. If you have trouble detecting these signals, pay particular attention to the feeling identification and communication exercise (Step 8) in chapter 7.

Once you have settled on a time and place, an agreement about getting started, and your time-out rules, write them down. (See Table 6.2 for an example.) Put this information somewhere accessible to both of you; this will prevent disagreements later if you forget the details of your arrangement.

STEP 3: KEEPING THINGS FRIENDLY

Now that you have created a setting for talking with your partner, you need to begin talking each day. Learning new skills takes time and practice. Thus, it is crucial that you and your partner not only work through each communication step in the book but also practice the skills during your talk times. It may be helpful to keep this book visible as a reminder to practice what you are learning. Mastering the skills is much more important than finishing the steps quickly.

At the start, choose your topics from those on the Inventory of Relationship Problems in chapter 4 that you both rated as least problematic (preferably those checked off as

Table 6.2　Planning for Practice Communication Sessions

Names _____

Time of day for talks _____

Place for talks _____

Length of time for talks (at least 15 minutes) _____

Clock we will use to time ourselves _____

_____

Who will remind after 2 minutes on Tuesday, Thursday, and Saturday

_____

Who will remind after 2 minutes on other days _____

Time-out signal _____

Where each partner goes during time-out _____

Length of time-out _____

minor difficulties); you will address the more serious issues a little later. Your purpose at first is just to get used to talking with each other and feeling comfortable doing so. In addition to starting with "cool" topics, there are other things that you can do to make conversation comfortable.

Couples sometimes unnecessarily "tag on" sarcastic or painful remarks to their communications. In the following conversation clip, some of the most common tag-ons are italicized.

> Maria:　You're late to our talk time, *as usual.*
>
> Jack:　*Don't nag.* I'll be there in a second.
>
> Maria:　*You're late because you only care about yourself.*
> I feel upset when I have to remind you.

This is the type of conversation that often results in an argument and leaves both partners feeling hurt and angry. Think how different the conversation would sound if the negative tag-ons were removed:

> Maria:　You're late to our talk time.
>
> Jack:　I'll be there in a second.
>
> Maria:　I feel upset when I have to remind you.

The edited conversation communicates all the necessary information between the partners without the hostility that frequently results in communication breakdowns. If you can edit out negative tag-ons, you will make your conversation times safer and more enjoyable.

Because both partners may have a well-ingrained habit of using negative tag-ons, it is important to be aware of what you say. Descriptions of the common types of negative tag-ons may help you recognize some that you use.

Sarcasm

Sarcasm is adding a word or phrase, using a tone of voice, or making a nonverbal gesture (e.g., rolling the eyes, sneering) to turn an otherwise positive or neutral remark negative —for example, "You're late to our talk time, *as usual*" or "I see that you washed the car, *finally.*" Sarcasm is often an indirect way to communicate anger or hurt feelings, but it tends to cause more problems than it solves.

Name-Calling

Statements like "Why don't you answer the phone, *you lazy slob?*" or "It makes me mad *that you are such a tyrant* when you discipline the kids" are a great way to anger your partner and start an argument that will leave both of you feeling bad. As with other negative tag-ons, you can drop them from your communication and still get your message across (try it in the two examples).

Character Assassination

Character assassination involves turning a complaint about your partner's behavior into a global judgment of him or her as a person—for example, "You parked your car in my spot *because you don't care about anyone but yourself*" or "*You're so frigid that* you don't give me a kiss when I walk in the door." Reread the examples without the italicized character assassinations and you can see how otherwise reasonable statements are rendered destructive and hurtful. The people making those complaints are hurting themselves because the partners are less likely to respond constructively to complaints that include character assassination. Because the message is filtered through hurt feelings, all the listener hears is the attack on his or her character.

Exercise 6.1 illustrates the use of character assassination in a conversation and lets you try your hand at eliminating it. If you want more practice editing out negative tag-ons, tape some of your conversations with your partner and then go back and listen to your own (not your partner's) statements. See if you can detect name-calling, sarcasm, or character assassination that you could edit out in the future.

Exercise 6.1   Conversation Illustrating Character Assassination

Partner 1

Use this exercise to practice editing out hurtful and unnecessary tag-ons. In the conversation, cross out every unnecessary word or phrase. You will know when you are done because the conversation will sound neutral or positive instead of angry and negative. The conversation is printed twice so that you and your partner can edit it independently and then compare answers.

Jack: For once in your life, could you keep the volume on the TV low enough that I can read the paper?

Maria: You could move to another room, but why would you ever do anything considerate for anybody?

Jack: Stop criticizing me, you bitch!

Maria: You don't like criticism because you're thin-skinned and arrogant.

Jack: Fine, I'll go to another room so the baby can have her way.

Maria: My oh my, you're so good to me that I can hardly stand it.

Version to Alter

Jack: For once in your life, could you keep the volume on the TV low enough that I can read the paper?

Maria: You could move to another room, but why would you ever do anything considerate for anybody?

Jack: Stop criticizing me, you bitch!

Maria: You don't like criticism because you're thin-skinned and arrogant.

Jack: Fine, I'll go to another room so the baby can have her way.

Maria: My oh my, you're so good to me that I can hardly stand it.

Partner 2

Use this exercise to practice editing out hurtful and unnecessary tag-ons. In the conversation, cross out every unnecessary word or phrase. You will know when you are done because the conversation will sound neutral or positive instead of angry and negative. The conversation is printed twice so that you and your partner can edit it independently and then compare answers.

Jack: For once in your life, could you keep the volume on the TV low enough that I can read the paper?

Maria: You could move to another room, but why would you ever do anything considerate for anybody?

Jack: Stop criticizing me, you bitch!

Maria: You don't like criticism because you're thin-skinned and arrogant.

Jack: Fine, I'll go to another room so the baby can have her way.

Maria: My oh my, you're so good to me that I can hardly stand it.

Version to Alter

Jack: For once in your life, could you keep the volume on the TV low enough that I can read the paper?

Maria: You could move to another room, but why would you ever do anything considerate for anybody?

Jack: Stop criticizing me, you bitch!

Maria: You don't like criticism because you're thin-skinned and arrogant.

Jack: Fine, I'll go to another room so the baby can have her way.

Maria: My oh my, you're so good to me that I can hardly stand it.

STEP 4: MAINTAINING A POSITIVE OUTLOOK

No situation is totally hopeless, but it can sometimes seem that way. As you learned in completing Step 1, you may need extra effort to see the positive features of your relationship if things are going badly. We have already noted the value of reminding yourself of the positive aspects of your relationship and having positive and realistic expectations. Another way to keep a positive outlook is to comment on the positive things your partner does, *especially when you are dissatisfied with something.* This involves learning two new skills: balancing what you say and making negative remarks specific rather than global.

Making Balanced Statements

When partners are unhappy, they often spend much of their time together arguing and exchanging criticisms. This steady stream of negative messages makes interactions unpleasant for both partners and may lead them to avoid each other. One major difference between happy and unhappy couples is that happy couples send out more positive messages than negative messages. It is very difficult to tally the number of positive and negative messages you give out. An easier way to make sure you and your partner are sending each other at least as many positive messages as negative ones is never to make a negative remark without balancing it with a positive one. This may sound strange at first, but it quickly becomes natural because it feels much better than straight criticism. Read the following statements and imagine how it would feel to hear each one from your partner.

Unbalanced: I wish you'd help set the table more often.

Balanced: I liked the way you helped me set the table last night, and I wish you'd do that more often.

Unbalanced: Every time I give an opinion, you tell me I'm wrong.

Balanced: I enjoy talking with you, and I'd like to talk with you more if you agreed with some of my opinions.

Unbalanced: I think your idea about spanking the kids when they misbehave is ridiculous.

Balanced: I agree with you that we need to do something about the kids' misbehavior, but I do not agree that spanking them will solve the problem.

To better understand why balancing messages is so effective, take another look at the model of communication presented in chapter 4. As we have said before, the way partners understand each other's behavior is filtered through their current feelings and thoughts. When a stream of negative communication becomes part of a relationship, the partners attend heavily to their own hurt and anger until these feelings color their perceptions of everything that happens in the relationship. They may even begin to pull back from the relationship to protect themselves. Each negative message causes more pain and withdrawal. In contrast, a balanced message contains something good and thus is easier to open up to. The positive aspects of the balanced message help the listener put aside the strong negative feelings that have made it impossible to evaluate the partner's messages evenhandedly. To put it simply, it feels much better to hear a balanced remark than an unbalanced one. When you balance your messages, your partner is more likely to listen to your criticism rather than just tuning out to avoid a painful communication.

Being Specific

You may be wondering how you can balance all of the messages you send. It is true that some negative messages cannot be balanced. In general, such messages tend to be too global and are therefore destructive rather than constructive. For example, it is hard to balance such messages as "I hate you," "You never do anything for me," "I always end up doing all the work," or "I don't like you, your friends, your family, or this crummy house." Such global criticisms are hurtful, are often ignored, and rarely produce any solution. If you want to improve your relationship, you will need to let your partner know about the specific problems. This means focusing on one complaint at a time rather than cataloging many or resorting to character assassination. It also means purging words like *always* and *never* from your complaint. A good general guideline is that if a complaint is impossible to balance, it is probably too broad and sweeping. Keep narrowing your complaints until you can balance them with something positive. For practice, try making the following global, unbalanced criticisms specific and balanced. You will know when you have done it because they will sound neutral rather than negative and critical when you say them out loud.

1. You never really loved me.

2. There is nothing about you that I like.

3. You are late for dinner on most nights of the week.

4. You haven't been spending enough time with the kids.

5. You always get things your way.

6. You said you would clean the house, but the kitchen is still a complete mess.

If you would like more practice making complaints specific, tape a few of your conversations with your partner. When you listen to the tapes, see whether you make broad, sweeping complaints using words like *always* and *never* or specific complaints that can be balanced. Also listen to see if you balance negative messages with positive messages. Practice balancing the negative messages you hear yourself saying on the tape.

STEP 5: AVOIDING ROADBLOCKS

Roadblocks are communication killers. They can instantly turn a productive conversation into an unproductive one—or simply end it altogether. Here we will review some common roadblocks you may encounter in your talk time. Being aware of them should help you overcome them. As you work through this chapter and the next one, you will be learning new skills that can replace any roadblocks you use now. Four common roadblocks are cross-complaining, interrupting, issuing ultimatums, and rehashing the past.

From Cross-Complaining to Treating One Problem at a Time

Cross-complaining is responding to a partner's complaint with a complaint of your own. In the following conversation each person is likely to feel that the partner does not understand or support him or her.

> Jose: I had a very tough day at work again.
>
> Michelle: Staying at home all day with the children is no
>   piece of cake.
>
> Jose: It's that new boss. I don't know what to do about him.
>
> Michelle: I feel bad about my situation. Every time I try to go out
>   during the day, the children act up. I feel trapped.

If either partner had instead simply said "Uh-huh" or something like "Yes, it's tough," the other would have felt validated and supported.

Sometimes cross-complaining takes the form of mutual criticism, often escalating in a spiral:

> Josh: You left the garage unlocked again. How many times do
>   I have to tell you to lock it after you park?
>
> Elena: At least my car isn't parked on the street like yours.
>
> Josh: The way you mistreat your car, it ought to be hidden so
>   the neighbors don't have to look at it.
>
> Elena: If you cared at all about the neighbors, you'd have invited
>   them over a long time ago. But you have to play hermit.

Perhaps all these complaints are justified, but it is clear that none of them will get resolved through this sort of exchange. Both Josh and Elena are simply trying to top each other's complaint. If their criticisms had been balanced (as explained in Step 4), this might not have happened: Josh's first complaint would not have felt like an attack to Elena, so she would not feel the need to return the attack.

At its most extreme, cross-complaining takes the form of "kitchen sinking." That is, people start discussing some point of dissatisfaction but end up complaining about almost everything they can think of. For you and your partner to resolve problems, you must focus on one thing at a time. If you make a complaint and your partner responds with another complaint, try responding by saying, "I think your complaint is important, and I would like to talk about it after we've discussed what I said." This balanced remark (or one roughly equivalent to it) can break the cycle of cross-complaining so you and your partner can slow down the action and handle one problem at a time.

From Interrupting to Taking Turns

Interrupting often goes hand in hand with cross-complaining. No one can listen and talk at the same time. Interruptions often result from fear that you will not get the last word or that you will listen to your partner but he or she will not then listen to you. If you have something important to say, try making a balanced comment such as "I'd appreciate it if you'd listen to me without interruption, and I'll do the same for you." Interruptions are likely to result in one or both partners trying to dominate the discussion. If this occurs, the dominated partner will probably end up feeling frustrated.

From Ultimatums to Requests

An ultimatum is a power play that one partner makes by raising the stakes suddenly, as in "Take out the damn garbage or I'll never speak to you again" or "If you don't come home right now, I'll be gone when you get here." Brinkmanship and threats have no place in a relationship that the partners are trying to improve. If you are serious about ending your relationship, the chapter on breakup and divorce (chapter 11) may be helpful. However, if you are committed to working on your relationship, you should realize that manipulative threats and ultimatums are extremely destructive *whether they work or not.* When they do not work, you end up looking foolish and communication deteriorates. When they do work, the results tend to be only short-term; your partner may respond with his or her own threats next time. In unhappy relationships such a pattern is quite common: Each partner tries to control the other with ultimatums and threats. Often this pattern leads to chains of escalating negative behavior that are broken only when one partner becomes so annoying or threatening that the other backs down. The one who backs down will almost surely harbor great resentment that can, over time, completely undermine the possibility of the relationship being repaired. Requests are likely to be far more useful than ultimatums in the long run, especially if you apply communication skills to discuss problem situations.

From Rehashing the Past to Living in the Present

The last roadblock, rehashing the past, is very hard for many couples to abandon. They refight the same fights over and over, and both partners are miserable. Remember an undeniable fact about the past: It's over. No matter who was right or wrong in an argument you had 6 months ago, the argument happened and can never be undone. If your relationship was unhappy in the past, dwelling on that unhappiness will likely make you feel worse about your relationship today. Any change that occurs will happen not in the past but in the present, with benefits in the future.

Some people feel that, in focusing on the present and the future, they are saying that everything past is unimportant or forgivable. That is not what it means to look away from the past. Any hurt or disappointment you experienced in the past was legitimate, but continuing to bring it up and dwell on it will not help you and your partner today. To look forward is to say, "Without any prejudgments, I'll try to give my partner the benefit of the doubt and work on the relationship with an open mind." It is easier to focus on the future with your partner if you have a vision of good things the future might bring. Exercise 6.2 should help you see some of those things and also help you feel enthusiastic about changing.

Exercise 6.2   Looking Into the Future

Sit down with your partner and discuss how you would feel, what you would think, and what you would do if your relationship were the way you wanted. Do not discuss what your partner should or would do; each of you should talk only about what benefits you expect from improvement in the relationship. The purpose of this conversation is to create a realistic and positive image of what the relationship could be like for each of you. The point of this exercise is to enjoy the idea of what might be, not to criticize how things are or what each partner is doing. If either of you starts feeling criticized, you may have to look into the future independently, reflecting on how each one would benefit from improvement in the relationship, and discuss it later.

STEP 6: NOTING YOUR PROGRESS

After you and your partner have worked through the first five steps and had at least a week of daily talk times, you are ready to look at your progress. The task is simply to reflect on what you have done. At this point, things may still be the same or only slightly different. However, whether you feel they are better or not, your relationship has already been enhanced in some ways. First, you are working together on this book. You have also increased your knowledge of both partners' communication backgrounds by discovering how gender and culture affect a relationship. Finally, you have become aware of some ways in which communication is filtered through feelings, expectations, and thoughts, and you have learned how to counter expectations and thoughts that adversely affect communication.

It is important to acknowledge your progress to yourself and to each other. Before your next scheduled conversation, each of you should make a list of the things that the other has done to try to improve the relationship. Begin the conversation by sharing the list with your partner. The goal of this exercise is to make your partner feel appreciated for the efforts he or she has made. You should also reward yourself. The fact that you have made it this far is in itself a cause for some celebration. Reinforcing or rewarding yourself for each step is appropriate and will help you make continuing progress.

There are two other things you can do before beginning the next chapter. First, you can enjoy sharing your improvements by reading to each other some of the things you have written in your relationship improvement diary (Step 1). Second, you can tape-record two talk times. Save the tapes, and listen to yourselves at the end of the next chapter to hear how much you have changed.

7

Learning to Communicate Effectively: Intermediate Steps

The previous chapter, on the basic steps, identified many behaviors (e.g., cross-complaining, name-calling) that should be stopped because they hinder communication. This chapter focuses on behaviors that need to be started or increased if communication is to improve. You will find these skills especially useful as you move beyond discussion of minor disagreements into deeper or more sensitive areas.

The intermediate steps, discussed in this chapter, are shown in Table 7.1. They will take longer than the basic steps. Plan to work through them slowly and thoroughly. Don't attempt more than one or two steps a week; most couples proceed more slowly than that. Remember, mastering the skills is much more important than finishing the chapter quickly. To get a sense of progress, you can tape-record your discussions regularly. You will know that you have mastered a skill—and can move on to the next step—when you hear yourself using the skill regularly on tape.

Some of the steps teach several related skills. If you want to focus on one skill at a time and thus complete the larger steps more slowly, that is perfectly acceptable. Your goal is a thoroughly and carefully improved relationship, not a hasty and haphazard repair job.

Table 7.1   Intermediate Steps for More Effective Communication

    7. Take responsibility for yourself.

    8. Attend to and communicate emotions.

    9. Check out your assumptions.

  10. Listen actively.

  11. Give behavior-effect feedback.

  12. Notice progress and reward yourself and your partner.

STEP 7: TAKING RESPONSIBILITY FOR YOURSELF

When a relationship is dissatisfying, it is common for each partner to feel that the other person is at fault. After all, who wants to be held responsible for a problem? Partners who are unhappy frequently make statements like "Things would be fine if only he would change" or "If she would stop making me drink, there wouldn't be a problem." Each partner blames the other—and then tries to change or fix the partner—and both partners are left feeling frustrated and helpless.

Although attributing relationship problems to your partner may make you feel better or give you a sense of being right, it also deprives you of your power to improve the relationship. If you assume no role in relationship difficulties, then you have no way to resolve them. In chapter 2, we advised you to think of your partner as an ally and collaborate with him or her to enhance the relationship. Part of this collaboration is letting your partner take responsibility for his or her own needs, actions, and feelings while you take responsibility for yours. This simple shift in focus can break deadlocks in the relationship because it is much easier for people to change themselves than to change others.

Using "I" Language

One way to take responsibility for the relationship is to use "I" language when describing your feelings, needs, expectations, and actions. Here are some examples:

With feelings: "You make me angry by coming home late" becomes "I get angry when you come home late."

With needs: "A marriage requires that both partners show physical affection" becomes "I need physical affection."

With expectations: "A good parent would spend more time with the children" becomes "I would like it if you spent more time with the children."

With actions: "You make me drink by nagging me so much" becomes "I drink when you nag me."

Say the above pairs of statements out loud and see how different they sound and feel. The statements without "I" language probably feel more blaming and attacking because they say that the speaker's opinions and feelings are objective facts or someone else's responsibility. In reality, we all are responsible for our own feelings, needs, actions, and expectations. What we think of as objective, irrefutable facts about relationships are often just our personal opinions. To admit this can be scary but also empowering: "I" language cannot be debated. Your partner can argue about whether or not he or she makes you angry but cannot argue with you when you say, "I am angry"—only you are qualified to make that statement. Your partner may disagree with you when you say, "A marriage requires physical affection" but can hardly argue with you if you say, "I need physical affection." You are the one who knows your own needs, expectations, and feelings, so when you use "I" language you are speaking with authority.

Focusing on Yourself

In addition to using "I" language, you can take more responsibility for your relationship by focusing on yourself and your own role in difficulties that arise. People often fail to see how they contribute to problems in the relationship. This is illustrated by a common pattern in unhappy marriages: The wife wants her husband to talk more about his feelings, thoughts, and experiences. The man is likely to be labeled by the woman (and perhaps by friends and counselors) as "distant," "afraid of intimacy," "unwilling to share," and many other terms that suggest the problem is entirely his. However, it is not that simple. The problem could be resolved if the man talked more about his inner life, but it could also be resolved if the woman allowed him to be silent when he wished to be silent.

Ideally, both partners would give in a little to resolve the problem, which is created both by the man's desire to keep his feelings to himself and by the woman's desire that he share his feelings. If the woman does not see her role in the problem, she will probably keep trying to change her less talkative partner; he will become irritated at the implication that the fault is entirely his and thus will resist all the more. The woman could break the cycle by recognizing and admitting her role. Rather than saying, "What do I have to do to get you to talk about your feelings? Why are you so distant and stone-faced all the time?" she could say something that acknowledges her contribution to the problem—for example, "It's important to me that we talk about feelings, and I can see that I've been nagging you about that. Would you be willing to talk to me more if I nagged you less?" The woman cannot change her husband, but she can change her own behavior. The man cannot stop his wife from nagging, but he can choose to talk more.

One way to apply this principle in your relationship is to open any discussion of a problem with an admission of your role in it. When you do this, your partner is less likely to feel blamed for the problem and will probably be more motivated to address the problem. Defusing the blame issue is a good way to initiate a problem-solving discussion because it increases the chances that you will focus on the problem rather than on who is at fault. We strongly recommend that, at the start of each problem-solving discussion, each partner state what he or she does to create or contribute to the problem. Exercise 7.1 will give you practice in thinking along these lines.

Exercise 7.1   Taking Responsibility

Both you and your partner should independently write about three problems in the relationship. Write a description of each problem, being sure to use "I" language when describing your own feelings, thoughts, and desires concerning the problem. For each problem, write about the role you play in perpetuating the problem. Describe only your own role. When you have written about three problems in the relationship, read your answers carefully to see if they include any statements that could be translated into "I" language or any information you could add to clarify your role in the problem.

STEP 8: ATTENDING TO AND COMMUNICATING EMOTIONS

As you know from chapter 4, emotions have considerable influence on communication in intimate relationships. This is true even for couples who never expressly talk about their feelings. Our emotions color what we see and how we interpret what our partners say. Consider the following scenario. Marlene has had a terrible day at work. Her boss criticized her performance, and she spilled coffee on her blouse. On the way home she was delayed in traffic for an hour on a hot afternoon. She reaches the door and stomps into the living room. Her husband greets her by asking, "How about some dinner?" Marlene yells, "Can't you see that I'm an hour late and I don't have time to wait on you hand and foot?" Her husband responds, "I can see that you're an hour late—that's why I made dinner. It's in the dining room." "Oh, I'm sorry, honey," says Marlene, "I didn't understand what you meant."

Marlene responded negatively to her husband's question about dinner because she was angry and upset over the day's bad experiences. Strong negative emotions, even if we are not aware of them, make us attend more to negative information and interpret ambiguous messages in a negative light. If Marlene had been in a good mood she might have interpreted her husband's question more positively, and the misunderstanding might not have happened.

Many people are unaware of their emotions and thus do not realize how their feelings change the ways in which they interpret communications. Once you become aware of your emotions, you will be able to see how they are affecting your perceptions of your partner. When you are in a bad mood, for example, you might realize that it is not the best moment to approach your partner about a major relationship problem. Moreover, if you are aware of your feelings, they can give you useful information about your relationship. By observing what you and your partner are doing when you feel happy, safe, contented, satisfied, and loving, you will know which activities to repeat in the future. By the same token, if you realize what actions or activities make you feel sad, scared, or angry, you will know what to avoid or work on in the future.

As you become more aware of your feelings, you can help your partner become more aware of them as well. By learning the verbal and nonverbal signs that you are having a particular feeling, your partner will be able to help you recognize your feeling by calling them to your attention—for instance, "You're pacing around the room—are you nervous?" In addition, if your partner is aware of your feelings, he or she will know when to ask about them and when to leave you alone.

Exercise 7.2 will help you learn to identify your feelings; it will also help you and your partner become aware of how you communicate feelings. Compare and discuss your responses. Pay attention to any sign that might indicate more than one feeling and discuss how such signs might be confusing to your partner (e.g., how can your partner tell whether your crying indicates joy or sadness?). Did you use much "I" language in listing the ways you communicate feelings? This exercise may be easier for women than for men because women tend to be more comfortable with their emotions.

Exercise 7.2   Identifying Feelings

Partner 1

You and your partner should independently complete the following sentences in as many ways as possible, then discuss. For example:

> I can tell that I am feeling anxious when *I have butterflies in my stomach; my palms sweat;*
> *I have a headache; the same thoughts keep running through my head over and over;*
> *I have stomach cramps; I have pain in my back and neck or in my chest.*

> My partner can tell that I am feeling anxious when *I pace back and forth; my voice quavers;*
> *I keep looking out the window; I suddenly ask if something is wrong; I say, "I feel anxious";*
> *I start cleaning the house; I drum my fingers on the table; I pour myself a drink; I cry.*

I can tell that I am feeling angry when _____

_____

_____

My partner can tell that I am feeling angry when _____

_____

_____

I can tell that I am feeling hurt when _____

_____

_____

My partner can tell that I am feeling hurt when _____

_____

_____

I can tell that I am feeling happy when _____

_____

_____

My partner can tell that I am feeling happy when _____

_____

_____

I can tell that I am feeling sad when _____

_____

_____

My partner can tell that I am feeling sad when _____

_____

_____

I can tell that I am feeling scared when _____

_____

_____

My partner can tell that I am feeling scared when _____

_____

_____

I can tell that I am feeling frustrated when _____

_____

_____

My partner can tell that I am feeling frustrated when _____

_____

_____

I can tell that I am feeling anxious when _____

_____

_____

My partner can tell that I am feeling anxious when _____

_____

_____

I can tell that I am feeling cared about when _____

_____

_____

My partner can tell that I am feeling cared about when _____

_____

_____

Partner 2

You and your partner should independently complete the following sentences in as many ways as possible, then discuss. For example:

I can tell that I am feeling anxious when *I have butterflies in my stomach; my palms sweat; I have a headache; the same thoughts keep running through my head over and over; I have stomach cramps; I have pain in my back and neck or in my chest.*

My partner can tell that I am feeling anxious when *I pace back and forth; my voice quavers; I keep looking out the window; I suddenly ask if something is wrong; I say, "I feel anxious"; I start cleaning the house; I drum my fingers on the table; I pour myself a drink; I cry.*

I can tell that I am feeling angry when _____

_____

_____

My partner can tell that I am feeling angry when _____

_____

_____

I can tell that I am feeling hurt when _____

_____

_____

My partner can tell that I am feeling hurt when _____

_____

_____

I can tell that I am feeling happy when _____

_____

_____

My partner can tell that I am feeling happy when _____

_____

_____

I can tell that I am feeling sad when _____

_____

_____

My partner can tell that I am feeling sad when _____

_____

_____

I can tell that I am feeling scared when _____

_____

_____

My partner can tell that I am feeling scared when _____

_____

_____

I can tell that I am feeling frustrated when _____

_____

_____

My partner can tell that I am feeling frustrated when _____

_____

_____

I can tell that I am feeling anxious when _____

_____

_____

My partner can tell that I am feeling anxious when _____

_____

_____

I can tell that I am feeling cared about when _____

_____

_____

My partner can tell that I am feeling cared about when _____

_____

_____

STEP 9: CHECKING OUT YOUR ASSUMPTIONS

As you saw from the model of communication presented in chapter 4, emotions are not the only influence on understanding (or misunderstanding) in a couple's communications. Thoughts also influence communication. When your partner talks to you, you actively interpret what he or she means, and you make judgments about your partner and the relationship. Often you make these judgments without realizing it. Sometimes these judgments and interpretations are valid, sometimes they are partly valid, and sometimes they are completely invalid. Because they are made privately by each partner they add an underlying, unspoken level to communication. This unspoken communication is illustrated in the following interaction between Grace and her husband Jerome. Grace is at home when Jerome comes home from work.

> Grace: *(Unspoken level of communication)* Jerome looks like he had
> a bad day. I hope he's OK.
> *(Spoken level of communication)* How are you, Jerome?
>
> Jerome: *(Unspoken level of communication)* She isn't really interested in
> hearing how I am. She's just asking because she feels obligated.
> *(Spoken level of communication)* You don't really want to know.
>
> Grace: *(Unspoken level of communication)* He won't tell me because he
> thinks I can't handle stress. He doesn't trust me at all.
> *(Spoken level of communication)* You think I'm so childish that
> I can't handle hearing that things are bad for you!
>
> Jerome: *(Unspoken level of communication)* I knew she didn't want to hear about
> my day! She just wants to complain about our relationship again.
> *(Spoken level of communication)* Let's just forget it.

Jerome and Grace cannot communicate effectively because they are incorrectly interpreting each other's motives and meanings. They each assume they know what the other means, but they never check out their assumptions. Both act as if they can read the partner's mind, with negative results.

How can couples keep the unspoken level of communication from sabotaging their communication? There are two steps in keeping your interpretations and judgments from doing harm. The first step is simply becoming aware of them. Many people do not realize that they inaccurately interpret their partner's communications, and thus they do not have the power to change their interpretations. The second step is testing your assumptions to see if they are valid. The only way to test your interpretations and judgments about your partner is to say them aloud—that is, make them part of the external world that you share with your partner. In the conversation we just heard, Jerome might have said, "Grace, I'm worried that you feel obligated to ask me about my day but are not really interested—is that true?" Grace could have told Jerome that her interest was genuine, and the whole argument could have been avoided. In testing your assumptions, be sure to use "I" language and avoid speaking like a mind reader (e.g., say, "I'm scared that you find me unattractive" rather than "You think I'm unattractive").

Exercise 7.3 will challenge you to supply the unspoken communications in a conversation and compare your assumptions with your partner's.

Exercise 7.3   Checking Out Assumptions

Partner 1

Olivia and Kirby are engaged in a discussion. As in all discussions, they are interpreting each other's behavior, but their unspoken thoughts are not printed. You and your partner should read the conversation and independently write what you think belongs in the blanks for "unspoken level of communication." In other words, write down the assumptions you make about each person's meanings, thoughts, and motives. When you are done, compare your answers.

Olivia: Well, I had another irritating conversation with our neighbor, Mrs. Miller, today.

Kirby: *(Spoken level of communication)* We've had this conversation before. I don't understand why you keep talking to her.

   (Unspoken level of communication) _____

   _____

Olivia: *(Spoken level of communication)* She's our *neighbor*, Kirby. Anyway, today she told me she was sorry that our house had been painted so poorly—can you believe that?

   (Unspoken level of communication) _____

   _____

Kirby: *(Spoken level of communication)* Well, if we had as much money as she does, maybe we could have hired a better painter. Why don't you tell her to mind her own business?

   (Unspoken level of communication) _____

   _____

Olivia: *(Spoken level of communication)* Well, I have to talk to someone during the day.

   (Unspoken level of communication) _____

   _____

Kirby: *(Spoken level of communication)* I've told you before that I don't have time to call you to chat when I'm at work. Why don't you join a church group or do volunteer work?

   (Unspoken level of communication) _____

   _____

Partner 2

Olivia and Kirby are engaged in a discussion. As in all discussions, they are interpreting each other's behavior, but their unspoken thoughts are not printed. You and your partner should read the conversation and independently write what you think belongs in the blanks for "unspoken level of communication." In other words, write down the assumptions you make about each person's meanings, thoughts, and motives. When you are done, compare your answers.

Olivia: Well, I had another irritating conversation with our neighbor, Mrs. Miller, today.

Kirby: *(Spoken level of communication)* We've had this conversation before. I don't understand why you keep talking to her.

   (Unspoken level of communication) _____

   _____

Olivia: *(Spoken level of communication)* She's our *neighbor*, Kirby. Anyway, today she told me she was sorry that our house had been painted so poorly—can you believe that?

   (Unspoken level of communication) _____

   _____

Kirby: *(Spoken level of communication)* Well, if we had as much money as she does, maybe we could have hired a better painter. Why don't you tell her to mind her own business?

   (Unspoken level of communication) _____

   _____

Olivia: *(Spoken level of communication)* Well, I have to talk to someone during the day.

   (Unspoken level of communication) _____

   _____

Kirby: *(Spoken level of communication)* I've told you before that I don't have time to call you to chat when I'm at work. Why don't you join a church group or do volunteer work?

   (Unspoken level of communication) _____

   _____

The exercise probably revealed that you and your partner do not interpret the same messages in the same way (this is true for almost all couples) and could benefit by telling each other about your assumptions. When partners share their assumptions with each other, usually the assumptions cause fewer difficulties.

STEP 10: LISTENING ACTIVELY

Unhappy couples frequently fail to listen to and validate each other. To validate what someone says is simply to communicate to the person that you hear what he or she says (whether you agree with it or not). The feeling that each partner's words are heard and acknowledged can be very helpful in discussions of topics that elicit disagreement. The two most common ways to validate a speaker are through paraphrasing and nonverbal signs.

Paraphrasing

Paraphrasing is saying to your partner what you think he or she has said. Paraphrasing lets your partner know that you are listening and lets you check out your assumptions. Partners often react to what they think they heard; this is often quite different from what actually was said. Paraphrasing prevents this from happening, as the following two examples show.

Conversation With No Paraphrasing

Tom: I feel like we've been working to improve
        our relationship for a long time.

Sheila: I'm about ready to leave also.

Tom: Well, then I'll leave too!

Conversation With Paraphrasing

Tom: I feel like we've been working on our relationship for a long time.

Sheila: You feel we've been working on our relationship for a long time.
        [paraphrases] Do you mean that you want to give up on it?
        [checks out assumption]

Tom: I can see why you'd say that I sound like I want to give up on it
        [paraphrases], but what I mean is that I'm proud of how long
        we've been able to stick with it. [clarifies]

Sheila: I'm glad to hear you're proud of how hard we have worked.
        [paraphrases] I am too.

Nonverbal Cues

Another way to validate your partner is through nonverbal cues. Making eye contact, nodding, and maintaining an open body posture can be a good way to let your partner know that you are listening, even if you say little more than an occasional "uh-huh." Also, if your partner uses particular nonverbal signs that make you feel that you are being heard, let your partner know about them now.

Exercise 7.4 will ask you to apply active listening to some imaginary conversations.

Exercise 7.4   Active Listening

Partner 1

Following are conversation clips in which one person is not validating the other. On the blank lines, write some paraphrasing statements or nonverbal behaviors the listener could use to validate the partner. Do the exercise independently, and then compare your results with your partner's.

Conversation 1

Alex: I had an upsetting conversation with your mother today.

Janine: I don't see why you can't get along with her.

Alternatives: _____

_____

Alex: I can't get along with her because she always criticizes me.

Janine: Well, maybe you need to have tougher skin.

Alternatives: _____

_____

Conversation 2

Rochelle: I really enjoy going to the art museum.

Danton: I can't see why; their collection is really poor.

Alternatives: _____

_____

Rochelle: It's just nice to get out of the house.

Danton: In this heat? No way!

Alternatives: _____

_____

Conversation 3

Celia: I'm worried that we're too strict with the kids.

Alvin: What do you know about how to raise kids?

Alternatives: _____

_____

Celia: I'm not an expert on how to raise children, but I could see how upset they were when we grounded them.

Alvin: They got what they deserved. If they don't like it that's too bad.

Alternatives: _____

_____

Partner 2

Following are conversation clips in which one person is not validating the other. On the blank lines, write some paraphrasing statements or nonverbal behaviors the listener could use to validate the partner. Do the exercise independently, and then compare your results with your partner's.

Conversation 1

Alex: I had an upsetting conversation with your mother today.

Janine: I don't see why you can't get along with her.

Alternatives: _____

_____

Alex: I can't get along with her because she always criticizes me.

Janine: Well, maybe you need to have tougher skin.

Alternatives: _____

_____

Conversation 2

Rochelle: I really enjoy going to the art museum.

Danton: I can't see why; their collection is really poor.

Alternatives: _____

_____

Rochelle: It's just nice to get out of the house.

Danton: In this heat? No way!

Alternatives: _____

_____

Conversation 3

Celia: I'm worried that we're too strict with the kids.

Alvin: What do you know about how to raise kids?

Alternatives: _____

_____

Celia: I'm not an expert on how to raise children, but I could see how upset they were when we grounded them.

Alvin: They got what they deserved. If they don't like it that's too bad.

Alternatives: _____

_____

STEP 11: GIVING BEHAVIOR-EFFECT FEEDBACK

Behavior-effect feedback is a way to let your partner know what effect he or she has on your feelings, thoughts, and actions. It is a tool for communication that lets you comment on your partner's behavior in a specific and nonjudgmental way. Giving someone feedback helps the person make connections between what is visible (behavior) and what cannot be seen (thoughts, feelings, and needs). Feedback is a structured way to share information about the relationship. Feedback takes this form: "When you [partner's behavior], I felt/thought/said/did [your reaction]." Table 7.2 lists several examples of behavior-effect feedback.

Feedback fits into the communication skills you learned earlier because it is specific and uses "I" language. Feedback should also be balanced. That is, if you give your partner a piece of negative feedback about a behavior you dislike, balance it with a piece of positive feedback. The subject of feedback should be your partner's behavior (what you can see). It is inappropriate to use feedback to mind read, as in "When you think that I'm a bad person, I get angry." Though awkward at first, feedback is valuable for learning to communicate more effectively. It tells you what you are doing well and what you could improve. It also lets you know that the skills you are learning are having an effect.

For practice in feedback, pay attention to what your partner does during your next scheduled talk time. At the end, give your partner balanced feedback about the communication. Do this following every scheduled conversation from now on.

Table 7.2   Examples of Behavior-Effect Feedback

When you say hello to me, I feel good.

When you cross your arms, I worry that you aren't listening.

When you paraphrase what I've said, I feel validated.

When you let me know that you're coming home late, I make dinner later and it's not a problem.

When you talk to me during my favorite TV show, I ignore what you say.

When you kiss and hug me, I feel sexually aroused.

STEP 12: NOTING PROGRESS AND REWARDING YOURSELVES

Change is not easy, and by now you and your partner have exerted considerable effort to improve your communication skills. We hope that this effort is paying off and that the changes you see in your relationship are rewarding in themselves. Even so, it is important to acknowledge these changes to yourself and your partner, even if they are less dramatic than you had hoped for. As we suggested at the end of the last chapter, you should again make a list of the efforts your partner has made to improve the relationship. Do this before your next scheduled conversation; begin the conversation by sharing your list with your partner and expressing your appreciation for his or her effort. Your support of each other's efforts will contribute to your progress. Finally, listen to the two tapes you made of your conversations as you worked on the previous chapter. Can you hear changes in the way you talk to each other now?

8 *Learning to Communicate Effectively: Advanced Steps*

Before you begin this chapter, make sure that you feel comfortable using the skills you have learned so far. It is very important that you continue validating, listening actively, being aware of your feelings and thoughts, and so on. Until you hear yourself consistently using the skills in the conversations you tape, it is probably best to postpone working on the advanced steps in improving communication.

In this chapter, we focus on ways to talk about areas of your relationship in which you have disagreement. Table 8.1 outlines the advanced steps that will be covered.

Table 8.1   Advanced Steps for More Effective Communication

13. Know when to problem solve.

14. Define the problem.

15. Solve or deal with problems.

16. Generate and evaluate solutions.

17. Make a contract.

18. Evaluate your progress.

STEP 13: KNOWING WHEN TO PROBLEM SOLVE

For many couples, attempts to problem solve result in communication breakdown and a sense of failure. This is because couples often stop using their communication skills when they approach areas of strong disagreement ("hot" topics). As you discovered in chapter 6, setting the stage for communication is an important step toward better communication. Similarly, setting the stage for problem solving is particularly important for improving your chances of resolving relationship difficulties. This section reviews some skills that will help you set the stage for successful problem solving.

Emotional Awareness

In Step 8, you learned how to identify emotions. At the beginning of each problem-solving session it is particularly important that you gauge both your own and your partner's mood. When people are experiencing intense emotions, they tend to misread other's intentions, become less rational, and have more difficulty reaching agreement with each other. All of these effects of strong emotion are counterproductive for a couple trying to solve a problem. If either of you is feeling strong emotion, this is not the time to try problem solving. Instead, turn to other activities that will help each of you calm down —for example, taking a time-out, talking and listening actively about the feelings each of you is experiencing, and the like. It is fine to problem solve on issues about which you have feelings, but the time to do it is when both partners are feeling fairly calm and rational. Exercise 8.1 will help you recognize the best times for problem solving.

Exercise 8.1   Knowing When to Problem Solve

Partner 1

Look over Exercise 7.2 again and review what each of you wrote. Then each of you should complete the following statements independently and compare your responses.

Some signs that I am having feelings that will prevent me from engaging in productive problem solving are . . .

_____

_____

_____

Some signs that my partner is having feelings that will prevent him or her from engaging in productive problem solving are . . .

_____

_____

_____

Some signs that I am in an emotional state that will promote effective problem solving are . . .

_____

_____

_____

Some signs that my partner is in an emotional state that will promote effective problem solving are . . .

_____

_____

_____

Partner 2

Look over Exercise 7.2 again and review what each of you wrote. Then each of you should complete the following statements independently and compare your responses.

Some signs that I am having feelings that will prevent me from engaging in productive problem solving are . . .

_____

_____

_____

Some signs that my partner is having feelings that will prevent him or her from engaging in productive problem solving are . . .

_____

_____

_____

Some signs that I am in an emotional state that will promote effective problem solving are . . .

_____

_____

_____

Some signs that my partner is in an emotional state that will promote effective problem solving are . . .

_____

_____

_____

Frame of Mind

Your thoughts can also detract from or promote problem solving. In the model of communication presented in chapter 4, we explained how your thoughts about your partner and your relationship can affect communication. If you are thinking of your partner as a collaborator, are seeing your relationship as having some positive features, are expecting progress to be made in your relationship, and are attributing good intentions to your partner, the conditions are excellent for problem solving. In contrast, if you are viewing your partner as an enemy, thinking that your relationship is bad and is unlikely to change, and believing that your partner has no interest in the relationship or does not care about you, it is not a good time to begin problem solving. First, attend to your negative thoughts, using the strategies outlined so far for countering them. Coming to a problem-solving session in a negative frame of mind is a good way to undermine the process. Exercise 8.2 will help you examine your frame of mind.

Exercise 8.2   Undermining Versus Promoting Problem Solving

Draw a line down the middle of a sheet of paper. In the left column make a list of things that might undermine problem solving by completing the following sentence in as many ways as possible:

Some things I might be thinking about myself, my partner, and our relationship that would undermine problem solving are . . .

In the right column list things that might promote problem solving by completing the following sentence:

Some things I might be thinking about myself, my partner, and our relationship that would promote problem solving are . . .

STEP 14: DEFINING THE PROBLEM

Doris and Leslie are talking at the dinner table.

Doris: You didn't pay any attention to me at the Wangs' party.

Leslie: That's not true—we stayed together for at least 15 minutes when we first came in. Anyway, I like getting a chance to talk with other people.

Doris: I like that too.

Leslie: Then I don't understand why you're complaining.

Doris: Well, I noticed you talked with the Rileys for almost half an hour.

Leslie: What's wrong with them?

Doris: Nothing, I like them very much.

Leslie: Then what are you complaining about?

Doris: I don't know exactly, it's just that something is bothering me.

Leslie: Well, if you can't tell me what I'm doing wrong, what am I supposed to do about it?

Doris and Leslie can't work productively together because they are not trying to solve the same problem. Leslie sees the problem as stopping whatever he is doing that makes Doris upset. Doris is not sure what the problem is. Maybe she is trying to say that she feels uneasy in social situations without Leslie by her side or that she feels she is less important to Leslie than other people are. In any case, she and Leslie have not clearly defined the problem. You can't work on a problem and agree on a solution unless you first come to an agreement about the problem. Defining the problem requires such skills as being specific, taking responsibility, and listening actively. It requires that both partners work together.

Let's see how Doris and Leslie might go about things differently.

Doris: You didn't pay any attention to me at the Wangs' party.

Leslie: When you say I didn't pay attention to you at the party [paraphrases], do you mean that you think I totally ignored you [checks out assumption]?

Doris: I understand that you feel I'm saying that you totally ignore me [paraphrases], but what I *am* saying is that I felt hurt that you spent less time with me than you did with other people [clarifies, uses "I" language]. I enjoyed the time you spent with me when we first got to the party [balances].

Leslie: I see that you're hurt [paraphrases]. I spend time with other people because I enjoy a chance to talk to other people at parties [takes responsibility for self, uses "I" language].

Doris: It's not your fault that I felt hurt [takes responsibility]. I understand that you enjoy talking to other people [paraphrases], but I also want us to spend more time together at parties [uses "I" language]. I feel as though I don't matter when we don't spend enough time together.

Leslie: You want us to spend more time together at parties [paraphrases]. I like the way we are at parties now [uses "I" language]. So it seems to me that we have different expectations about how much attention to pay to each other, and so we disagree on how much time to spend together at parties [checks out assumption].

Doris: Yes, we seem to have different expectations, and we don't agree on how much time to spend together at parties [paraphrases].

Doris and Leslie together have clearly defined the problem, and they can now start working on it. They have agreed on a description of the problem (they have different expectations, and they disagree about how much time to spend together at parties) and have communicated their feelings about the problem (Leslie likes the way things are now, but Doris is hurt by the status quo).

Typically, a good problem definition meets five criteria:

1. It is mutually agreed upon. Both partners have input into definition of the problem, and they make clear through paraphrasing that both understand the problem in the same way.

2. It outlines each partner's role in the problem. One partner is not disparaged or blamed for the problem or made responsible for solving it. Both partners must admit that they contribute to the problem.

3. It includes a simple and specific description of the problem. The problem is not so vague or global (i.e., "There is a general sense of unease in our marriage" or "We don't enjoy each other enough") that it is hard to know where to start solving it. The definition must be specific enough that both partners can easily understand what the problem is. The easiest way to make a problem specific is to mention examples or specific things each partner does that cause difficulties.

4. It describes each partner's feelings about the problem. Partners should briefly express their feelings using "I" language.

5. It includes something positive. Problem definitions should be balanced, including positive elements as well as negative ones—for example, "I like the time we spend together at parties, but we disagree on how much of that kind of time we want." Mentioning the positive features surrounding a problem helps the listener hear about the problem without feeling criticized. Following are examples of problem definitions: Some are better than others.

Example 1

Poor: You don't care about our relationship. [This statement is poor because it blames one partner, includes nothing positive, and is vague and global.]

Slightly better: I feel unloved in our relationship. [This statement is better because it uses "I" language, states a feeling, and does not blame; however, it is still not specific enough and includes no positives.]

Much better: I enjoy the time we spend together. So when we go to a party and you talk with other people more than with me, I feel unloved. [This statement is much better because it specifies a behavior, does not blame, admits that both partners are part of the problem, includes something positive, and states a feeling. Of course, the other partner must agree on this definition before it is complete.]

Example 2

Poor: We just don't get along anymore. [This statement is poor because it is very vague and global, includes no positives, and does not address feelings.]

Slightly better: Since Margie was born, we seem to bicker with each other every day. [This statement is slightly better because it narrows the problem to a particular time in the relationship and specifies a behavior that is causing problems.]

Much better: I'm upset because ever since Margie was born, we argue over bills at the end of each month. I liked the way we used to work together on bills. [This statement is much more specific and includes a feeling statement. It is also balanced. Again, it needs to be confirmed by the other partner.]

Example 3

Poor: Our sex life is lousy. [This statement is vague and contains no positives; neither partner takes responsibility.]

Slightly better: I've been enjoying sex less lately because you don't touch me enough when we make love. [This statement narrows the definition and uses "I" language; however, it blames one person and is totally negative.]

Much better: Since you were assigned the night shift at work, I've being enjoying sex less because we have less time for lovemaking. I liked it better when we had more time for sex because you touched me more and that made me feel good. [This statement is much more specific, includes something positive, and does not blame the partner.]

You now have some idea of what constitutes a good problem definition. Exercise 8.3 will give you practice in defining problems.

Exercise 8.3   Defining Problems

Select a topic from your list of problems to discuss and try to define it (not *solve it*) *with your partner. Use your active listening skills to reach a definition that meets the five criteria outlined earlier. Try this with several problems on your list. When you reach agreement, write down your definitions. As a reminder, we have summarized the features of good and bad problem definitions in Table 8.2.*

Table 8.2 Features of Good and Bad Problem Definitions

Good problem definitions

1. Are mutually agreed upon
2. Outline each partner's role in the problem
3. Include a simple and specific description of the problem
4. Include a description of each partner's feelings about the problem
5. Include something positive

Bad problem definitions

1. State only one partner's view
2. Are accusatory and blaming
3. Tend to be general and vague
4. Simply list each person's gripes
5. Focus only on the negative

STEP 15: SOLVING VERSUS DEALING WITH PROBLEMS

These two couples have difficulties of different sorts.

Couple 1

Clausell and Bernice have been married for 5 years. Four weeks ago, Bernice's mother died. Bernice is frequently sad and tearful, even though Clausell tries to cheer her up. Lately, they both find themselves too exhausted to go out and have fun together.

Couple 2

Pat and Karen have been living together for 2 years, and they plan on staying together because they are both very happy in their relationship. On graduating from college, both received attractive offers for jobs in cities that are 20 miles apart. Neither wants to turn down the offer, yet they both want to live together in the same house.

Both couples face problems, but the problems are of different kinds. Some problems are amenable to practical solutions, whereas others are not. Bernice and Clausell's problem results from something that cannot be changed. Bernice's mother is dead, and Bernice is experiencing normal feelings of grief, which have an impact on the relationship. Obviously, because death cannot be reversed, the problem cannot be solved in a practical sense. Nevertheless, the problem can be dealt with: Clausell can actively listen to Bernice's feelings and support her until she completes the grieving process and the relationship returns to normal.

Pat and Karen's problem, in contrast, can be solved in a practical sense. One of them can commute from home to the other city, or the couple can live at a geographical midpoint and both can commute. Of course, they may still need to deal with feelings about their living arrangement, but their problem can be largely solved in a practical way.

These two problems illustrate the difference between dealing with and solving a problem. Though Clausell and Bernice may do some practical problem solving (e.g., setting aside time to talk each day), most of their work lies in dealing with feelings about a problem. Karen and Pat's situation requires a different emphasis: Though they need to address their feelings to some extent, most of their work lies in reaching a practical decision about living arrangements.

When attempting to problem solve, you must be aware of the kind of problem you are facing. Some problems do not require many practical changes but do require that partners support each other. Typically, these problems mean coping primarily with feelings. Other problems may be solved quickly, easily, and practically. These problems primarily involve actions rather than feelings.

Partners frequently disagree about which kinds of problems require solutions and which require dealing with feelings. One fairly common pattern in heterosexual relationships involves the man's trying to solve problems practically while the woman tries to deal with them emotionally. A woman in this situation often believes that the man does not want to listen to her feelings but rather wishes to "solve" them and make them vanish. The man often feels that the woman merely wants to complain rather than solve the problem that is causing the trouble in the first place.

A crucial aspect of problem solving is telling your partner honestly whether you think the problem should be solved, dealt with, or both. The easiest way to do this is to make statements using "I" language. For example, you might say, "I just need you to listen to how I felt when the car wouldn't start—I'd rather worry about how to fix it later" or "I don't really care which weekend we go to your mother's—I just want to arrange it now so I won't have a schedule conflict later." As with other skills you have learned, verbalizing your perception of a problem advances communication by making something that is private and known only to you a part of the shared world of your relationship.

Many problems are entirely practical (e.g., choosing a movie, deciding what time to eat) or entirely emotional (e.g., needing kind words after a disappointment, adjusting to the emotional shock of turning 40), but others have both emotional and practical dimensions. A good example lies in the preparation for marriage. Couples anticipating marriage deal with intense feelings of fear, joy, and love; they also face many practical problems, such as the list of wedding guests, the financial arrangements, the type of ceremony, and the location of the wedding. When facing a problem that has both emotions to be dealt with and practical solutions to enact, always be clear about which part of the process you are addressing. Miscommunication is likely when one partner is trying to solve the problem rationally while the other is trying to share feelings about it. If you are unsure what is happening at the moment, ask your partner: "Are we talking about how we feel now, or do you want to try to think up practical solutions?" or "I feel that we have had a chance to express our feelings, and I want to move on to looking for a solution—is that OK with you?" In general we suggest dealing with feelings first—particularly if they are strong—because people are usually better at solving practical problems when their feelings have been heard and validated.

Exercise 8.4 will ask you to judge whether certain problems should be solved or simply dealt with.

Exercise 8.4   Solving Versus Dealing With Problems

Partner 1

You and your partner should rate each problem on the list independently, following the instructions. Then compare your answers. If your two sets of scores are consistently different, you should take extra care to clarify the way you view problems when you attempt problem solving together.

Assign each problem a number from 1 to 5. The numbers have the following meanings:

1 = The problem is completely practical and can be solved.

2 = Some feelings may need to be dealt with, but the problem is mostly practical.

3 = The problem will require equal amounts of practical problem solving and dealing with emotions.

4 = The problem may require a little practical problem solving but mostly must be dealt with emotionally.

5 = The problem has no practical solution, and all that we can do is deal with the problem.

Problems

_____ 1. What clock to use to start prearranged talk times

_____ 2. Who will do the dishes

_____ 3. How to handle a child who won't go to bed on time

_____ 4. How to increase feelings of affection in the relationship

_____ 5. What kind of car to buy

_____ 6. How much physical affection to display in public

_____ 7. What to do when one partner is laid off from work

_____ 8. Whom to invite to a party

_____ 9. How much time to spend with in-laws

_____ 10. When to have children

_____ 11. Whether or not to use birth control and what kind to use

Partner 2

You and your partner should rate each problem on the list independently, following the instructions. Then compare your answers. If your two sets of scores are consistently different, you should take extra care to clarify the way you view problems when you attempt problem solving together.

Assign each problem a number from 1 to 5. The numbers have the following meanings:

1 = The problem is completely practical and can be solved.

2 = Some feelings may need to be dealt with, but the problem is mostly practical.

3 = The problem will require equal amounts of practical problem solving and dealing with emotions.

4 = The problem may require a little practical problem solving but mostly must be dealt with emotionally.

5 = The problem has no practical solution, and all that we can do is deal with the problem.

Problems

_____   1. What clock to use to start prearranged talk times

_____   2. Who will do the dishes

_____   3. How to handle a child who won't go to bed on time

_____   4. How to increase feelings of affection in the relationship

_____   5. What kind of car to buy

_____   6. How much physical affection to display in public

_____   7. What to do when one partner is laid off from work

_____   8. Whom to invite to a party

_____   9. How much time to spend with in-laws

_____   10. When to have children

_____   11. Whether or not to use birth control and what kind to use

STEP 16: GENERATING AND EVALUATING SOLUTIONS

Once you and your partner have defined the problem and agreed to work on solving it, you can start working toward a solution. During this process, you should resist the temptation to redefine the problem or bring up new problems. A good way to start your search for a solution is to break down the process into two steps—brainstorming and evaluation. Brainstorming is simply generating as many possible solutions—however unusual or ridiculous—as you can. You may hesitate to mention certain solutions for fear that they will not work or that your partner will reject them out of hand. In fact, however, if none of your solutions is ridiculous, you are not letting yourself go enough to benefit from brainstorming. You'll have time to evaluate the alternatives later.

Here is an example of brainstorming by Frank and Louise, a middle-aged married couple. Louise is angry because Frank never helps her do the laundry. She nags Frank about it, and this makes him angry. The couple defines the problem as follows: "Though Frank helps with the dishes and other housework, he never does the laundry, which makes Louise angry. Frank is angry because Louise nags him about the laundry." They brainstorm these alternatives:

1. Frank and Louise will send the laundry to the cleaner's.
2. Frank and Louise will not do their laundry at all but instead will get used to wearing dirty clothes.
3. Louise will continue to do the laundry and stop nagging Frank.
4. Frank will do all the laundry from now on to make up for Louise's doing it herself for so long.
5. Frank will do the laundry every other week. Louise will stop nagging Frank.
6. Each partner will do his or her own laundry.
7. Frank will pay Louise to do his laundry.
8. Frank will leave the house whenever he is nagged about the laundry.

Another couple, Jackie and Bob, have a different problem. Bob is bisexual and has had several sexual affairs with men over the course of the marriage. Jackie feels hurt and is afraid that Bob will contract the AIDS virus. They brainstorm these alternatives:

1. Bob will never have another affair.
2. Bob will have affairs only with women.
3. Jackie will have affairs of her own.
4. Bob will continue to have affairs with men but will begin practicing safer sex.
5. Bob will have close friendships with other men but not have sex with them.
6. Bob and Jackie will go to sex therapy together to work on the problem.
7. Bob will have no male friends.
8. Bob will associate with gay friends only if Jackie is around.

Exercise 8.5 will ask you to practice brainstorming about another problem.

Exercise 8.5 Brainstorming

Here is a couple with a problem. After reading the problem definition, each of you should generate at least 10 possible solutions. Some of them should be ridiculous or impractical.

Nora and Sal have been dating for a year. Both want to get married, but their families always bicker with each other, and they are afraid to bring the families together for a wedding because they do not want their big day ruined.

List your solutions separately, then compare your lists.

Evaluation takes place after all possible solutions have been listed. You can discard some solutions right away because you both agree that they are silly or involve some changes neither of you wants. For example, Frank and Louise can quickly agree that Solution 2 is out because they both want clean clothes, and Solution 1 is out because they both want to spend their money on other things. Once you have eliminated the obvious items, you will be left with a few potential solutions to discuss, using your listening skills. Those possibilities can be refined or combined into a solution that will work.

Once you have generated a solution, how do you know whether or not it will work? Effective solutions depend on collaboration and compromise. Collaboration means that both partners help each other to achieve whatever they have agreed on. For example, if Frank agrees to do the laundry every other week, Louise can agree to stop nagging him and thank him when he does the laundry. If your solution involves change on the part of your partner, ask yourself, "What can I do differently to help my partner change?" A good solution does not demand that one partner change to please the other but that both partners work together to change the relationship and make it better for both.

The other feature of a good solution is compromise. It is hard to get exactly what you want in a relationship, but you can frequently get some of what you want if you are willing to give your partner the same. Frank will probably not do the laundry all the time as Louise would like, but he may be willing to do it some of the time. Frank cannot have things exactly as he would like either, but he can get his wife to stop nagging and also still get his laundry done for him half the time. You may be surprised how much easier it is to change if you know your partner is changing too. Your partner will be much more likely to give in a bit if you do the same. Exercise 8.6 is an exercise in compromise.

Exercise 8.6 Compromising

Look over the problems you indicated in Exercise 4.1 (see Questionnaire 3). Write down your ideal solution for each problem and what you would be willing to settle for. These two things should be clearly different. Use this list for reference as you engage in problem solving with your partner. Remind yourself that you can give in some and still come away satisfied.

STEP 17: MAKING A CONTRACT

Once you and your partner have come up with a solution through problem definition, brainstorming, and evaluation, you should put it into a written contract. A contract is a clear and specific agreement between partners about some change you are going to make in your relationship. Some couples feel that writing their agreements down is silly or overly legalistic—yet consider the advantages. When we must put something in writing, we are forced to be clear about what we mean. We also have something to refer to in case we forget or misinterpret an agreement. Finally, writing something down with a partner often strengthens our commitment to honor the promises we have made.

When you make a written agreement with your partner, be sure that it includes specific behaviors. If you don't, misunderstandings will result. A couple who contracts to something vague like "Jerry will be nicer to Kinsha" is likely to run into difficulty: Jerry may think being nicer involves taking out the trash, whereas Kinsha may think it means kissing her good night. On the other hand, if Jerry and Kinsha write a contract that says, "Jerry will take the trash out to the dumpster every Wednesday and Saturday night," there is no chance of misunderstanding or disagreement over whether or not the contract has been fulfilled.

Similarly, couples should not make contracts to change feelings and thoughts because these things are not equally easy for both partners to observe and determine if the contract is being honored (we always know our own thoughts and feelings better than we do those of others). If the couple contracts that "Kinsha will make Jerry feel that his work is important," Kinsha will be unable to tell whether or not Jerry is having such a feeling; she also may not know how to induce it. A better contract would include specific behaviors—for example, "When Jerry comes home from work and talks about his day, Kinsha will listen actively, using paraphrasing and empathy, for at least 5 minutes." If one partner is not sure what behaviors help induce certain feelings and thoughts, the other partner can help by giving behavior-effect feedback (e.g., "When you talk to me about my job, I feel important"). These specific behaviors, unlike feelings or thoughts, are easily seen and monitored by both partners. Both can thus agree on whether or not the contract is being carried out. Here are some examples of good and bad contracts:

Contract 1

Bad: Enrico will be more emotionally expressive around Lee.

Good: At least once a day, Enrico will express his emotions about something that has happened that day. Lee will listen actively to what Enrico says.

Contract 2

Bad: Molly will help Rollo get the kids to bed.

Good: At 7:45 each night Molly will check to make sure that both of the children have brushed their teeth and are in their pajamas. At 8:00 she will tell them to go to bed. Rollo will agree with Molly in front of the children that it is time for bed and will go upstairs with them, tuck them in, and kiss them good night.

Contract 3

Bad: Maria will be more sexy around Carlos and make him feel more aroused.

Good: At least one night a week Maria will initiate sexual activity such as kissing, hugging, petting, and/or intercourse. Before, during, or after sexual activity, both she and Carlos will talk about what they enjoy about sex and what they find attractive in each other.

Contract 4

Bad: Cris will believe that Rich is handling the finances correctly.

Good: Cris will not tell Rich that he is incompetent at handling money. Rich will show Cris the bank statements at the end of each month and explain them to Cris.

Building in Reminders

In drawing up a contract, it is often helpful to build in some reminder of the changes to be made. Even with the best of intentions, partners often fall into old habits simply because the habits are familiar. You can help yourselves interrupt these familiar patterns by setting up reminders. For example, you might post a contract on the refrigerator or put up a sign that only you will understand (a man who is trying to express more love and appreciation for his wife might draw a heart on his date book). In addition, you can facilitate progress by specifying some behavior that one partner can use to make change easier for the other. For example, your contract might say, "Belinda will not smoke in Jim's presence, and Jim will thank her for it" or "When Harry says something loving, Bea will hug him and tell him that she appreciates him."

The features of good problem solutions and contracts are summarized in Table 8.3; Exercise 8.7 will give you a chance to practice making good contracts.

Table 8.3   Features of a Good Problem Solution or Contract

1. Focuses on specific behaviors

2. Outlines ways in which each partner can change

3. Specifies ways in which each partner can help the other change

4. Reflects a compromise between the partners

5. Is available to both partners (best if each has a written copy)

Exercise 8.7   Producing Good Contracts

The following contracts are poor because they do not address specific behaviors and do not include ways that partners can help each other make the desired changes. With your partner, discuss the weaknesses of each contract and revise it. You can assume anything you like about the relationships in each example, as long as the result is a good contract.

1. Tom will be a better host to Pat's friends.
2. Rachel will make an effort to be more supportive of Alex.
3. Keith will not drink so much.
4. Lilly will befriend Joe's mother.
5. LaBradford will worry less.

STEP 18: EVALUATING YOUR PROGRESS

You have now completed the chapters on learning to communicate effectively, and it is time to evaluate your progress. As you recall from chapter 4, the only way to improve communication is by changing behavior. Thus, a starting point is to consider the behaviors that occur between you and your partner during communication. Exercise 8.8 will help you determine whether your communication behaviors have improved.

Another way to evaluate your progress in communication is to repeat some of the questionnaires you used in chapter 4 to assess the state of your relationship at that point. In Exercise 8.9, you will use the Communication Patterns Questionnaire (Questionnaire 2 in chapter 4) to look for changes in your patterns of communication.

Exercise 8.10 is an overall evaluation. You will use the Marital Adjustment Test and the Modified Positive Feelings Questionnaire (Questionnaires 1 and 7 from chapter 4) to reevaluate your satisfaction with the relationship and your feelings within the relationship. Because these are two important factors that influence and are influenced by behavior—and because behavior is the means for changing communication—we ask you to reexamine them now.

Compare your responses to these questionnaires with the responses you gave the first time around. The measures in Exercise 8.10 tend to be fairly stable over time, and you should not be disappointed if your scores on them have not changed dramatically. Still, now that you have completed the communication skills chapters, you will find it useful to make a before-and-after comparison of your answers.

Whatever the degree of change you have managed to bring about in your relationship, you need to consolidate your gains and make every effort to maintain them. Chapter 9 discusses ways to do this and shows how you can benefit by using your new skills in other relationships.

If you and your partner have made a sincere and concerted effort to work through chapters 6 through 8 and you still see no change in your communication, you may need more assistance than this book can offer. We recommend that you seriously consider consulting a professional counselor.

Exercise 8.8   Changes in Communication Behaviors

Partner 1

The following are communication behaviors that occur during problem-solving discussions. For each item, decide whether the behavior in your relationship has remained the same or improved. Your responses on this exercise will point to the things that have changed in your communication with your partner and the things you still need to work on. At your next scheduled communication time, you and your partner should discuss each item on the list and, using the skills you have learned, come to an agreement about any behaviors that still need to be changed.

Same   **Improved**

☐   ☐   My partner is pessimistic about solving the problem.

☐   ☐   My partner is calm and relaxed in discussing the problem.

☐   ☐   My partner brings up problems that are unrelated to the one we are discussing.

☐   ☐   My partner focuses on how things might be better in the future.

☐   ☐   My partner does not listen fully to what I am saying.

☐   ☐   My partner does not offer constructive solutions to the problem.

☐   ☐   My partner takes some responsibility for the problem.

☐   ☐   My partner interrupts me when I am speaking and does not allow me to express my opinions.

☐   ☐   My partner is honest and open with his/her feelings about the problem.

☐   ☐   My partner focuses on the problem we are discussing.

☐   ☐   My partner criticizes me and my views of the problem.

☐   ☐   My partner does not express his/her real feelings about the problem.

☐   ☐   My partner allows me to express my opinions.

☐   ☐   My partner blames me or holds me responsible for the problem.

☐   ☐   My partner offers constructive solutions to the problem.

☐   ☐   My partner listens closely to what I am saying.

☐   ☐   My partner is tense and anxious in discussing the problem.

Same	**Improved**	
☐	☐	My partner is supportive of me and my views of the problem.
☐	☐	My partner focuses on bad things from the past.
☐	☐	My partner is optimistic about solving the problem.
☐	☐	I am pessimistic about solving the problem.
☐	☐	I am calm and relaxed in discussing the problem.
☐	☐	I bring up problems that are unrelated to the one we are discussing.
☐	☐	I focus on how things might be better in the future.
☐	☐	I do not listen fully to what my partner is saying.
☐	☐	I do not offer constructive solutions to the problem.
☐	☐	I take some responsibility for the problem.
☐	☐	I interrupt my partner when he/she is speaking and do not allow him/her to express his/her opinions.
☐	☐	I am honest and open with my feelings about the problem.
☐	☐	I focus on the problem we are discussing.
☐	☐	I criticize my partner and his/her views of the problem.
☐	☐	I do not express my real feelings about the problem.
☐	☐	I allow my partner to express his/her opinions.
☐	☐	I blame my partner for the problem.
☐	☐	I offer constructive solutions to the problem.
☐	☐	I listen closely to what my partner says.
☐	☐	I am tense and anxious in discussing the problem.
☐	☐	I am supportive of my partner and his/her views of the problem.
☐	☐	I focus on bad things from the past.
☐	☐	I am optimistic about solving the problem.

Partner 2

The following are communication behaviors that occur during problem-solving discussions. For each item, decide whether the behavior in your relationship has remained the same or improved. Your responses on this exercise will point to the things that have changed in your communication with your partner and the things you still need to work on. At your next scheduled communication time, you and your partner should discuss each item on the list and, using the skills you have learned, come to an agreement about any behaviors that still need to be changed.

Same   **Improved**

☐   ☐   My partner is pessimistic about solving the problem.

☐   ☐   My partner is calm and relaxed in discussing the problem.

☐   ☐   My partner brings up problems that are unrelated to the one we are discussing.

☐   ☐   My partner focuses on how things might be better in the future.

☐   ☐   My partner does not listen fully to what I am saying.

☐   ☐   My partner does not offer constructive solutions to the problem.

☐   ☐   My partner takes some responsibility for the problem.

☐   ☐   My partner interrupts me when I am speaking and does not allow me to express my opinions.

☐   ☐   My partner is honest and open with his/her feelings about the problem.

☐   ☐   My partner focuses on the problem we are discussing.

☐   ☐   My partner criticizes me and my views of the problem.

☐   ☐   My partner does not express his/her real feelings about the problem.

☐   ☐   My partner allows me to express my opinions.

☐   ☐   My partner blames me or holds me responsible for the problem.

☐   ☐   My partner offers constructive solutions to the problem.

☐   ☐   My partner listens closely to what I am saying.

☐   ☐   My partner is tense and anxious in discussing the problem.

Same   **Improved**

☐   ☐   My partner is supportive of me and my views of the problem.

☐   ☐   My partner focuses on bad things from the past.

☐   ☐   My partner is optimistic about solving the problem.

☐   ☐   I am pessimistic about solving the problem.

☐   ☐   I am calm and relaxed in discussing the problem.

☐   ☐   I bring up problems that are unrelated to the one we are discussing.

☐   ☐   I focus on how things might be better in the future.

☐   ☐   I do not listen fully to what my partner is saying.

☐   ☐   I do not offer constructive solutions to the problem.

☐   ☐   I take some responsibility for the problem.

☐   ☐   I interrupt my partner when he/she is speaking and do not allow him/her to express his/her opinions.

☐   ☐   I am honest and open with my feelings about the problem.

☐   ☐   I focus on the problem we are discussing.

☐   ☐   I criticize my partner and his/her views of the problem.

☐   ☐   I do not express my real feelings about the problem.

☐   ☐   I allow my partner to express his/her opinions.

☐   ☐   I blame my partner for the problem.

☐   ☐   I offer constructive solutions to the problem.

☐   ☐   I listen closely to what my partner says.

☐   ☐   I am tense and anxious in discussing the problem.

☐   ☐   I am supportive of my partner and his/her views of the problem.

☐   ☐   I focus on bad things from the past.

☐   ☐   I am optimistic about solving the problem.

Exercise 8.9   Changes in Patterns of Communication

COMMUNICATION PATTERNS QUESTIONNAIRE

Partner 1

Please indicate the extent to which you agree or disagree with the following statements concerning the disagreements and conflicts that arise between you and your partner. We are interested in how you and your partner typically deal with problems in your relationship. Please rate each item on a scale of 1 (= very unlikely) to 9 (= very likely).

WHEN SOME PROBLEM IN THE RELATIONSHIP ARISES:

	Very unlikely								Very likely
1. Both members avoid discussing the problem.	1	2	3	4	5	6	7	8	9
*2. Both members try to discuss the problem.	1	2	3	4	5	6	7	8	9
3. My partner tries to start a discussion while I try to avoid a discussion.	1	2	3	4	5	6	7	8	9
4. I try to start a discussion while my partner tries to avoid a discussion.	1	2	3	4	5	6	7	8	9

DURING A DISCUSSION OF A RELATIONSHIP PROBLEM:

	Very unlikely								Very likely
1. Both members blame, accuse, and criticize each other.	1	2	3	4	5	6	7	8	9
*2. Both members express their feelings with each other.	1	2	3	4	5	6	7	8	9
3. Both members threaten each other with negative consequences.	1	2	3	4	5	6	7	8	9
*4. Both members suggest possible solutions and compromises.	1	2	3	4	5	6	7	8	9
5. My partner nags and demands while I withdraw, become silent, or refuse to discuss the matter further.	1	2	3	4	5	6	7	8	9
6. I nag and demand while my partner withdraws, becomes silent, or refuses to discuss the matter further.	1	2	3	4	5	6	7	8	9

Note. From *Communication Patterns Questionnaire* by A. Christensen and M. Sullaway, 1984, Los Angeles: Unpublished manuscript, University of California. Copyright 1984 by the authors. Adapted by permission.

		Very **unlikely**								**Very** **likely**
7.	My partner criticizes while I defend myself.	1	2	3	4	5	6	7	8	9
8.	I criticize while my partner defends himself/herself.	1	2	3	4	5	6	7	8	9
9.	My partner threatens negative consequences and I give in or back down.	1	2	3	4	5	6	7	8	9
10.	I threaten negative consequences and my partner gives in or backs down.	1	2	3	4	5	6	7	8	9
11.	My partner calls me names, swears at me or attacks my character.	1	2	3	4	5	6	7	8	9
12.	I call my partner names, swear at him/her, or attack his/her character.	1	2	3	4	5	6	7	8	9

AFTER A DISCUSSION OF A RELATIONSHIP PROBLEM:

		Very **unlikely**								**Very** **likely**
*1.	Both feel each other has understood his/her position.	1	2	3	4	5	6	7	8	9
2.	Both withdraw from each other after the discussion.	1	2	3	4	5	6	7	8	9
*3.	Both feel that the problem has been solved.	1	2	3	4	5	6	7	8	9
4.	After the discussion, both try to be especially nice to the other.	1	2	3	4	5	6	7	8	9
5.	My partner tries to be especially nice, acts as if things are back to normal, while I act distant.	1	2	3	4	5	6	7	8	9
6.	I try to be especially nice, act as if things are back to normal, while my partner acts distant.	1	2	3	4	5	6	7	8	9

SCORING INSTRUCTIONS: For our purposes, add your ratings on those items with an asterisk (*) before the item number. This is your Mutual Constructive Communication Score.

MUTUAL CONSTRUCTIVE COMMUNICATION SCORE _____

Partner 2

Please indicate the extent to which you agree or disagree with the following statements concerning the disagreements and conflicts that arise between you and your partner. We are interested in how you and your partner typically deal with problems in your relationship. Please rate each item on a scale of 1 (= very unlikely) to 9 (= very likely).

WHEN SOME PROBLEM IN THE RELATIONSHIP ARISES:

	Very unlikely								**Very likely**
1. Both members avoid discussing the problem.	1	2	3	4	5	6	7	8	9
*2. Both members try to discuss the problem.	1	2	3	4	5	6	7	8	9
3. My partner tries to start a discussion while I try to avoid a discussion.	1	2	3	4	5	6	7	8	9
4. I try to start a discussion while my partner tries to avoid a discussion.	1	2	3	4	5	6	7	8	9

DURING A DISCUSSION OF A RELATIONSHIP PROBLEM:

	Very unlikely								**Very likely**
1. Both members blame, accuse, and criticize each other.	1	2	3	4	5	6	7	8	9
*2. Both members express their feelings with each other.	1	2	3	4	5	6	7	8	9
3. Both members threaten each other with negative consequences.	1	2	3	4	5	6	7	8	9
*4. Both members suggest possible solutions and compromises.	1	2	3	4	5	6	7	8	9
5. My partner nags and demands while I withdraw, become silent, or refuse to discuss the matter further.	1	2	3	4	5	6	7	8	9
6. I nag and demand while my partner withdraws, becomes silent, or refuses to discuss the matter further.	1	2	3	4	5	6	7	8	9

		Very unlikely								Very likely
7.	My partner criticizes while I defend myself.	1	2	3	4	5	6	7	8	9
8.	I criticize while my partner defends himself/herself.	1	2	3	4	5	6	7	8	9
9.	My partner threatens negative consequences and I give in or back down.	1	2	3	4	5	6	7	8	9
10.	I threaten negative consequences and my partner gives in or backs down.	1	2	3	4	5	6	7	8	9
11.	My partner calls me names, swears at me or attacks my character.	1	2	3	4	5	6	7	8	9
12.	I call my partner names, swear at him/her, or attack his/her character.	1	2	3	4	5	6	7	8	9

AFTER A DISCUSSION OF A RELATIONSHIP PROBLEM:

		Very unlikely								Very likely
*1.	Both feel each other has understood his/her position.	1	2	3	4	5	6	7	8	9
2.	Both withdraw from each other after the discussion.	1	2	3	4	5	6	7	8	9
*3.	Both feel that the problem has been solved.	1	2	3	4	5	6	7	8	9
4.	After the discussion, both try to be especially nice to the other.	1	2	3	4	5	6	7	8	9
5.	My partner tries to be especially nice, acts as if things are back to normal, while I act distant.	1	2	3	4	5	6	7	8	9
6.	I try to be especially nice, act as if things are back to normal, while my partner acts distant.	1	2	3	4	5	6	7	8	9

SCORING INSTRUCTIONS: For our purposes, add your ratings on those items with an asterisk (*) before the item number. This is your Mutual Constructive Communication Score.

MUTUAL CONSTRUCTIVE COMMUNICATION SCORE _____

Exercise 8.10   Overall Evaluation

THE MARITAL ADJUSTMENT TEST

Partner 1

1. Check the dot on the scale below which best describes the degree of happiness, everything considered, of your present marriage. The middle point, "Happy," represents the degree of happiness which most people get from marriage, and the scale gradually ranges on one side to those few who are very unhappy in marriage, and on the other, to those few who experience extreme joy or felicity in marriage.

    •   •   •   •   •   •   •

| Very unhappy | Happy | Perfectly happy |

State the approximate extent of agreement or disagreement between you and your mate on the following items. Please respond to each item.

	Always agree	Almost always agree	Occasionally disagree	Frequently disagree	Almost always disagree	Always disagree
2. Handling family finances	☐	☐	☐	☐	☐	☐
3. Matters of recreation	☐	☐	☐	☐	☐	☐
4. Demonstrations of affection	☐	☐	☐	☐	☐	☐
5. Friends	☐	☐	☐	☐	☐	☐
6. Sex relations	☐	☐	☐	☐	☐	☐
7. Conventionality (right, good, or proper conduct)	☐	☐	☐	☐	☐	☐
8. Philosophy of life	☐	☐	☐	☐	☐	☐
9. Ways of dealing with in-laws	☐	☐	☐	☐	☐	☐

Note. From "Short Marital-Adjustment and Prediction Tests: Their Reliability and Validity" by H. J. Locke and K. M. Wallace, 1959, *Marriage and Family Living, 21,* p. 252. Copyrighted 1959 by the National Council on Family Relations, 3989 Central Avenue N.E., Suite 550, Minneapolis, MN 55421. Reprinted by permission.

10. When disagreements arise, they usually result in:

Husband giving in ☐   Wife giving in ☐   Agreement by mutual give and take ☐

11. Do you and your mate engage in outside interests together?

All of them ☐   Some of them ☐   Very few of them ☐   None of them ☐

12. In leisure time do you generally prefer:

To be "on the go" ☐   To stay at home ☐

Does your mate generally prefer:

To be "on the go" ☐   To stay at home ☐

13. Do you ever wish you had not married?

Frequently ☐   Occasionally ☐   Rarely ☐   Never ☐

14. If you had your life to live over, do you think you would:

Marry the same person ☐   Marry a different person ☐   Not marry at all ☐

15. Do you confide in your mate?

Almost never ☐   Rarely ☐   In most things ☐   In everything ☐

For scoring instructions, see chapter 4, pages 44–45.

MARITAL ADJUSTMENT TEST TOTAL SCORE _____

Partner 2

1. Check the dot on the scale below which best describes the degree of happiness, everything considered, of your present marriage. The middle point, "Happy," represents the degree of happiness which most people get from marriage, and the scale gradually ranges on one side to those few who are very unhappy in marriage, and on the other, to those few who experience extreme joy or felicity in marriage.

•   •   •   •   •   •   •

Very   Happy   Perfectly

unhappy   happy

State the approximate extent of agreement or disagreement between you and your mate on the following items. Please respond to each item.

	Always agree	Almost always agree	Occasionally disagree	Frequently disagree	Almost always disagree	Always disagree
2. Handling family finances	☐	☐	☐	☐	☐	☐
3. Matters of recreation	☐	☐	☐	☐	☐	☐
4. Demonstrations of affection	☐	☐	☐	☐	☐	☐
5. Friends	☐	☐	☐	☐	☐	☐
6. Sex relations	☐	☐	☐	☐	☐	☐
7. Conventionality (right, good, or proper conduct)	☐	☐	☐	☐	☐	☐
8. Philosophy of life	☐	☐	☐	☐	☐	☐
9. Ways of dealing with in-laws	☐	☐	☐	☐	☐	☐

10. When disagreements arise, they usually result in:

    Husband giving in ☐   Wife giving in ☐   Agreement by mutual give and take ☐

11. Do you and your mate engage in outside interests together?

    All of them ☐   Some of them ☐   Very few of them ☐   None of them ☐

12. In leisure time do you generally prefer:

    To be "on the go" ☐   To stay at home ☐

    Does your mate generally prefer:

    To be "on the go" ☐   To stay at home ☐

13. Do you ever wish you had not married?

    Frequently ☐   Occasionally ☐   Rarely ☐   Never ☐

14. If you had your life to live over, do you think you would:

    Marry the same person ☐   Marry a different person ☐   Not marry at all ☐

15. Do you confide in your mate?

    Almost never ☐   Rarely ☐   In most things ☐   In everything ☐

For scoring instructions, see chapter 4, pages 48–49.

MARITAL ADJUSTMENT TEST TOTAL SCORE _____

MODIFIED POSITIVE FEELINGS QUESTIONNAIRE

Partner 1: Assessment of Feeling

Below is a list of questions about various feelings between people in a relationship. Answer each one of them in terms of how you generally *feel about your partner, taking into account the last few months. The rating you choose should reflect how you* actually *feel, not how you think you should feel or would like to feel.*

Please answer each question by choosing the best number to show how you have generally been feeling in the past few months. Choose only one number for each question.

1	2	3	4	5	6	7
Extremely negative	**Quite negative**	**Slightly negative**	**Neutral**	**Slightly positive**	**Quite positive**	**Extremely positive**

1. How do you feel about your partner as a friend to you? 1 2 3 4 5 6 7
2. How do you feel about the future of your relationship? 1 2 3 4 5 6 7
3. How do you feel about having a relationship with your partner? 1 2 3 4 5 6 7
4. How do you feel about your partner's ability to put you in a good mood so that you can laugh and smile? 1 2 3 4 5 6 7
5. How do you feel about your partner's ability to handle stress? 1 2 3 4 5 6 7
6. How do you feel about the degree to which your partner understands you? 1 2 3 4 5 6 7
7. How do you feel about your partner's honesty? 1 2 3 4 5 6 7
8. How do you feel about the degree to which you can trust your partner? 1 2 3 4 5 6 7

The following nine items are in the form of statements rather than questions. However, please complete them in the same manner, remembering to base your responses on how you generally *feel about your partner, taking into account the last few months.*

1. Touching my partner makes me feel 1 2 3 4 5 6 7
2. Being alone with my partner makes me feel 1 2 3 4 5 6 7
3. Having sexual relations with my partner makes me feel 1 2 3 4 5 6 7
4. Talking and communicating with my partner makes me feel 1 2 3 4 5 6 7
5. My partner's encouragement of my individual growth makes me feel 1 2 3 4 5 6 7
6. My partner's physical appearance makes me feel 1 2 3 4 5 6 7
7. Seeking comfort from my partner makes me feel 1 2 3 4 5 6 7
8. Kissing my partner makes me feel 1 2 3 4 5 6 7
9. Sitting or lying close to my partner makes me feel 1 2 3 4 5 6 7

SCORING INSTRUCTIONS: Obtain a total score by adding the scores for all items.

POSITIVE FEELINGS QUESTIONNAIRE TOTAL SCORE _____

Note. Information about the Positive Feelings Questionnaire appears in "Assessment of Positive Feelings Toward Spouse" by K. D. O'Leary, F. D. Fincham, and H. Turkewitz, 1983, *Journal of Consulting and Clinical Psychology, 51,* 949–951. Adapted by permission of the authors.

Partner 2: Assessment of Feeling

Below is a list of questions about various feelings between people in a relationship. Answer each one of them in terms of how you generally *feel about your partner, taking into account the last few months. The rating you choose should reflect how you* actually *feel, not how you think you should feel or would like to feel.*

Please answer each question by choosing the best number to show how you have generally been feeling in the past few months. Choose *only one number* for each question.

1	2	3	4	5	6	7
Extremely negative	**Quite negative**	**Slightly negative**	**Neutral**	**Slightly positive**	**Quite positive**	**Extremely positive**

1. How do you feel about your partner as a friend to you?   1 2 3 4 5 6 7
2. How do you feel about the future of your relationship?   1 2 3 4 5 6 7
3. How do you feel about having a relationship with your partner?   1 2 3 4 5 6 7
4. How do you feel about your partner's ability to put you in a good mood so that you can laugh and smile?   1 2 3 4 5 6 7
5. How do you feel about your partner's ability to handle stress?   1 2 3 4 5 6 7
6. How do you feel about the degree to which your partner understands you?   1 2 3 4 5 6 7
7. How do you feel about your partner's honesty?   1 2 3 4 5 6 7
8. How do you feel about the degree to which you can trust your partner?   1 2 3 4 5 6 7

The following nine items are in the form of statements rather than questions. However, please complete them in the same manner, remembering to base your responses on how you generally *feel about your partner, taking into account the last few months.*

1. Touching my partner makes me feel   1 2 3 4 5 6 7
2. Being alone with my partner makes me feel   1 2 3 4 5 6 7
3. Having sexual relations with my partner makes me feel   1 2 3 4 5 6 7
4. Talking and communicating with my partner makes me feel   1 2 3 4 5 6 7
5. My partner's encouragement of my individual growth makes me feel   1 2 3 4 5 6 7
6. My partner's physical appearance makes me feel   1 2 3 4 5 6 7
7. Seeking comfort from my partner makes me feel   1 2 3 4 5 6 7
8. Kissing my partner makes me feel   1 2 3 4 5 6 7
9. Sitting or lying close to my partner makes me feel   1 2 3 4 5 6 7

SCORING INSTRUCTIONS: Obtain a total score by adding the scores for all items.

POSITIVE FEELINGS QUESTIONNAIRE TOTAL SCORE _____

CHAPTER

9

Maintaining Your Progress and Communicating With Others

Before you start this chapter, it is important to be clear about your progress in developing better communication skills. Exercise 9.1 will help you and your partner decide if you are ready to work on maintaining good communication and using your communication skills with others.

If you have made satisfactory progress, you may already be thinking about how you're going to use the time you formerly spent sorting out miscommunications. In fact, it is tempting to stop reading here. However, we urge you to resist this temptation. Couples who stop working on their relationships at this point usually find that their improvements are not lasting. Sliding back into past communication patterns is easy, and a continued effort is needed to avoid old habits that took a long time, perhaps years, to establish. We therefore begin by discussing two important aspects of nurturing a relationship: maintaining your progress and preventing backsliding or relapse.

MAINTAINING PROGRESS

Like a plant that needs regular watering, your relationship needs continual nurturing. Minor caretaking now and then can save you some major work later. But how can you know what to do for your relationship? The answer sounds easy: Continue applying the skills you have already learned to improve your communication. In practice, this can be more difficult than it sounds.

The key to maintaining your progress is to incorporate the changes in your communication into your everyday life. To illustrate this process, let's use the analogy of gardening. Before you start a garden, you need to make many decisions: where to situate your garden for optimal sun and shelter, what kinds of seeds to use, when to plant, and when to water and cultivate. For the experienced gardener these decisions may be so natural that they are made subconsciously, and growing plants may be relatively easy. However, for the inexperienced gardener—or the experienced one who has let things slide—the decisions require a conscious effort. However they are made, these decisions affect the quality of the gardening experience. For instance, planting seeds in a too-shady area could result in long hours of transplanting, and caring for the garden could become more burdensome than enjoyable.

Exercise 9.1   Assessing Your Progress

Partner 1   Yes   No

1. Have you found it difficult to make progress?   ☐   ☐

   If yes, in what areas? _____

   _____

2. Have you skipped exercises or had trouble completing them?   ☐   ☐

   If yes, which chapter's exercises? _____

   _____

3. Have you had difficulty practicing the exercises in any chapter?   ☐   ☐

   If yes, which chapters? _____

   _____

4. Have your efforts been unsuccessful?   ☐   ☐

   If yes, what has stopped you from making them successful?

   _____

   _____

5. Does it seem impossible for you and your partner to make progress?   ☐   ☐

   If yes, in what areas? _____

   _____

6. Are you considering ending your relationship?   ☐   ☐

SCORING

A. If you answered yes to Question 1 only, you are probably ready to begin reading this chapter. In fact, the areas you listed may be good topic areas for exercises in this chapter. Feel free, however, to review the chapters most relevant to the areas of difficulty before going on.

B. If you answered yes to Question 2, 3, 4, or 5, we suggest that you review the chapters you listed and the exercises in those chapters.

C. If you answered yes to Question 6, please consult chapter 11, "What If It Seems Hopeless?"

Partner 2   Yes   No

1. Have you found it difficult to make progress?   ☐   ☐

   If yes, in what areas? _____

   _____

2. Have you skipped exercises or had trouble completing them?   ☐   ☐

   If yes, which chapter's exercises? _____

   _____

3. Have you had difficulty practicing the exercises in any chapter?   ☐   ☐

   If yes, which chapters? _____

   _____

4. Have your efforts been unsuccessful?   ☐   ☐

   If yes, what has stopped you from making them successful?

   _____

   _____

5. Does it seem impossible for you and your partner to make progress?   ☐   ☐

   If yes, in what areas? _____

   _____

6. Are you considering ending your relationship?   ☐   ☐

SCORING

A. If you answered yes to Question 1 only, you are probably ready to begin reading this chapter. In fact, the areas you listed may be good topic areas for exercises in this chapter. Feel free, however, to review the chapters most relevant to the areas of difficulty before going on.

B. If you answered yes to Question 2, 3, 4, or 5, we suggest that you review the chapters you listed and the exercises in those chapters.

C. If you answered yes to Question 6, please consult chapter 11, "What If It Seems Hopeless?"

So it is with relationships. Incorporating communication skills into your daily life is the key to maintaining good relationships. You need to invest some time now in deciding how to integrate your newly acquired skills into your life. One of the first steps is to set aside times for communication with your partner. In our experience, very few couples who have been together for a while have times when they can sit down and simply talk to each other for 15 minutes. To improve communication, a couple must change this circumstance. Quite simply, you cannot learn communication skills without having the time to communicate. Similarly, without the opportunity for continued practice, you are unlikely to maintain your communication skills.

Dedicating specific times to communication is a good start toward maintaining progress, but it is not sufficient. You will need to assess the strengths and weaknesses of your communication and build in exercises to help consolidate your gains. For example, if a major problem for one partner was listening to the other person, perhaps one talk session a week could be devoted to a formal exercise designed to improve this skill (e.g., paraphrasing; see Step 10). There are many ways to incorporate communication skills into your daily life. The way you do this is perhaps less important than the mere fact that you do it. Be aware, however, that it requires a conscious effort. Do not put off the effort; the task will only get harder as time passes.

PREVENTING BACKSLIDING OR RELAPSE

All couples have problems with communication at one time or another, and it is unrealistic to assume that you'll never experience setbacks. Techniques such as paraphrasing or using "I" language may seem silly or unnecessary at first, but they can help you clarify feelings, wishes, and expectations when used appropriately. By anticipating future sources of miscommunication and making plans to deal with them now, you can prevent miscommunications. Further, by recognizing the warning signs of a communication breakdown, you'll be able to prevent yourselves from backsliding or relapsing into those previously comfortable, but not always effective, communication habits.

Let us return to the gardening analogy. We know that dry soil or browning leaves are sure signs of trouble. The attentive gardener immediately takes steps to correct the problem at the source. Often, having learned from previous failures, the gardener anticipates and plans for potential troubles. By attending regularly to the plants, the gardener can carry out a previously prepared plan at the appropriate time when trouble signs appear. For example, plants need more water in extremely hot weather, and they may need shelter from extreme cold. However, the gardener can accommodate those needs only by listening to the weather forecast daily. It is not enough to know what to do; the gardener must also know when to do it. Both advance planning and daily monitoring are essential for a thriving garden.

Although relationships don't literally dry up or turn brown, they do exhibit trouble signs. Whether these signs point to a stressful event, a communication breakdown, or both, you'll want to plan for them and monitor your relationship so that you will be able to forestall trouble. To begin, you may want to ask yourselves what circumstances or events might be trouble signs in your relationship. Keep in mind that these signs may not always be cause for alarm—they could have a perfectly reasonable explanation. For some, a trouble sign might be simply the observation that the partner is less supportive than usual. For others, it may be that the partner is extremely quiet or very boisterous. Trouble signs may also be linked to particular situations, such as financial difficulties or visits from relatives.

In summary, to prevent backsliding into old communication habits, you should:

1. Identify trouble signs.
2. Track the situations in which they are most likely to occur.
3. Know when these signs do indeed indicate trouble for you and your partner.
4. Devise a plan to deal with trouble once you see the signs.

PLANNING FOR MAINTENANCE

Studying the following situations can help you develop a concrete, systematic maintenance program. As you complete the exercises interspersed with these examples, you'll get practice in identifying good ways to prevent backsliding. Later, we'll suggest how you can generate additional ideas for maintaining your gains.

Situation 1

Chester: I think that continuing this communication stuff is unnecessary. It seems so unnatural. Besides, there's no way I'll be able to talk with you every night at 9:00 o'clock about my day at work.

Kate: Does this mean that you don't want to tell me about work anymore?

Chester: No. It's just that basketball season is starting, and I don't want to break from games to talk with you. It's not that I don't care about you, just that a game gets my mind off my problems at work.

Obviously, the 9:00 P.M. time is no longer useful for Chester and Kate. What should they do? Take a few moments with your partner to discuss how you would handle this situation, then read on to find out what Chester and Kate decided.

Kate: Chester, would it be better to talk about your work day at dinner? That's a time when we don't have other things we want to do.

Chester: Yes. OK. I'm just so used to our talking at 9:00 P.M. that I didn't think of another time.

Kate: Good. And maybe this way, you won't have to wait for several hours before talking about what's on your mind.

Like Chester and Kate, many couples become accustomed to a particular daily routine. In this case, something that disrupted the routine could have stopped the couple from communicating altogether; they needed to establish a new routine. What possible problems can you foresee with the time you have set aside for communication each day? What can you do to avoid such problems?

Situation 2

Mark: When did your parents say they're coming to visit?

Darleen: They said they'll be in town next week for my niece's first birthday.

Mark: That's nice. Where are they staying?

Darleen: Well, they'd like to stay with us.

> Mark: With us? How long do they expect to be here?
>
> Darleen: Only a week this time.
>
> Mark: A week! Darleen, you know I'll be arguing about money with your mom by the end of the first day. Why is it that you never consult me when your parents come into town? You can talk to me about anything else, but when it comes to your parents . . .
>
> Darleen: Fine, now you're accusing me of being inconsiderate. You don't understand!

Apparently, a visit from Darleen's relatives is a particularly stressful event for both Mark and Darleen. Although they can talk about other matters, they have no plan for keeping the communication lines open regarding a visit from Darleen's relatives. This is a communication breakdown in response to a stressful event. Exercise 9.2 will help you become aware of stressful events in your own relationship.

Exercise 9.2   Stressful Events

Make a list of events that might place significant stress on your relationship and lead to communication breakdowns. Then try to answer the following questions: Do you have plans for dealing with the added pressure of these events? How do you anticipate handling these situations? What can you do now to make future events less stressful? We strongly recommend that you set aside 15 minutes to discuss these questions with your partner.

Even the couples who communicate best sometimes have difficulties. When communication problems do arise, it is important to recognize them early and try to solve them quickly. Often, it can be difficult to recognize communication relapses because you are focusing on the troubling issue at hand. Exercise 9.3 will prepare you to recognize backsliding.

Exercise 9.3   Backsliding

Each partner should complete the following sentence in as many ways as possible:

We're on the road to a communication breakdown when . . .

Combine your answers into one list. Now try to make a plan to deal with backsliding. Under the list you have compiled write the following:

If any one of these occurs, we're backsliding. Our plan for backsliding is to . . .

Complete the sentence by writing in your plan for backsliding. Post your list where both of you will have easy access to it.

Situation 3

Elaine: You know, after we worked through that book, I thought that we wouldn't have any more problems.

Carl: Is there a problem? Can we talk about it later? I'm late for a softball game.

Elaine: That's just it. When we were working with that book, all I wanted was for you to take time to talk to me. I'm not sure that's enough anymore.

Carl: Really, honey, I'm late for my game. You said if I told you why I couldn't talk to you at a certain time, you'd understand and wait until later.

Although Carl and Elaine previously reached an agreement concerning their expectations for the relationship, it appears that Elaine's expectations are changing. When one person begins to develop new expectations for the partner or the relationship, what worked before may no longer be effective. All couples go through changes. Dealing effectively with these changes—and with the expectations arising from the changes—is crucial to a good maintenance program. How will you know if your expectations for your relationship have changed? If they change, will you be able to tell your partner? How will you do so? How would you respond if your partner told you that his or her expectations had changed? Exercise 9.4 addresses these questions.

Exercise 9.4   Changing Expectations

First, list some possible ways in which your expectations might change. Next, review the questions in the last paragraph as they relate to your new set of expectations. How might your relationship change, given these new expectations? What would you do, given the new expectations? You should each do this exercise independently, then discuss your answers.

Situation 4

Karen: What's the matter, Doug?

Doug: Oh, I can't see eye to eye with this new guy at work. No matter what I do, I always end up making him upset.

Karen: What happens?

Doug: Well, he asks me a question and I answer it. For example, the other day he asked how the computer works. I said, "You turn on this switch and the power comes on." But then he gave me this strange look and walked away. I honestly thought that he wanted to know where the switch was.

Karen: That sounds frustrating. Have you tried to understand what he was asking about before you answer? You know, it wasn't so long ago that you misinterpreted what I was asking.

Doug: You mean, use the stuff from that book at my work?

Karen: Yes, and look . . . you're doing it right now with me and we seem to understand each other.

Doug: Hmm, I guess I could try that. But won't it seem kind of weird?

Many people think that using the skills they've learned through this book may seem odd outside their couple relationship. However, making those skills a more natural part of your life is one way to make further progress in your relationship. In addition, as you bring your skills to other settings, they become easier to use and can lead to better relationships with coworkers, friends, children, and parents. Later in the chapter, we'll look more closely at the use of communication skills in other relationships. Right now, Exercise 9.5 will get you started in applying your skills more broadly.

Exercise 9.5   Using Your Skills in Other Relationships

Make a list of other relationships in which you could apply your communication skills. Try practicing your skills in each of these relationships over the next several days. See whether you notice any differences.

A Focus on the Positive

You may have noticed that the four situations portrayed earlier all focused on problem solving. However, by completing the exercises, you've discovered that you need not wait for a problem to arise before working on your relationship. A good maintenance program requires more than simply preparing yourself for difficult future situations. You also need to focus on the present. A very easy way to focus on maintaining your relationship at present is to include positive behaviors in your maintenance program. By devoting some time to doing positive things with your partner each day, you'll keep your relationship healthy and have fun at the same time.

Developing good, positive behavior habits will help you and your partner to be positive toward each other and gain more satisfaction from your relationship. However, you should vary the kinds of positive things you do in your relationship and do them in moderation. Doing only one positive thing for your partner, or overdoing that one thing, could affect your relationship negatively. Taking your partner out to dinner, for example, could be seen as a very positive gesture. However, doing only this—and nothing else—every day not only might diminish the pleasure but also might send the wrong message to your partner. He or she might think that you are not willing to change other behaviors or that you think such actions are sufficient for a satisfactory relationship. Putting all your time and energy into an occasional big investment (such as an entire night out together) may not be ideal either. Instead, try varying the small, positive things you do.

In choosing positive activities, consider your partner's preferences—and your own. For instance, you may decide to say one nice thing to your partner each day, take turns planning weekly outings, treat yourselves to an occasional night away from the kids, or set aside time to relax by yourselves each evening. The same activities are not necessarily positive for all couples, and the activities need not represent major investments of time and energy to be valuable. Do what works for you and your partner.

Table 9.1 lists some ways to generate ideas for positive behaviors to bring into your relationship. Some couples have difficulty coming up with ideas at first. These are only suggestions to get you started. However, we do emphasize the importance of using positive behaviors to maintain a good relationship.

Table 9.1   Ways to Generate Ideas for Positive Behaviors

1. Observe other couples. What positive things do you see them do? Would those things be useful in your relationship?

2. Make a list of small actions that you think would make your partner feel good. Ask your partner to read the list and tell you if he or she would appreciate your doing the things that you listed. Ask your partner to add items to the list. Now you can choose something special to do for your partner each day.

3. Play a grab bag game with your partner. Each of you should make a list of things that make you feel good and cut the items into separate pieces of paper. Draw one of your partner's ideas each day and carry it out.

4. Do something spontaneous for your partner. Afterward, find out whether your partner liked it and whether it would be good to repeat sometime in the future.

5. Plan a shared activity that both you and your partner would enjoy.

6. Give your partner feedback when he or she does something you like.

Making It Easy

We've discussed the importance of incorporating your maintenance program into your daily routine. But what does that mean in practical terms? The answer depends on what your daily life is like and how your maintenance program will suit it. Exercise 9.6 is designed to help you integrate that program into your routine.

Exercise 9.6   Your Week

You'll need three pens—black, blue, and red. Using the black pen, complete Schedule 1 for the days on which you work. Include only those activities that you engage in without *your partner — for example, work, hobbies, exercise classes, spectator sports, and the like. (If you don't work outside the home, complete the schedule for Monday through Friday.)*

Now, with the blue pen, write in activities that you share with your partner—for example, eating breakfast, preparing dinner, walking the dog, and so on.

Next, with the red pen, add the activities that you've been doing as you've worked through the communication exercises in this book. The more they overlap with other activities in your routine the better. If some communication activities don't overlap with other activities, work with your partner to make them overlap with the activities entered in blue ink. In some cases this may be impossible; that's all right. Try instead to think of a shared activity that would overlap with your communication exercise.

As you fill in these schedules, you may find that you have nothing listed for certain times of day. That is no problem. Use your free times to reward yourself or your partner for the work you've put into your relationship that week. It may be a good idea to vary your free time activities according to the events of the week. These unscheduled times provide an additional opportunity to incorporate some positive behaviors into your relationship.

Now, repeat the process for your days off (typically, with Schedule 2). How are the schedules similar? How are they different? What do they tell you about developing your maintenance plan?

Partner 1

Schedule 1: Monday Through Friday

Time	Monday	Tuesday	Wednesday	Thursday	Friday
6:00 A.M.					
7:00 A.M.					
8:00 A.M.					
9:00 A.M.					
10:00 A.M.					
11:00 A.M.					
Noon					
1:00 P.M.					
2:00 P.M.					
3:00 P.M.					
4:00 P.M.					
5:00 P.M.					
6:00 P.M.					
7:00 P.M.					
8:00 P.M.					
9:00 P.M.					
10:00 P.M.					
11:00 P.M.					
Midnight					

Schedule 2: Weekend

Time	Saturday	Sunday
6:00 A.M.		
7:00 A.M.		
8:00 A.M.		
9:00 A.M.		
10:00 A.M.		
11:00 A.M.		
Noon		
1:00 P.M.		
2:00 P.M.		
3:00 P.M.		
4:00 P.M.		
5:00 P.M.		
6:00 P.M.		
7:00 P.M.		
8:00 P.M.		
9:00 P.M.		
10:00 P.M.		
11:00 P.M.		
Midnight		

Partner 2

Schedule 1: Monday Through Friday

Time	Monday	Tuesday	Wednesday	Thursday	Friday
6:00 A.M.					
7:00 A.M.					
8:00 A.M.					
9:00 A.M.					
10:00 A.M.					
11:00 A.M.					
Noon					
1:00 P.M.					
2:00 P.M.					
3:00 P.M.					
4:00 P.M.					
5:00 P.M.					
6:00 P.M.					
7:00 P.M.					
8:00 P.M.					
9:00 P.M.					
10:00 P.M.					
11:00 P.M.					
Midnight					

Schedule 2: Weekend

Time	Saturday	Sunday
6:00 A.M.		
7:00 A.M.		
8:00 A.M.		
9:00 A.M.		
10:00 A.M.		
11:00 A.M.		
Noon		
1:00 P.M.		
2:00 P.M.		
3:00 P.M.		
4:00 P.M.		
5:00 P.M.		
6:00 P.M.		
7:00 P.M.		
8:00 P.M.		
9:00 P.M.		
10:00 P.M.		
11:00 P.M.		
Midnight		

COMMUNICATING WITH OTHERS

In chapter 1 we raised some questions about Cinderella and Prince Charming. Did they have any friends, or did they live isolated in their castle? Did Cinderella's relationships with her stepmother and stepsisters continue after the story ended? If so, did those relationships improve or worsen? We may also wonder if Cinderella and Prince Charming had any children. If so, how was their family life? Did Cinderella and Prince Charming hold jobs? If so, how did they relate to their coworkers? Did the couple get along with the prince's parents?

Although a fairy tale couple can find a happy ending without reference to other people, our lives are affected in profound ways by others. A couple's happiness can often be influenced by external relationships, especially with children and in-laws. Here we will discuss the application of your communication skills to other types of relationships, such as those with friends, coworkers, in-laws, and children.

In the previous section, we asked you to use your communication skills with people other than your partner to help yourself maintain your progress and make these skills part of your daily life. You may have found it difficult to apply newly learned skills with others who had not read this book and thus were not following the same set of rules for good communication. How can you overcome this difficulty?

The key to successful communication is to use your skills to establish a common ground between you and the other person. People generally like to feel that they have been heard and understood; they can get this feeling by talking with a skilled communicator, whether or not they themselves possess good communication skills. For you, establishing common ground might mean discussing similar or shared experiences; such conversation can result in an improved environment for communication about other topics. Establishing common ground may sometimes involve trying to share what you know about the rules of good communication as well as the messages you are trying to convey (e.g., you could say that you have found paraphrasing helpful and would like to use it to make sure you are understanding the other person correctly). Of course, it can be frustrating to try to communicate effectively with someone who is unaware of good communication practices or who shares no interest in your topic. Just do your best to adapt your skills to each situation and person.

Friends and Coworkers

The relationships in which you most likely can use your communication skills are those with friends and coworkers. By practicing good communication you will not only improve the relationships but will also find that your skills will gradually become more natural and easier to use. It is important to keep practicing until good communication is a habit. Like other habits, this one takes time to establish.

Many people find that they tend to favor certain skills in their relationships. To examine how you use various skills in different relationships, complete Exercise 9.7 with friends and/or coworkers.

Exercise 9.7   Knowing Your Skills

On each of the next 3 days, choose a different person with whom you will use your skills. Keep a log of the skills that you actually used in your conversations, and note other skills that you could have used but did not. The entries in your log should include the following information:

1. Person chosen for conversation

2. Topic of conversation

3. Communication skills used

4. Additional skills that might have been used

At the end of the 3 days review this log and ask yourself these questions: "Are there skills that I tend to favor? Are there skills that I use less often? Are some skills easier to apply than others? Do friends and coworkers respond differently when I use communication skills? Is it easier to practice good communication with certain people? If so, why? What can I do to make it easier to use communication skills?" Next time you speak with these people, try varying the skills that you use. Do you notice a difference?

In-Laws

Although good communication alone does not guarantee a perfect relationship with in-laws, using your communication skills to clarify and facilitate conversations can be helpful, especially if the relationship causes discomfort for you. Moreover, ongoing use of your skills in your communication with relatives can help you and your relatives better understand one another and defuse conflicts, should they arise. Remember Mark and Darleen, who had a communication breakdown because of an upcoming visit from Darleen's parents? In the conversation, Darleen stated that her parents would "like to stay with them." But what if Darleen's parents actually would prefer to stay in a hotel but did not say so for fear of hurting their daughter's feelings? Or what if Darleen's father suggested staying with the young couple so that he could persuade Mark to go golfing with him more often? Either scenario would shed a different light on the parents' request to stay with Mark and Darleen. In fact, Mark and Darleen might have avoided a communication breakdown if Mark had communicated directly with Darleen's parents.

If you have in-laws, complete Exercise 9.8. It is designed to help you avoid communication breakdowns like Mark and Darleen's.

Exercise 9.8 Using Your Skills With In-Laws

Partner 1

1. Who usually speaks to your spouse's relatives?

   I ☐   My spouse ☐   Both of us ☐

2. Who usually speaks to your relatives?

   I ☐   My spouse ☐   Both of us ☐

3. List times when you have had difficulty communicating with relatives, what happened, and the communication skills you used.

Date/occasion	What happened	Skills used
_____	_____	_____
_____	_____	_____
_____	_____	_____
_____	_____	_____

4. List communication skills that could have clarified the issue.

   _____   _____   _____

5. Think about an upcoming encounter with relatives. What communication skills do you plan to use with your relatives at that time?

   Skills to use

   _____

   _____

   _____

Partner 2

1. Who usually speaks to your spouse's relatives?

   I ☐   My spouse ☐   Both of us ☐

2. Who usually speaks to your relatives?

   I ☐   My spouse ☐   Both of us ☐

3. List times when you have had difficulty communicating with relatives, what happened, and the communication skills you used.

Date/occasion	What happened	Skills used
_____	_____	_____
_____	_____	_____
_____	_____	_____
_____	_____	_____

4. List communication skills that could have clarified the issue.

   _____   _____   _____

5. Think about an upcoming encounter with relatives. What communication skills do you plan to use with your relatives at that time?

   Skills to use

   _____

   _____

   _____

Children

Until now, we have been discussing communication among adults. Communication with children is important as well, but it requires that you adapt your skills according to the child's age. Communication with adolescents more closely resembles communication among adults. Therefore, we will focus on using your communication skills with children of preschool and elementary school age.

The Communication Alphabet

Following are some guidelines that can be helpful in communicating with children. We have listed them using a "communication alphabet."

A: **A**void distractions. Children find it difficult to focus on a conversation when distractions are present. If possible, find a quiet place to talk and turn off the television or stereo. However, do not expect a child to sit in a chair to talk with you as an adult might. Some shared activity, such as drawing or playing with clay, can set the stage for conversation without serving as a distractor.

B: **B**egin sentences with positives instead of negatives. For example, "I would like you to set the table" replaces "I don't want you going out before you set the table." By beginning sentences with positives, you will gain more cooperation from a child and eliminate defensive feelings.

C: **C**onvey your communications **C**almly, **C**learly, **C**oncretely, and **C**ompletely. Be brief and to the point. Long-winded or verbose communications only confuse children with short attention spans. Being relaxed, enunciating well, and giving examples can help you to convey your entire message.

D: **D**emonstrate good communication. Children learn best by watching others. As you use your communication skills with other adults and with children, children will learn and practice them with you.

E: Establish **E**ye contact. Make eye contact with children when speaking to them. You will communicate better if you face children and are physically close to them when speaking. Teach children to do the same with peers and adults.

F: Provide **F**eedback. Give children a mixture of praise and constructive criticism about their communications. Make sure the feedback is clear and specific, focusing on actions, not on the children themselves. For example, you may want to try saying, "Jimmy, can you look at Justin when you wish him a happy birthday?" instead of "Jimmy, talk properly to Justin." Communicate your approval when a child does something well. Whenever possible, try to avoid correcting a child in front of peers or other adults to spare the child unnecessary embarrassment.

G: **G**ain and keep children's attention by a method appropriate to their age. To gain the attention of an elementary school child, try using an attention-getting phrase before making a statement—for example, "Next" or "Now we will . . ." With younger children, you may need to call the child's name or tap him or her on the shoulder. To keep a child's attention during communication, try changing accompanying activities (i.e., drawing, eating) as you talk, or change topics of conversation more often than you would with adults. If the child appears tired or frustrated, take a break.

H: Encourage good **H**abits. Teach children good communication habits. Taking turns, not interrupting others, and respecting other people's feelings are habits that children can easily learn and understand. Like other habits, children can make them a part of everyday life.

I: Use **"I"** statements. Teach children that feelings always belong to someone and that people should begin their sentences with the word "I" when discussing their own feelings. Demonstrate this by saying, for example, "I get angry when you throw your toys" instead of "You make me angry."

J: **J**oin your child in using good communication, and talk often. Build conversation time into your daily schedule. The child can then expect and look forward to your conversations.

K: **K**neel or sit on the floor when speaking to younger children. Not only does this help you to enter a child's world, it also helps you to see the world from a child's perspective.

L: Keep **L**anguage simple. Avoid using words that are unfamiliar to the child. If you're not familiar with a word the child uses, ask him or her to explain it to you. For children who have difficulty with the variety of question words (why, who, where, when), simplify your questions by making them "what" questions. For example, "who" becomes "what person," "where" becomes "what place," and "when" becomes "what time."

M: **M**odify your communication as the child grows. What works with a 3-year-old may no longer work with a 6-year-old. Also, gear your expectations to the abilities and capabilities of the child as he or she develops.

N: **N**ever give back-handed compliments such as "It's about time you cleaned up your room" or "That's nice. Why can't you do that more often?" (Such comments are taboo for adults, too.) They send mixed messages of criticism and praise, not effective feedback.

O: Give **O**ne direction at a time. Saying, "I want you to clean the table, set it, and then put your clothes away" in a single sentence can be confusing, especially for younger children. You will get better results if you communicate only one request at a time.

P: **P**raise children to show them they are appreciated. For example, saying, "I like it when you take the clothes out of the dryer without my asking" can improve the environment for communication.

Q: **Q**uestion children gently, allowing time for them to answer. A child may take a while before responding, particularly if the question is not easily understood.

R: **R**epeat what children say to clarify that you have understood. You may wish to paraphrase instead of repeating literally; "parroting" is a behavior that many children use to tease others. Also, have children repeat instructions you have given. Not only does this clarify that you have been heard correctly, it also can help the child remember what you said.

S: **S**tick with what you say. Children need to know that your words can be counted on. If you're unsure of something, either keep it to yourself or tell the child you are unsure so that he or she will not develop unrealistic expectations.

T: **T**ell stories as a way to explain difficult or abstract issues. For example, use "Little Red Riding Hood" to illustrate the dangers of talking to strangers.

U: **U**se references to time in casual conversations to help children situate what is going on around them. For younger children, this may mean talking about events in relation to small time periods such as morning, lunchtime, afternoon, after dinner, or before bed.

V: **V**erbalize feelings to help children develop better communication. Help children to label their feelings with words other than *good, nice,* or *bad.* Try *excited, happy,* and *sad* instead. Also, tell children clearly that you may not know how they are feeling if they do not tell you.

W: **W**atch other adults when they talk to children, and have children observe other children their ages as they talk to peers or adults. Many parents find that they can learn a great deal from the way other parents speak to their children, and many children learn best from watching their contemporaries.

X, Y, & Z: **EX**ude **Y**outhful **Z**eal. Make communicating fun for children. For instance, a visit to the zoo is a great way to spark conversation and have fun in the process. Playing simple games like "Simon Says" is also an enjoyable way to practice communication skills with children.

Exercise 9.9 asks you to apply these principles for communicating with children.

Exercise 9.9   Using the Communication Alphabet

Try out the communication alphabet with a child in your life. It's much harder than it looks. How well did it work? What was easy? What required more effort?

Just as no person is entirely separate from and unaffected by others, no relationship exists in isolation. How well you communicate with others can influence how well you get along with your partner. By using your communication skills with everyone in your world, you will make those skills more natural and integrate them into your daily habits. After a while you'll probably find yourself using them automatically.

10 *Special Topics: Dual Careers, Spirituality, and Sex*

This chapter addresses three issues of concern to many couples: dual careers, spirituality, and sex. If you have problems with your partner in any of these three areas, or simply wish to learn more about them, we invite you to read the appropriate sections.

CARING FOR A DUAL-CAREER MARRIAGE

Until fairly recently, it was unusual for a woman to be both married and employed. However, economic realities and the women's liberation movement have combined to reverse the situation: Today about half of American wives work outside the home. The rise of the dual-career relationship has produced new benefits and new problems for modern couples. Negotiating this new territory presents a challenge for many. In this section we will discuss four common problem areas for two-career couples: unrealistic expectations, sex role pressure, childrearing, and moving or commuting.

Unrealistic Expectations: Can You Really Have It All?

Cultural images can be hard to live up to. Through magazines, television, and film, popular culture has offered us an idealized image of the contemporary American couple. She is beautiful and efficient, a successful professional, loving mother, energetic house-keeper, and supportive companion. He works late at the office, is respected in his field, and finds time to be a loving and totally attentive father and spouse. This image is appealing because it suggests that our fantasies can be realized. We can devote enormous amounts of time and energy to our partners, our children, our jobs, and ourselves without shorting anything or anyone. It is a seductive fantasy—but that is all it is.

If there is one thing all couples have in common, it is that they have 24 hours of time each day. Because the amount of time is finite, it is impossible to "have it all." Ten hours on the job is by definition that many hours less with your partner or family. A night out with your partner is one less night spent working, studying, enjoying your own company, or taking care of your children. Many people in dual-career relationships try to deny this reality and end up running themselves ragged. Yet it is easy to understand their denial: The alternative is making choices, which can be a painful and sobering process. How you make these choices, and what you choose, says a great deal about you and your relationship.

If you delay making choices and setting priorities with your partner, life may eventually take the choices away from you. Consider, for example, partners who put off deciding whether and when to have children: As they approach the end of the child-bearing years, the choice may be forced on them at an inconvenient time in their lives. Similarly, job offers and promotion opportunities may slip by because people are not in a position to accept them. We cannot recommend strongly enough that you and your partner discuss your expectations for career, children, and family before the passage of time brings you to a state of crisis.

Although evaluating your own and your partner's priorities in life is an ongoing and fluid process, Exercise 10.1 will help you get started.

Exercise 10.1   Priorities

On a piece of paper draw two circles, one for you and one for your partner. Divide your own circle like a pie chart to show how you would like to spend your time. You can create as many slices as you want, but you should include childrearing (if you have children), career development, time spent with your partner, and time spent alone (reading, exercising, thinking, just relaxing, etc.). After dividing up your own time, cut the second pie to show how you would like your partner to spend his or her time.

Figure 10.1 shows sample charts drawn by a woman named Vanna for herself and her husband, Patrick. Vanna expects to devote most of her time and energy to her professional life, so she assigned 60% of the circle to her career. She does not want to invest much time in raising children (10% of the pie), but she wants to have an intimate relationship with her husband (25%). She does not feel she needs much time for her own development (5%). Vanna hopes that Patrick will devote most of his energy (65%) to his career, help out with the children (10%), spend a fair amount of time with her (25%), and require no time to be alone (0%).

Each of you should independently fill out pie charts for you and your partner, then compare and discuss your results.

You may wish to repeat this exercise at later points in your relationship; your responses might change over time. You may also wish to use the exercise for short-term planning (e.g., "What will we do this summer?") or longer term planning (e.g., "How will we structure our lives until our child enters kindergarten?").

Sex Role Pressure

As dual-career relationships have become more common, there has been less pressure on men and women to embrace traditional roles. Still, that pressure has not been eliminated. The images of modern couples prevalent in the popular media reveal our culture's hesitancy to abandon traditional roles. Men and women are portrayed engaging in non-traditional behaviors in addition to, not instead of, fulfilling traditional roles.

Figure 10.1 Sample Priority Charts

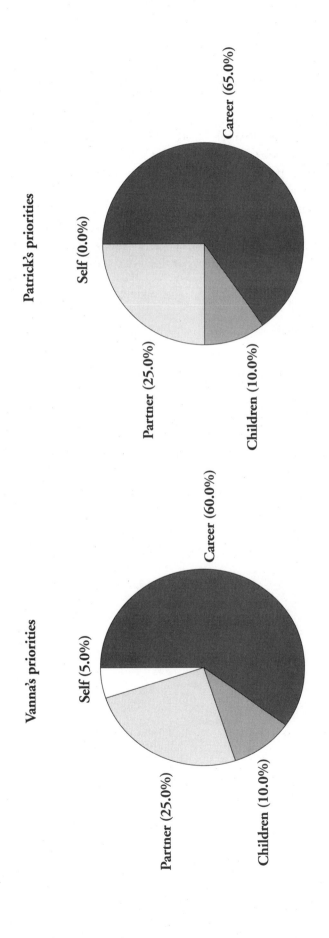

Some couples say and believe that they do not want a traditional relationship, with the man working and the woman in the home, yet their behavior reinforces traditional gender roles. This does not mean that they are hypocritical. Rather, they simply are unaware of the extent to which the ideas and behaviors associated with traditional roles permeate all relationships in our culture. Like the air we breathe, traditional gender roles surround us, but their effects can be difficult to see. For example, a husband who sincerely wants his marriage to be egalitarian may nonetheless feel anxious if his wife earns as much money as he does; at some level beyond his awareness, he may believe that the man should be the primary breadwinner. Similarly, a woman who wants an egalitarian marriage may nonetheless feel envy when her daughter, after falling and scraping a knee, yells, "I want my daddy!" Without realizing it, this mother may still believe that children should be closer to their mothers than to their fathers. Even if you truly believe that the traditional gender roles are not for you, you may detect inconsistencies in your behavior and feelings that suggest otherwise. It takes careful self-observation to discover if this is the case. Exercise 10.2 is an exercise in self-observation.

Exercise 10.2   Beliefs About Traditional Sex Roles

Partner 1

Following is a list of beliefs about traditional sex roles. For each one, indicate how much you agree or disagree with the statement. Then answer the questions about behaviors and feelings that accompany each role. You may find that the beliefs you express are not completely consistent with your behaviors and feelings. If so, it does not mean that you are dishonest. It simply means that—like many others—you may not be aware of everything you think, feel, and do. You and your partner should do the exercise independently, then compare results.

Belief 1: A clean house is a woman's responsibility.

Strongly disagree ☐   Disagree ☐   Agree ☐   Strongly agree ☐

Behavior to watch: Do you and your partner spend equal amounts of time doing housework, or does the woman do more?

Feelings to watch: If the house is a mess, does the woman feel responsible while the man feels angry at the woman for not cleaning up?

Belief 2: The man's career is more important than the woman's.

Strongly disagree ☐   Disagree ☐   Agree ☐   Strongly agree ☐

Behaviors to watch: Does the man listen to his partner talk about her career as much as she listens to him talk about his? Do you go to more social functions connected to the man's career than functions connected to the woman's?

Feelings to watch: How would you feel (or how do you feel) if the woman earned as much as or more money than the man? How would you feel about moving to a new city to advance the woman's career as compared to moving for the sake of the man's career?

Belief 3: The woman has primary responsibility for the children.

Strongly disagree ☐   Disagree ☐   Agree ☐   Strongly agree ☐

Behavior to watch: When your child gets sick, is the woman usually the one who takes off work and stays home?

Feelings to watch: Does the woman feel more guilt about not being home than the man does? Does the man feel as comfortable as the woman in being emotionally and physically warm with his children?

Partner 2

Following is a list of beliefs about traditional sex roles. For each one, indicate how much you agree or disagree with the statement. Then answer the questions about behaviors and feelings that accompany each role. You may find that the beliefs you express are not completely consistent with your behaviors and feelings. If so, it does not mean that you are dishonest. It simply means that—like many others—you may not be aware of everything you think, feel, and do. You and your partner should do the exercise independently, then compare results.

Belief 1: A clean house is a woman's responsibility.

Strongly disagree ☐   Disagree ☐   Agree ☐   Strongly agree ☐

Behavior to watch: Do you and your partner spend equal amounts of time doing housework, or does the woman do more?

Feelings to watch: If the house is a mess, does the woman feel responsible while the man feels angry at the woman for not cleaning up?

Belief 2: The man's career is more important than the woman's.

Strongly disagree ☐   Disagree ☐   Agree ☐   Strongly agree ☐

Behaviors to watch: Does the man listen to his partner talk about her career as much as she listens to him talk about his? Do you go to more social functions connected to the man's career than functions connected to the woman's?

Feelings to watch: How would you feel (or how do you feel) if the woman earned as much as or more money than the man? How would you feel about moving to a new city to advance the woman's career as compared to moving for the sake of the man's career?

Belief 3: The woman has primary responsibility for the children.

Strongly disagree ☐   Disagree ☐   Agree ☐   Strongly agree ☐

Behavior to watch: When your child gets sick, is the woman usually the one who takes off work and stays home?

Feelings to watch: Does the woman feel more guilt about not being home than the man does? Does the man feel as comfortable as the woman in being emotionally and physically warm with his children?

Childrearing

The arrival of children is often the one development that puts greatest pressure on a dual-career couple. If you and your partner have decided never to have children, it should be quite possible for both of you to have successful, challenging careers. However, because over 90% of Americans eventually marry and most American marriages result in children, the topic of balancing two careers with the demands of childrearing deserves attention.

In most relationships, the conflict between career and children is felt more keenly by the woman. Because women are the ones who become pregnant, women's careers are inevitably interrupted in the period surrounding childbirth. There are social constraints as well. Women who pursue full-time careers instead of being full-time mothers are likely to experience both internal and external pressure to give up their jobs.

Some of the guilt many working women feel is due to a belief that the child of a working mother cannot grow up to be psychologically healthy. A great deal of research in the social sciences has shown that this belief is unfounded. Obviously, if both parents are so involved in their careers that they have no time for their child, the child's development will suffer. Normally, however, some positive developments can take place when a mother works outside the home: The father can become more actively involved in parenting, with benefits for both father and children. Also, daughters of working mothers can see that they have a broad array of options for their own futures.

As we mentioned earlier, the real demon in two-career relationships is not that both partners work but that time is finite. Children—especially young ones—take a great deal of time, even if day care and sitters are available. The question you and your partner must answer is "Where will we get the time needed for child care?" Some couples cut down on social activities, and others move from full-time to part-time work. In some cases, one partner stops working to raise children full time. The right solution is whichever one you and your partner agree on. As with other choices, you are likely to be more satisfied if you carefully set your priorities in advance rather than simply waiting to see what suffers as a result of the demands of parenthood.

Exercise 10.3 should get you started in the right direction. It deals with your expectations and ideas about children, and it will help you examine your priorities.

Exercise 10.3   Expectations About Children

Partner 1

Answer the questions independently, then compare your answers with your partner's.

1. The ideal number of children for me is: 0   1   2   3   4   5   6+

2. As a result of our having children, I expect
   - ☐ myself to spend less time on career.
   - ☐ my partner to spend less time on career.
   - ☐ both myself and my partner to spend less time on career.
   - ☐ neither myself nor my partner to spend less time on career.

3. As a result of our having children, I expect
   - ☐ my daily routine to be greatly changed.
   - ☐ my partner's daily routine to be greatly changed.
   - ☐ both my own and my partner's daily routines to be greatly changed.
   - ☐ neither my own nor my partner's daily routine to be greatly changed.

4. Raising children takes time. List three things you do now that you could eliminate or abbreviate in order to leave more time for parenting. Make a similar list for your partner.

   Three things I could eliminate or cut down on:

   _____

   _____

   _____

   Three things I think my partner could eliminate or cut down on:

   _____

   _____

   _____

Partner 2

Answer the questions independently, then compare your answers with your partner's.

1. The ideal number of children for me is: 0   1   2   3   4   5   6+

2. As a result of our having children, I expect
   ☐ myself to spend less time on career.
   ☐ my partner to spend less time on career.
   ☐ both myself and my partner to spend less time on career.
   ☐ neither myself nor my partner to spend less time on career.

3. As a result of our having children, I expect
   ☐ my daily routine to be greatly changed.
   ☐ my partner's daily routine to be greatly changed.
   ☐ both my own and my partner's daily routines to be greatly changed.
   ☐ neither my own nor my partner's daily routine to be greatly changed.

4. Raising children takes time. List three things you do now that you could eliminate or abbreviate in order to leave more time for parenting. Make a similar list for your partner.

   Three things I could eliminate or cut down on:

   _____

   _____

   _____

   Three things I think my partner could eliminate or cut down on:

   _____

   _____

   _____

   _____

Moving and Commuting

If both you and your partner have careers, you are more likely to have conflicts about where to live. You may both receive attractive job offers from separate parts of the country, or one of you may be transferred to another locality. Resentments often arise in such situations. If one partner accepts career setbacks to follow the other to a new job, both partners may feel that the follower's life and career are less important. The person making the career move may feel that an air of recrimination hangs over the relationship, as if a debt has been incurred that can never be paid off.

One reason such tensions arise is that careers are rarely equal. One partner usually earns more, is in a more respected line of work, or has more seniority on the job. So, unless a couple is so well off that they need not consider earnings, one partner's career is in reality more important to the couple because it brings in more of the money that pays the bills. A move made for the sake of the better paying job merely highlights the reality: The couple needs one job more than the other. For the partner in the less remunerative job, this highlighting of financial status can be embarrassing and uncomfortable, especially if that partner is male (recall the sex role expectations discussed in the previous section).

How can a couple minimize the conflict surrounding relocation? If you move for the sake of your partner's better paying job, it may be helpful to remind yourself that it was not your partner who set the wage scales of your respective occupations. Although it is understandable for you to wish that your job commanded a higher salary and to communicate your disappointment to your partner, it is not realistic to hold your partner personally responsible for salary differences. If you blame your partner for things he or she cannot control, you are likely to receive resentment rather than support as you make a sacrifice that is necessary for the survival of the couple.

If your partner has moved so that you could pursue your career, you can ease the transition by attending to two fears that are likely to arise in your partner's mind. Your partner may fear that you consider his or her career unimportant and may also worry that the relationship is less important to you than it is to him or her—that is, to the one who is moving to keep the relationship intact. To calm these fears, you should consistently and clearly express your appreciation of your partner and the relationship. In the hustle and bustle of a move it is easy to neglect relationship maintenance, but maintenance is well worth the effort. Your purpose in expressing appreciation is not to relieve guilt (your partner is responsible for his or her own decision to move) but to calm fears, convey affection, and keep your relationship solid during the transition to a new life.

Some couples choose an alternative to moving jointly to the location of one partner's job: They live in separate places and "commute to the relationship." Some couples even raise families under such circumstances. The advantage of this arrangement is that both partners can actively pursue their careers. On the other hand, the partners generally have limited time together and may spend considerable money on phone calls and travel.

The issues that arise when one partner moves for the sake of the other's career can arise in commuting relationships if the commuting is not shared equally. One partner may end up doing most of the commuting, particularly if social contacts are more developed in one location. If you find this pattern leading to resentment, you may need to balance things out by scheduling social events in the commuting partner's location or making a contract for regular visits to both locations.

If you are in a commuting marriage, you will probably encounter a certain amount of societal disapproval. Some people, typically those with traditional attitudes about work and family, believe that if a commuting marriage were really good, one of the participants would give up the job and follow the partner. People holding those views may verbally or mentally label you as "unable to commit," "prone to infidelity," and "afraid of intimacy." Encountering prejudice is an unavoidable consequence of trying something nontraditional. It may help to remind yourself that your commuting is proof of your commitment to your relationship. Your willingness to incur considerable inconvenience to stay together speaks to your maturity and commitment. If you were not invested in your relationship, you would be more likely to end it and look for someone else closer to home.

ENHANCING THE SPIRITUAL DIMENSION OF YOUR RELATIONSHIP

Spirituality encompasses more than religious activities that take place in churches, synagogues, and mosques. It also involves a couple's values, philosophy of life, and beliefs about what—if anything—transcends human existence. If you and your partner share a spiritual outlook, it can add a dimension to the relationship—a sense that the relationship is part of a greater design that transcends the two of you. However, if you have markedly different spiritual outlooks, the result can be tension in the relationship, particularly if you have children whom both of you wish to educate in accordance with your views.

Many couples find that the closer they get to each other, the more their sense of spirituality grows. This can happen even if spiritual concerns are not directly discussed. It is no coincidence that the key word in this book, *communication*, is related to the religious terms *commune* and *communion*. All these words derive from the same root and mean, essentially, "to come together into one." Building intimate connections with your partner as you share the joys and disappointments of life is a direct route to spiritual growth. The greater the intimacy with your partner, the greater your capacity to feel connected to your soul, higher power, deity, or God (however you identify your sense of spirituality). As your sense of spiritual trust grows, you will also find it easier to be vulnerable with your partner; this makes your relationship more intimate. Thus, intimacy and spirituality can enrich each other.

Handling Spiritual Differences

With the rise of interfaith marriage and geographic mobility, as well as the decline of traditional religion, many people find themselves with partners who have markedly different outlooks on life. Partners may belong to different denominations or sects within the same religion, or they may practice completely different religions. One partner may be religious and the other agnostic or atheist. Couples handle these differences in a number of ways, some of which work better than others.

Some couples decide to ignore the differences, ruling out discussion of religion or spirituality. As a short-term solution, this may be adequate. However, if the relationship is an enduring one, the couple will eventually face events that force them to consider spiritual issues: for instance, how to deal with the aging and death of parents, how to respond to tragedies, what values to inculcate in children, how to find meaning in life, and how to cope with one's own mortality. When a couple cannot discuss questions that are basic to human existence, a sense of barrenness may develop in the relationship. The couple who has considered spirituality before milestone events occur will be better prepared to deal with them, even if the partners differ in their spiritual views.

Proselytizing is another approach to dealing with spiritual differences. One partner pities or judges the other and pressures the partner to convert to his or her own faith. This approach tends to be ineffective. Few people want to hear that their entire outlook on life is inadequate, particularly from a partner. When one partner tries to impose spiritual beliefs on the other, deep resentment can develop and can permanently damage the relationship. Even for people who do not consider themselves religious, spiritual beliefs, when threatened, can prove to be surprisingly important—sometimes to the surprise of both partners. Because spirituality can be so important, you should try hard to be tolerant of your partner's views.

We recommend a third approach to handling spiritual differences. Rather than trying to change each other's minds or ignoring the issue of spirituality, you can share your spiritual views as a way for both of you to explore your spirituality and possibly create new spiritual meanings in your relationship. As in any interaction, communication skills can make this process much easier. You need not have the same theological views to agree on values. It is not unusual to see a relationship in which one partner is a Christian who endorses such values as kindness and honesty and the other partner is a nonreligious humanist who holds precisely the same values. Couples who disagree at first may find that they can create a common ground in which they can both believe. The very act of creating such common ground can enrich the spiritual dimension of a relationship.

Even if you and your partner cannot agree about spiritual concerns, you can profit from discussions of spirituality. If you use the communication skills you have learned, such discussions are likely to increase your understanding of each other and make both of you feel that your views are respected.

Enhancing Spirituality

Some couples, especially young ones, have no disagreements about spirituality because neither partner has paid much attention to that aspect of life. If that is your situation, you may find great rewards in consciously trying to develop a spiritual dimension in your relationship, particularly as you and your partner grow older.

One way to heighten your sense of spirituality is to take advantage of important life events, good or bad, by talking with your partner about what they mean to both of you. A baby arrives, a war breaks out, we get married, a friend becomes gravely ill, our child has a brush with the law, we turn 40 or 50, we retire, our parents move into a nursing home—such events raise questions like "Why am I here?" "Is there a God?" "Where am I going with my life?" and "What does life mean, anyway?" Rather than ponder these questions in solitude, use your communication skills to discuss them with your partner. Even negative events provide opportunities to develop the spiritual dimension of your relationship.

You and your partner may also wish to seek spiritual experiences together. The most common way to do this is to join a religious organization. However, for some couples, organized religion is not attractive or even an option. There are numerous alternatives that you can explore together in order to enhance the spiritual dimension of your relationship: These include praying, meditating, celebrating religious holidays, receiving pastoral counseling, and attending marital enrichment courses. Many couples also find spiritual communion in nature. Watching the sun creep over the horizon, seeing a bird feed its young, climbing to the top of a mountain, or sitting quietly by a stream can be a magical experience for a couple, engendering both awe at the world and a sense of connection to it. Lovemaking can also be a time for partners to share a sense of spiritual togetherness, reflected in the old saying "As the flesh becomes one, so too does the soul." Finally, many couples experience a deep sense of spiritual unity through childbirth and childrearing.

Exercise 10.4 is designed to help you and your partner improve your communication about spiritual matters.

Exercise 10.4   Enhancing Communication About Spirituality

Find a quiet time and discuss some of the questions in the list: Use your communication skills to facilitate the discussion.

1. What comes to mind when you hear the word *God*?

2. In what ways do you feel your relationship honors your values and your outlook on life?

3. Have there been any moments in your relationship when you felt connected to something that transcended human existence?

4. Were you brought up in an organized religion? If so, in what ways was this experience good? In what ways was it bad?

5. What values do you think children need to learn?

6. If you learned that you were going to die tomorrow, would you have regrets about the way you have lived?

7. Has your relationship changed any of your beliefs and values?

8. Do you feel that you understand your partner's outlook on life?

9. Does your religion give you any guidance on how to have a good relationship?

DEALING WITH SEXUAL DIFFICULTIES

Many people are surprised to learn that most couples experience dissatisfaction with their sexual relationships at some time. Because sex is a topic that makes many people uncomfortable, a couple with sexual difficulties may mistakenly gather that they are unique and that there must be something terribly wrong with their relationship. This feeling of isolation and anxiety can exacerbate the problem.

Another unfortunate consequence of the unwillingness in our culture to discuss sex openly is that couples often fail to get accurate information about common sexual behavior and therefore incorrectly conclude that their own sexual behavior is abnormal. For instance, some people in intimate relationships believe that masturbation is an indication that the couple's sexual relationship is unfulfilling. In reality, even people in highly satisfying sexual relationships masturbate. Another common myth is that sexual difficulties must be a symptom of some deeper flaw in a relationship. Sometimes relationship problems and sexual problems are linked, but sexual difficulties also emerge in otherwise satisfying and happy relationships.

Following are some other common sexual myths. If you have heard and believed these myths, you may be relieved to read the accurate information that follows each myth. As an additional source of helpful information about sexuality, we recommend the series of *Joy of Sex* books (listed in the bibliography at the end of chapter 12).

Common Sexual Myths

Myth: The larger the penis, the greater the pleasure for both partners.

Fact: Penis size has little or no relationship to a couple's sexual satisfaction.

Myth: Couples who are middle-aged and older have little or no sexual interest.

Fact: Although the frequency of sexual activity declines with age, most couples are sexually active through their 60s and 70s, and many couples are active in their 80s and 90s.

Myth: Inability to sustain an erection (impotence) is always a sign of psychological problems.

Fact: Impotence often has a biological cause, including aging and alcohol consumption.

Myth: "Good girls" get married but don't enjoy sex.

Fact: In a survey of 93 married couples, 86% of the wives said that they "nearly always" or "usually" felt pleasure and were sexually aroused when having sex with their husbands. All 93 of the wives reported feeling pleasure and being sexually aroused at least some of the times when they had sex with their husbands.

Myth: All good sex involves intercourse.

Fact: Most couples derive sexual pleasure from touching and stroking each other, whether intercourse occurs or not. It is also common for men and women to differ in their emphasis on intercourse. Some people may feel sexually satisfied by lovemaking that does not include intercourse.

Myth: All good sex is spontaneous.

Fact: Couples who schedule a time for sex tend to find the anticipation arousing.

Myth: A man should not have to ask a woman what she likes sexually. He should just know how to satisfy her.

Fact: People vary enormously in what they find sexually rewarding. The only way for a man to know what a woman likes is for the couple to talk about it.

Myth: Fantasies during sex are a sign of perversion.

Fact: It is common for people to fantasize during sex.

Myth: Most couples experience simultaneous orgasm through intercourse.

Fact: Some women never experience orgasm through intercourse, and others experience it infrequently. Even if a woman regularly has orgasm through intercourse, she and her partner may not reach orgasm at the same time.

Sex, Communication, and Sexual Dysfunction

Many people feel that communication about sex is somehow different from communication about other aspects of a relationship and that it therefore must be handled in some special, totally different way. However, our clinical experience suggests that the communication skills outlined in this book work just as well with sexual matters as with other topics. If you doubt this, consider that in many ways sex is like any other important subject you would discuss with your partner: You have expectations to make clear, values to express, feelings to share, and compromises to work out. Although it may seem unromantic to apply communication skills to discuss your sexual relationship, the rewards can be great. You may learn to be a better lover for your partner; likewise, your partner may become a better lover for you. Further, for many couples, an atmosphere of trust and open communication enhances the ability to relax and enjoy sex.

It is particularly important to keep communicating about sex when problems develop. Even if communication alone will not solve the problem, it will probably help both of you deal with the problem. The following are some sexual dysfunctions that you and your partner may encounter. If any of these difficulties persists in your relationship for more than a month despite open communication about the problem, you may wish to find a book dealing with sexual problems or to consult a doctor or sex therapist. (Remember, even when you seek outside help, continue communicating and supporting each other.)

Rapid Ejaculation

Sometimes a man will ejaculate before either partner is ready—for example, just before or immediately after penetration. In many cases, rapid ejaculation occurs because the man feels pressure to perform, experiences stress and anxiety, or feels guilt or shame about sex. Acceptance and open communication between partners can do much to alleviate this problem. Blaming or complaining often increases the man's anxiety, making premature ejaculation even more likely in the future.

Some men develop a habit of ejaculating quickly because they masturbate to orgasm rapidly. In such a case, the man can prevent premature ejaculation with his partner by changing the way he masturbates. The following exercise is intended to help a man increase the time it takes to reach orgasm by increasing ejaculatory control.

Lie on your back and, either alone or with your partner's help, stimulate your penis. Focus your attention on the sensations in your penis as you are stimulating yourself or are being stimulated. When you become highly aroused, the stimulation should be stopped immediately. If you are doing this exercise with your partner, decide in advance on a signal you can use to stop the stimulation. Don't wait until ejaculation is inevitable to stop the stimulation. Let the arousal subside—which may take up to a minute or two—then resume stimulation of the penis. After stopping three times, continue the last round of stimulation to orgasm. This exercise is most effective when done regularly (at least three times a week) and when done with a partner.

Pain During Sex and Vaginismus

This category of dysfunction includes pain felt by a woman in the vagina, ovaries, or cervix during intercourse and pain felt by a man in the penis or testes during intercourse or ejaculation. If the woman is not aroused during intercourse, the pain may result from insufficient lubrication in the vagina. Increasing the time spent in sexual activity before penetration may help increase vaginal lubrication. In many cases, pain experienced by either partner indicates a physical problem such as sexually transmitted disease or viral infection. Most such diseases and infections can be detected and treated by a doctor.

Pain during intercourse can also be caused by vaginismus, or spasms of the vaginal walls. These painful spasms decrease the size of the vagina, making intercourse painful or impossible. Although treatment of vaginismus can take time and effort, the results are generally quite good. If you have this problem, we suggest that you seek the aid of a sex therapist.

Sexually Transmitted Diseases

A couple's degree of concern about AIDS, herpes, gonorrhea, and syphilis depends on the nature of their relationship. If you are in a relationship that is not monogamous, if you and/or your partner have had other sexual partners in the past, or if you and/or your partner have used intravenous drugs, you need to discuss sexually transmitted diseases, drawing on your communication skills. You need not give detailed accounts of your sexual histories; simple statements such as "I have always practiced safer sex" or "I had a blood test and found out that I am free of sexually transmitted diseases" can suffice.

Early in a relationship, discussion of issues related to sex can be awkward. If such a discussion has yet to occur in your relationship, we urge you to practice safer sex with your partner. Sometimes this can be uncomfortable—for instance, if your partner is uneasy about condom use—but the discomfort is small compared to the costs of sexually transmitted disease (which in the era of AIDS can include death).

Impotence

It is very common for a man to be unable to sustain an erection at some point in his life. For many men, the problem is ongoing. Sometimes impotence is a one-time result of stress, overconsumption of alcohol, or performance anxiety, and some reassurance from a partner can keep impotence from becoming a major problem. Ongoing impotence has a number of potential causes, many of which are biological. Your doctor may be able to help determine the cause of the difficulty.

Absence of Orgasm

Although sex need not always result in orgasm, a problem arises if one or both partners wish to reach orgasm but cannot. Sometimes a man is unable to ejaculate, even long after vaginal penetration. This condition, known as retarded ejaculation, can be treated by a sex therapist. It is far more common for women to have difficulty reaching orgasm. Some women never experience orgasm, and others can achieve it only in a particular fashion, such as through masturbation or oral sex. For orgasm to occur, a person must first be sexually aroused. Thus, lack of orgasm can result if the couple does not spend enough time on arousing activities (such as kissing, caressing, etc.) before intercourse. Although many women never experience orgasm through intercourse, extended foreplay makes orgasm more likely. Lonnie Barbach's book *For Each Other: Sharing Sexual Intimacy* offers much information and many exercises for couples who wish to expand the female capacity for orgasm and sexual pleasure in general (see the bibliography at the end of chapter 12).

Boredom

For couples who have been together a number of years, boredom and lack of interest in sex can become a significant problem. One reason this happens is that couples fall into sexual routines, having sex at a particular time in a particular way. Of course, any routine will turn boring eventually, so the challenge for couples who wish to keep their sex lives exciting is to vary the routine. Here are some things you can do to bring some variety into your sex life.

1. Using your communication skills, discuss what you like about sex with your partner. Let your partner know what he or she does that you like, as well as specific things that would increase your sexual satisfaction.

2. Go on a date together. Plan on having sex afterward so that you can enjoy the anticipation. Dress attractively and flirt during dinner. Consider seeing a romantic or sexual movie after dinner.

3. Check into a hotel one night instead of staying home.

4. Spend some time sharing sexual fantasies. Use your communication skills to help both of you feel comfortable.

5. Select a book on sex and read it together. See if the book suggests any new activities or sexual positions that you would like to try.

11 *What If It Seems Hopeless? Breakup or Divorce*

Every couple has problems now and then. Some of these problems can be successfully resolved; others cannot. When the problems are persistent and overwhelming, the couple may need to consider whether the best course of action is to dissolve the relationship. This chapter, which addresses the difficult issues faced by the couple contemplating a breakup, will help you weigh the advantages and disadvantages of ending your relationship. If you decide that it is in your best interest to terminate the relationship, you should pay close attention to the last part of this chapter. It provides some specific information for people ending legally sanctioned relationships (e.g., marriage) as well as some guidelines for helping children understand and adjust to the changes typically associated with the end of a relationship.

To clarify your own position, begin by answering the following questions independently of your partner. Questions have been selected and modified from the Marital Instability Index.*

1. Even people who get along quite well with their partners sometimes wonder if their relationship is working out. Have you ever thought your relationship might be in trouble?

2. Has the thought of getting a divorce or separation crossed your mind in the past 3 years?

3. Have you discussed divorce or separation with a close friend?

4. Have you or your partner ever seriously suggested the idea of divorce or separation within the last 3 years?

5. If you are married, did you talk about consulting an attorney?

If you answered yes to Question 1, you are not alone. In fact, research shows that approximately one person in two typically answers yes to this question and that it is quite common for people to wonder if their relationships might be in trouble (Booth, Johnson, & Edwards, 1983). "Yes" answers to Questions 2 through 5 are less common. If you

---

*From "Measuring Marital Instability" by A. Booth, D. Johnson, & J. N. Edwards, 1983, *Journal of Marriage and the Family, 45*, p. 392. Copyrighted 1983 by the National Council on Family Relations, 3989 Central Avenue N. E., Suite 550, Minneapolis, MN 55421. Reprinted by permission.

answered yes to two or more of these questions, we recommend that you continue reading this chapter.

WHEN THE GOING GETS ROUGH

Does the fact that you are thinking about ending your relationship mean that you and your partner should part? Not necessarily. Feeling that a breakup might be in the cards is quite different from deciding that your relationship is over. All too often, when difficulties arise, a couple concludes that the relationship is no longer viable. These decisions tend to be made when partners are in a highly emotional state and cannot problem solve effectively. A time of emotional stress is usually not a good time to determine if a relationship is truly over. Stephanie and Pablo's situation illustrates this point.

Stephanie: I'm really upset about that stunt you pulled the other day. It hurt me. I'd like to talk to you about where our relationship is going.

Pablo: Hey, I already apologized for that, and I feel bad that you got hurt. Your insecurity really gets to me. If you can't handle it, that's your problem and you need to deal with it. So maybe we'd be better off without this.

Stephanie: So, you think you'd be better off without me? I'm tired of you saying this whenever we disagree on something. You couldn't handle a week alone. I bet you couldn't even fix yourself a TV dinner.

Pablo: What I was talking about was being better off without this discussion. But fine. Let's talk. And while we're at it . . . I bet that I could cook and clean better than you any day. You know, now that we're talking about our relationship, I think I'd be better off without your constant nagging. I'm fed up with these arguments. Yeah, I'd probably be better off alone.

Stephanie: I just wish you'd stop playing these games. Either you are in this relationship or you're not in it. Make up your mind!

Stephanie and Pablo are allowing their strong feelings to guide their discussion. In fact, the discussion has heated up to the point where they have said some quite serious, damaging things about the future of their relationship. Yet, as we noted in the chapters on communication skills, important decisions should not be made during times of intense emotion. Stephanie started the discussion because she was concerned about her relationship with Pablo. Similarly, at the beginning of the discussion, Pablo appeared concerned about Stephanie's feelings and their effect on the relationship. Because of the intense feelings on both sides, the discussion escalated until the end of the relationship was on the table.

In the communication chapters, we discussed the effects of feelings on behaviors and thoughts. A couple's feelings at a time of difficulty can strongly influence their judgments about whether or not the relationship is worth continuing. If you are in a serious relationship, ending it could have a dramatic impact on your life, especially if the relationship is legally binding. We urge you to examine how your feelings during difficult times may be influencing your thoughts about ending your relationship. To begin, complete Exercise 11.1.

Exercise 11.1   Feelings That Could Affect a Decision About Breakup or Divorce

Partner 1

In the list of feelings, circle those that you are currently experiencing with regard to your relationship. Then ask yourself how each feeling you circled might affect your decision to end the relationship.

Affectionate	Afraid	Agitated	Alone	Angry
Annoyed	Bitter	Bored	Cautious	Cheerful
Content	Cooperative	Critical	Daring	Desperate
Destroyed	Devoted	Disagreeable	Discouraged	Enraged
Fearful	Free	Friendly	Frightened	Furious
Glad	Happy	Hopeless	Hostile	Hurt
Impatient	Irritated	Jealous	Kind	Lost
Loving	Lucky	Mad	Mean	Meek
Miserable	Nervous	Obliging	Offended	Outraged
Panicked	Patient	Peaceful	Pleasant	Polite
Powerful	Quiet	Rejected	Resentful	Sad
Safe	Secure	Shaky	Shy	Sociable
Strong	Stubborn	Sympathetic	Tense	Terrified
Thoughtful	Timid	Trapped	Turned on	Understanding
Unsociable	Upset	Vexed	Warm	Weak
Wild	Worrisome			

Partner 2

In the list of feelings, circle those that you are currently experiencing with regard to your relationship. Then ask yourself how each feeling you circled might affect your decision to end the relationship.

Affectionate	Afraid	Agitated	Alone	Angry
Annoyed	Bitter	Bored	Cautious	Cheerful
Content	Cooperative	Critical	Daring	Desperate
Destroyed	Devoted	Disagreeable	Discouraged	Enraged
Fearful	Free	Friendly	Frightened	Furious
Glad	Happy	Hopeless	Hostile	Hurt
Impatient	Irritated	Jealous	Kind	Lost
Loving	Lucky	Mad	Mean	Meek
Miserable	Nervous	Obliging	Offended	Outraged
Panicked	Patient	Peaceful	Pleasant	Polite
Powerful	Quiet	Rejected	Resentful	Sad
Safe	Secure	Shaky	Shy	Sociable
Strong	Stubborn	Sympathetic	Tense	Terrified
Thoughtful	Timid	Trapped	Turned on	Understanding
Unsociable	Upset	Vexed	Warm	Weak
Wild	Worrisome			

WHY DO PEOPLE END THEIR RELATIONSHIPS?

Most people experience the breakup of a relationship at some point in their lives; however, the reasons behind those breakups vary widely. Some couples cite unrealistic expectations or misperceptions as leading to their breakups. Others fault communication difficulties or unsatisfying relationships. Still others say that they have simply grown apart and no longer have similar interests or values.

Men and women tend to differ in the complaints they cite as leading to the dissolution of relationships. Lack of communication and affection are cited by one woman out of two; one woman in three reports a lack of shared interests; and one in four women cites alcoholism, physical abuse, or extramarital sex as factors contributing to breakup. Although among men one in six cites alcoholism or infidelity as a cause of breakup, most men tend to see nagging, whining, and fault finding as behaviors leading to the termination of their relationships. The causes cited differ with the type of relationship and the people involved, but the result is clear: a permanent dissolution of a relationship as a consequence of the partners' inability to solve a problem. Some problems are not amenable to solution, and some problems—such as a long history of mutually destructive behavior involving physical violence—may not be worth solving. For couples who face unsolvable problems or problems that may not be in their interest to solve, ending the relationship is a reasonable alternative.

Breakups and Society

The rise in divorce rates shows that breaking up of "lifetime" relationships has become increasingly common in our society. Over 95% of Americans get married, and about 50% of marriages end in divorce. In fact, about one of every four marriages ends in divorce within 3 years. In comparison, in the 1920s only one of seven marriages ended in divorce (Bornstein & Bornstein, 1986). Life-style changes have considerably altered people's attitudes toward the ending of relationships, and the attitudinal shift is one reason the divorce rate has risen so rapidly.

Not too long ago, people were excommunicated from churches when they divorced. Divorcees were shunned, and words such as *adultery, mental or physical cruelty,* and *desertion* were typically associated with divorce proceedings. Today we have no-fault divorces, which eliminate the need for one spouse to prove the other guilty of an offense in order to obtain a divorce. The existence of irreconcilable differences is sufficient for a divorce to be granted. The no-fault legislation has dramatically increased the ease and convenience with which legally sanctioned relationships can be ended. It has also had considerable impact on society's views of divorce and breakup. Most important, it has diminished some of the hostility and blame that surround the ending of relationships.

In addition to legislative changes, role models in our society have also shaped new attitudes about the termination of relationships. Actors' and actresses' multiple marriages and breakups make the headlines of supermarket tabloids. Billionaires and athletes openly discuss the dissolution of relationships as well as the formation of new ones. Even politicians and television evangelists now talk publicly about their relationships. As a result of our society's increased openness, a chance at a new relationship has become an accepted alternative for couples unable to reconcile their differences.

WHAT ARE THE EFFECTS OF BREAKUP OR DIVORCE?

For many people, separation brings a new and meaningful second chance. At the same time, it also brings many unexpected changes. Feelings of loneliness, depression, anxiety, guilt, and failure can abound. The need to come to terms with being single can be accompanied by growing disorganization in everyday life. Moreover, a separation or divorce affects the lives of others, including children, mutual friends, coworkers, and in-laws.

Changes in Your Life Routine

Many changes in life's routine follow a separation or a divorce. There is an unoccupied place at the dinner table; there is no rush for the shower in the morning; there is no one to come home to after a good or bad day at work. Consider how your daily life would be different if you ended your current relationship. How would it be better? How might it be worse? Exercise 11.2 will help you visualize the changes.

Exercise 11.2   Daily Schedule

Partner 1

To get an idea of the likely changes in your life, complete the following daily schedule by writing in your activities for today. Start with "The alarm clock went off" and include each activity (e.g., brushing your teeth, making coffee, eating breakfast, taking the kids to school, driving to work, conducting your work activities, lunching with a colleague, etc.). Next, using a different color pen, circle the activities that would change in some way following a separation, breakup, or divorce (the activities need only be different, not better or worse). The number of circled activities will suggest how much your daily life would change if your relationship ended.

Today is _____

6:00 A.M.   _____

6:30 A.M.   _____

7:00 A.M.   _____

7:30 A.M.   _____

8:00 A.M.   _____

8:30 A.M.   _____

9:00 A.M.   _____

9:30 A.M.   _____

10:00 A.M.   _____

10:30 A.M.   _____

11:00 A.M.   _____

11:30 A.M.   _____

Noon   _____

12:30 P.M.   _____

1:00 P.M.   _____

1:30 P.M.   _____

2:00 P.M.   _____

2:30 P.M.   _____

3:00 P.M. _____

3:30 P.M. _____

4:00 P.M. _____

4:30 P.M. _____

5:00 P.M. _____

5:30 P.M. _____

6:00 P.M. _____

6:30 P.M. _____

7:00 P.M. _____

7:30 P.M. _____

8:00 P.M. _____

8:30 P.M. _____

9:00 P.M. _____

9:30 P.M. _____

10:00 P.M. _____

10:30 P.M. _____

11:00 P.M. _____

11:30 P.M. _____

Midnight _____

Partner 2

To get an idea of the likely changes in your life, complete the following daily schedule by writing in your activities for today. Start with "The alarm clock went off" and include each activity (e.g., brushing your teeth, making coffee, eating breakfast, taking the kids to school, driving to work, conducting your work activities, lunching with a colleague, etc.). Next, using a different color pen, circle the activities that would change in some way following a separation, breakup, or divorce (the activities need only be different, not better or worse). The number of circled activities will suggest how much your daily life would change if your relationship ended.

Today is _____

6:00 A.M. _____

6:30 A.M. _____

7:00 A.M. _____

7:30 A.M. _____

8:00 A.M. _____

8:30 A.M. _____

9:00 A.M. _____

9:30 A.M. _____

10:00 A.M. _____

10:30 A.M. _____

11:00 A.M. _____

11:30 A.M. _____

Noon _____

12:30 P.M. _____

1:00 P.M. _____

1:30 P.M. _____

2:00 P.M. _____

2:30 P.M. _____

3:00 P.M.   _____

3:30 P.M.   _____

4:00 P.M.   _____

4:30 P.M.   _____

5:00 P.M.   _____

5:30 P.M.   _____

6:00 P.M.   _____

6:30 P.M.   _____

7:00 P.M.   _____

7:30 P.M.   _____

8:00 P.M.   _____

8:30 P.M.   _____

9:00 P.M.   _____

9:30 P.M.   _____

10:00 P.M.   _____

10:30 P.M.   _____

11:00 P.M.   _____

11:30 P.M.   _____

Midnight   _____

A breakup or divorce will also affect your financial situation. Many couples who have lived together experience a decline in standard of living following a separation: Two households cost more to maintain than one. Also, married people usually pay lower taxes than do single people. Women are usually more subject to a decline in income following separation. Statistically speaking, 5 years after the termination of such a relationship, a woman's income typically covers just 94% of her standard of living prior to separation; for a man, by contrast, the figure is 130% (Duncan & Hoffman, 1985).

To find out how a change in income will affect your life, complete Exercise 11.3.

Exercise 11.3   Monthly Expenses

Partner 1

_____   Rent or mortgage

_____   Utilities (electricity, gas, water, garbage, sewer, phone, cable TV)

_____   Food

_____   Child care

_____   Automobile (gas, repairs)

_____   Medical expenses

_____   Insurance (medical, auto, life)

_____   Travel

_____   Leisure activities

_____   Loans

_____   Taxes

_____   TOTAL EXPENSES

_____ – _____ = _____

  [current income]   [total expenses]   [net balance]

Partner 2

_____   Rent or mortgage

_____   Utilities (electricity, gas, water, garbage, sewer, phone, cable TV)

_____   Food

_____   Child care

_____   Automobile (gas, repairs)

_____   Medical expenses

_____   Insurance (medical, auto, life)

_____   Travel

_____   Leisure activities

_____   Loans

_____   Taxes

_____   TOTAL EXPENSES

_____ – _____ = _____
[current income]   [total expenses]   [net balance]

If the exercise shows that you'll be in the red, you have reason for concern. However, the purpose of the exercise is not to start you on financial planning but to give you an idea of how your life-style may change if you dissolve your relationship. If you are married and want to initiate financial planning, remember to include alimony, child support, court costs, attorney's fees, and so on in your estimates.

Changes in You

Following a separation, there will also be changes in your self-concept: You will need to make the transition from seeing yourself as part of a couple to seeing yourself as single. Will you date? Will friends you and your partner knew as a couple still be available to you? Can you cope with your friends' associating with your ex-partner? Will you be lonely? Can you make new friends? Questions like these cause anxiety for many people considering separation or divorce. To help allay some of this anxiety, take 10 minutes to imagine yourself as single. Exercise 11.4 will guide you.

If you were single, would there be people who could ease your transition to singleness? If so, who would they be?

Exercise 11.4   Questions About Life as a Single Person

Partner 1

Consider the questions and answer all that apply.

1. What is my life like during the day on Monday through Friday?

2. What are my evenings like?

3. What are my weekends like?

4. What are holidays like?

5. How do I spend time with my children?

6. What do I do in my leisure time?

7. Whom do I talk to on the phone?

8. Whom do I visit?

9. What places do I go? Am I alone? Whom am I with?

Next, write down what you liked and disliked about being single.

I liked: _____

_____

_____

I disliked: _____

_____

_____

Partner 2

Consider the questions and answer all that apply.

1. What is my life like during the day on Monday through Friday?

2. What are my evenings like?

3. What are my weekends like?

4. What are holidays like?

5. How do I spend time with my children?

6. What do I do in my leisure time?

7. Whom do I talk to on the phone?

8. Whom do I visit?

9. What places do I go? Am I alone? Whom am I with?

Next, write down what you liked and disliked about being single.

I liked: _____

_____

_____

I disliked: _____

_____

_____

Changes for Others

Separation or divorce also affects the lives of people outside the couple. Children are perhaps the most affected as loved ones move away, traditions are lost, and routines are disrupted. Because half of the children born today will experience the divorce of their parents by the time they are 18, we'll focus on the actions parents can take to help children understand and adjust to the changes associated with divorce. Although the remainder of the chapter specifically deals with divorce, many of the issues discussed are relevant to other types of breakup.

Children's reactions to parental separation or divorce vary considerably. Some children exhibit problem behaviors such as acting out at home or school or isolating themselves from other children; such difficulties are particularly evident during the first 2 years following a divorce. Other children adjust to the changes quite successfully. Table 11.1 lists some common reactions seen in children of divorced parents. If such difficulties become severe or persist, you may want to consult a professional who works with children.

Table 11.1   Common Reactions of Children in Response to Divorce

Although the following reactions may be seen in children of all ages, X's mark ages at which the reactions are most common.

Reaction	Preschool child	Elementary school child	Adolescent
Anxiety	X	X	X
Sadness	X	X (7–8 years)	X
Grieving	X	X (7–8 years)	
Anger	X	X (9–10 years)	X
Embarrassment		X (9–10 years)	X
Loneliness		X (9–10 years)	X
Low self-esteem	X	X	X
Depression	X	X	X
Bed wetting	X	X	
Acting much younger	X	X	
Isolation from peers		X	
Academic difficulties		X	X
Aggression	X	X	X

As soon as you know that you are separating permanently, it is important to start preparing your child for what may come. Expect to see some changes in your child's behavior as you do this, and make a plan to handle these changes. To begin, you will need to use the communication skills outlined in this book to address some special issues. (See chapter 9 for pointers on communicating with children.) Remember to use language and ideas that are appropriate to your child's age.

Begin by explaining that there will be changes in your house, that you may move, and that you or your partner will not be living in the home anymore. Children must understand that the changes are not their fault. Most children are aware of the increased tension or arguments that typically precede the end of a relationship. Explain how these conflicts are related to difficulties that have nothing to do with your child. Also make clear that, despite the changes, both parents still love the child. Stress that the separation or divorce is final (if that is the case) so that the child will not entertain false hopes of a reunion. You may also want to focus on the positive by-products of a separation or divorce—for instance, the child may have two places to celebrate birthdays and holidays and may have more time alone with each parent. If you know your custody arrangements, discuss them with your child. Make a calendar to help a preschool or elementary-age child understand visitation and joint custody. If appropriate, prepare the child for questions from others, who may ask what life is like with each parent or which parent the child would prefer to live with. Emphasize that you will still love your child no matter how he or she answers these questions.

As legal processes advance, tell your child about any new developments that might change arrangements that you have discussed earlier. At this time you may also want to help your child see that he or she is not alone in coping with the ending of a parental relationship. Point out well-adjusted children whose parents are no longer together, and encourage your child to talk about his or her own experiences with those children. Also encourage—but do not pressure—your child to talk with both parents about feelings regarding the divorce. Table 11.2 summarizes the issues that should be discussed at various points with children of different ages.

Books that you might read with your child or make available to him or her are another helpful resource. For the preschool child, we recommend *I Have Two Families*, by Doris Helmering. For elementary school children, reading *A Dinosaur's Divorce*, by Laurene and Marc Brown, is likely to stimulate discussion. Adolescents may benefit by reading *How to Get It Together When Your Parents are Coming Apart*, by Arlene Richards and Irene Willis. Finally, you might find assistance in *The Parent's Book About Divorce*, by R. A. Gardner. These and other titles are listed in the bibliography appearing in chapter 12. Check your local library for additional resources.

Table 11.2   Guide for Discussions With Children

KEY

P = Preschool child
E = Elementary school child
A = Adolescent

When	**What to do**
You're aware that you're separating	Explain that it is not the child's fault, both parents still love the child, there may be changes in routine, both parents will not be living together. Expect changes in behavior and develop appropriate plans for dealing with behavior (P, E, A).
The process begins	Discuss possible changes in residence (P, E) or attending a new school and making new friends (E, A). Focus on positive aspects such as having two places to celebrate holidays (P, E) or having more time alone with each parent (P, E, A). Prepare the child for any possible involvement in the legal process (E, A), such as questions from an attorney and the like. Encourage discussion and questions with both parents (P, E, A).
The process advances	Advise the child on new developments (P, E, A). Explain custody arrangements, if you know them (P, E, A) and use a calendar to explain them (P, E). Read about divorce with the child (P, E) or suggest some reading (A). Encourage the child to talk to well-adjusted peers about feelings and/or reactions (E, A). Continue to encourage discussion with both parents (P, E, A). Emphasize the finality of the process (E, A).

COMMUNICATION IN DIVORCE

Many couples are unaware that divorce or separation can require a great deal of communication at a time when the partners may not wish to communicate with each other. Communication at this time can become quite stressful. In fact, conflict between ex-spouses frequently increases after divorce. To understand more about the role of communication in the ending of a relationship, let's follow Elizabeth and John as they proceed with a divorce.

Elizabeth and John Starr have been married for 3 years. Each has been married once previously. They have 3 children. Ed is 10 years old and is Elizabeth's son by her previous marriage. Jane, age 6, is John's daughter by his previous marriage. John, Jr., is Elizabeth and John's 18-month-old son.

Elizabeth contacted an attorney 2 weeks ago to start the divorce proceedings. She told her attorney that she was no longer happy in her marriage and did not wish to remain in it. However, she is very worried that she will not be able to support herself and the children on her current salary.

John contacted an attorney last week, citing a similar reason for wanting a divorce. He is less concerned about being able to support himself; however, he tells his attorney that he does not want his wife to "take him to the cleaners."

Notice how Elizabeth and John are both communicating with and becoming dependent on attorneys. Each circumstance must be described to the attorney, the options discussed, and so on. For people who may be "fed up" with the marriage this process can be difficult, although communication skills can facilitate it. Furthermore, Elizabeth and John's case is somewhat unusual: The decision to divorce is not always mutual.

A Choice of Process

In the traditional adversarial divorce process, each lawyer tries to obtain the best possible settlement for his or her client. Face-to-face communication is kept to a minimum; most issues are handled through the lawyers. However, the pain, suffering, and financial burdens associated with litigation should not be underestimated. Spouses relinquish much control by handing matters over to lawyers, who then engage in an adversarial process that favors the partner with the greater financial resources. Decisions about alimony, division of property, child support, and custody are made by a judge, and the outcome can be unsatisfactory to one partner or both. For example, a parent seeking custody may be taking a chance the judge will award it to the other parent. Also, court-ordered child support awards average less than the amount estimated as necessary for raising a child at the poverty level. Furthermore, there is no guarantee that the ex-spouse will actually make the child support payments. Fewer than half of such payments are made in full, and some 20% of custodial mothers receive no payments at all.

Those who do not favor the adversarial process have the choice of pursuing divorce mediation, which is becoming a popular alternative to litigation. In mediation the spouses meet with an impartial third party—a mediator—with the goal of reaching a settlement that is satisfactory to both parties. Mediation is attractive because it offers the opportunity for a win-win outcome rather than producing a winner and a loser as litigation does. Although divorce mediation does not guarantee that both partners will be satisfied with the results, it does give the partners more control over decisions than they would have in the traditional adversarial process. There is some evidence that both husbands and wives believe that they get what they want through mediation, an outcome not produced by litigation. On the other hand, the degree of control enjoyed by parties in mediation could lead to agreements that a spouse later regrets. This is not surprising considering the emotional turmoil surrounding a divorce; people may make concessions simply to be done with the process, or they may reach agreements that are not workable. It is therefore wise to have an attorney examine an agreement reached though mediation before it is ratified by a judge. Divorce mediation requires substantially more cooperation, negotiation, and communication than does litigation. Use of communication skills can make it go more smoothly. Still, mediation is no panacea; it may be unsuitable for many couples, especially if there is a marked difference in the power exerted by the two partners. Table 11.3 lets you compare the features of mediation and of the traditional adversarial divorce process.

Table 11.3   Summary of Divorce Processes

	Adversarial process	**Divorce mediation**
Goal	Presentation of best case for each party to allow judge to reach a settlement	Mutual agreement
Who participates?	Spouses, attorneys, judge	Spouses, mediator, and/or attorney
Who decides?	Judge	Spouses and mediator (judge ratifies agreement)
Costs	Attorney fees, court costs	Mediator's fee and/or attorney's fee
Communication	Limited	Necessary
Outcome	No guarantees	No guarantees

Exercise 11.5 uses the situation of Elizabeth and John Starr, described earlier, to help you visualize the process of divorce and understand the role of communication in the process.

Exercise 11.5   Examining the Divorce Process

Elizabeth and John have decided to pursue divorce mediation. Consider the following questions and answer them on a separate sheet of paper.

1. What is the best way to decide child custody in this situation?

   Should John, Jr., and Ed live with John, Sr.?

   Should Jane live with Elizabeth?

   Should all the children live with one parent?

   Should joint custody be pursued? If so, how?

   List all possible arrangements. How many are there?

2. How will visitation privileges be handled?

   What are the possible options?

3. From Elizabeth's perspective, devise a yearly plan for where the children should spend holidays and vacation periods.

   Devise another plan from John's perspective.

4. Suppose that John's income is $30,000 per year and Elizabeth's is $20,000.

   Who should pay child support and/or alimony and how much?

   What would be a fair settlement?

5. What would be one way to divide the property between John and Elizabeth?

   What would be some other alternatives?

6. Consider the two holiday and vacation plans you devised in answer to Question 3. What communication skills would be helpful in resolving this issue?

7. If you are considering a divorce, what issues would be important to you?

8. Consider the present status of your relationship. Would the traditional adversarial process or divorce mediation better help you achieve your goals?

After the Divorce

Although divorce is stressful, most men and women adjust reasonably well within 2 to 3 years to the changes their new lives bring. For some people, however, additional stressors related to economic concerns, emotional and social difficulties, or specific life events can make the adjustment more difficult. After the divorce, you should try to keep communication channels open between you, your spouse, and your children. In some cases, discussions about remarriage, stepparents, and blended families may be appropriate. Although communicating with your ex-spouse may seem difficult, it can make dealing with post-divorce matters much easier. Further, your children will deal with the divorce better if they see that their parents can communicate effectively; watching parents continue to argue and fight can be very stressful for children, even when the parents are no longer married.

This chapter has briefly covered some of the many issues that arise when couples break up or divorce. If you are seriously considering ending your relationship, you may want to read about these issues in greater detail. A useful book on the subject, listed in the bibliography in chapter 12, is *The Divorce Book*, by Matthew McKay, Peter Rogers, Joan Blades, and Richard Gosse. Whatever choice you make, you will be better off if you have evaluated your options. You may continue in the relationship with renewed commitment and excitement, or you may have begun the important work of rebuilding your life as a single person.

CHAPTER
12 *Conclusion*

FOR COUPLES

As you have discovered, making—and keeping—a relationship healthy and fulfilling requires work. However, the sort of intense effort that you have exerted in working though this book may not be necessary all the time. If the skills you have learned and practiced are now a natural part of your communication, preserving the fruits of your hard work may only require setting aside time to monitor your relationship at regular intervals. At those times you may need to return to this book or engage in some refresher exercises.

Although this book addresses important skills, it is not an exhaustive guide for improving communication or relationships. Moreover, couples sometimes need outside help in improving their relationships. Because we may all have trouble accurately assessing what is happening in our relationships, the more objective perspective of a third person can sometimes be valuable. If your relationship is still not satisfactory to you, consider pursuing other options—for instance, a visit to your local self-help group (some communities have self-help centers that maintain listings of such groups) or a consultation with a mental health professional or member of the clergy. The bibliography at the end of this chapter suggests readings that may interest you if you want to know more about specific topics covered in this book.

FOR PEOPLE WHO WORK WITH COUPLES

Although this book is a guide to better communication, it also parallels the therapy process. Kanfer and Schefft (1988) have outlined a conceptual framework for therapy comprising seven phases, shown in Table 12.1. In this section, we provide the rationale for the structure of the book by explaining how specific sections correspond to the stages of therapy as described by Kanfer and Schefft.

Phase 1: Role Structuring and Creation of a Therapeutic Alliance

Mirroring the therapy process, chapter 1 begins by helping each partner to define his or her role in the change process and to learn about our goals for guiding change. Immediately, the reader is identified as an expert on his or her difficulties: The reader is asked to decide whether or not this book is appropriate for bringing about change. A short screening summary, resembling one likely to be used at an intake, helps the partners decide on an appropriate course of action. Like an intake session, the first chapter informs the couple about what they can expect from the book and makes clear that, if the book falls short of their expectations, they have the option of seeking alternative

Table 12.1   The Seven Phases of Therapy

Phase 1: Role structuring and creation of a therapeutic alliance

Phase 2: Development of a commitment for change

Phase 3: Behavioral analysis

Phase 4: Negotiation of treatment objectives and methods

Phase 5: Implementation of treatment and maintenance of motivation

Phase 6: Monitoring and evaluation of progress

Phase 7: Maintenance, generalization, and termination of treatment

Note. Adapted from *Guiding the Process of Therapeutic Change* by F. H. Kanfer and B. K. Schefft, 1988, Champaign, IL: Research Press.

resources. In the process of role definition, our expectations for the partners are specified early. The reader is notified that simply reading the book (like simply attending therapy) will not be sufficient to bring about change; instead, change will require work on the reader's part, and this work may not always be easy. Besides giving each partner responsibility for his or her own change, we stress the importance of exercises (the equivalent of between-session assignments) in the change process. The necessity of a commitment to change is introduced here, as is the need to be prepared for setbacks. A short exercise, a mood enhancement task in which the couple is asked to recall some fond memories, completes the first phase of therapy by building hope and motivation in the reader.

Phase 2: Development of a Commitment for Change

Chapter 2 is devoted to this second phase of therapy, development of a commitment for change. It concludes with an agreement symbolizing that commitment. The chapter begins by establishing a working collaborative set. Thoughts that stop cooperation are challenged so that they will not detract from the collaborative set later in the process. We discuss incentives for change in detail to increase the reader's motivation to enter the commitment to change. Through prompting to consider the positive consequences of that commitment—such as maintaining one's investment in a relationship, learning about communication differences between men and women, learning more about oneself, learning how to enhance communication in other relationships, and achieving overall relationship enhancement—the reader begins developing realistic goals for the relationship, goals that the book will help him or her attain.

Phase 3: Behavioral Analysis

The goal of chapters 3, 4, and 5 is to help readers understand communication in their relationships. We approach the behavioral analysis from a broad perspective that includes the affective, cognitive, and cultural contexts of behavior. Because we address a variety of relationships, possible behavioral differences affecting relationships and communication styles receive considerable emphasis in these three chapters. We hope that through behavioral analysis of several types of relationships, readers will learn both to observe the communication behaviors most relevant to their own relationships and to observe communication behaviors from a variety of perspectives. For example, behavioral analysis of communication rules used by men and women (chapter 5) prompts readers not only to examine miscommunications in a sample conversation but also to observe their own communications, as well as those with people of the opposite gender.

Chapter 4 lays some common ground for all readers. Communication is explained with respect to the speaker, the listener, the intended message, and the encoded message. By breaking the communication process into its components, we guide the couple toward refining and restating problem areas, much as a therapist might do in therapy. Consideration of the thoughts, feelings, and behaviors that affect communication, as well as the background each partner brings to a relationship, provides a framework for understanding how miscommunications occur. Readers are encouraged to discover areas of communication difficulty that are specific to the relationships of concern. Further, by learning to make these observations for themselves, readers will be able to identify communication problem areas in future relationships. This process sets up themes that are explored later and encourages generalization, as in therapy.

In the use of this book, as in therapy, continued assessment throughout the process of change is necessary to monitor improvement. Chapter 4 includes a number of self-report instruments designed to help partners assess their relationship in specific terms; these instruments provide a baseline measure of the relationship. At the end of chapter 8, following completion of the chapters on communication skills, readers are referred again to these measures for an assessment of their progress.

Phase 4: Negotiation of Treatment Objectives and Methods

As in any therapy, firm ground rules and well-defined goals are needed if a positive outcome is to be obtained. In chapter 6, readers are encouraged to set the stage for future work. They designate a time and place for communication, establish rules for getting started, and decide how and when to implement communication time-out. These steps are imperative if the couple is to avoid miscommunication as they begin working together on their relationship; they are the same steps many therapists use in structuring between-session assignments. Chapter 6 also emphasizes the importance of realistic expectations. As in therapy, expecting too much too soon can lead to setbacks or early termination. Addressing expectations up front can help readers sustain their motivation.

Chapter 6 also defines some very specific objectives for the reader. These include keeping things friendly, maintaining a positive outlook, and avoiding roadblocks. These steps enable partners to build a collaborative set and lay the groundwork for future effort on more difficult communication issues. Successful completion of relatively easy exercises can help reduce resistance to change. Moreover, successful completion encourages people to attempt further changes. As in therapy, continued evaluation of the couple's progress is incorporated into this chapter.

Phase 5: Implementation of Treatment and Maintenance of Motivation

The communication steps taught in chapters 6, 7, and 8 are the core of our intervention for enhancing communication. Chapter 6 lays the groundwork for continued improvement. Chapters 7 and 8 include exercises that gradually progress in difficulty and allow the couple to move beyond discussions of minor disagreements. Like therapy, this part of the book encourages couples to master one skill at a time so that the use of skills becomes automatic. In addition, rewards are foreseen for the use of each new skill so that learning, overlearning, and maintenance of these skills will result. The learning of intermediate skills is monitored at the end of chapter 7.

After mastering the intermediate skills, readers proceed to chapter 8 and the problem-solving skills. Although many couples want to jump to this section as soon as they enter an agreement to work on the relationship, we hold these skills until relatively late in the intervention. As in therapy, addressing a difficult aspect of the relationship without laying the necessary groundwork is not desirable and may even do more harm than good, particularly if highly emotional material is involved. Couples are advised to begin this chapter only when they have observed themselves consistently using the skills learned earlier.

The exercises in chapter 8 guide the couple toward satisfactory experiences in problem-solving by activating the problem-solving process in small stages. This structure allows the couple to complete each step successfully, enhancing their communication skills as they keep conflicts from getting out of hand. For many couples, small changes in the problem-solving approach are striking. Noticing these changes typically provides the continued motivation necessary for future work. Continued work on problem solving in chapter 8 helps the couple make problem-solving behaviors automatic and integrate them naturally into their communicative life.

Phase 6: Monitoring and Evaluation of Progress

Step 18 of chapter 8 begins the sixth phase of therapy: monitoring and evaluation of progress. Some of the measures from chapter 4 are repeated so that the couple can compare the present state of their relationship to the way it was before they worked through the communication chapters. In addition, chapter 9 lets the couple evaluate their progress before they begin working on maintenance and generalization.

Phase 7: Maintenance, Generalization, and Termination of Treatment

As in therapy, long-term treatment efficacy depends on maintenance of progress and establishment of natural reinforcers in the readers' life for the generalization of desired behaviors. Although these goals are the focus of chapters 9 and 10, readers were prepared earlier to anticipate continued work after completion of the communication skills chapters. Readers should not be surprised that we encourage them to avoid backsliding, continue focusing on positives, use their communication skills with others outside the primary relationship, and use those skills to deal with special topics such as sex and spirituality. In fact, the motivated couple has probably already begun to initiate relapse prevention before reading chapter 9. In any case, these chapters offer a good review of the couple's path toward change, highlighting ways to minimize future communication difficulties. As in therapy, this process prepares the reader for the eventual end of the intervention.

Like many therapy endings, the conclusion of our book reviews of the process and suggests further information and referral sources. Chapter 11 may be considered a referral source for couples who have found it in their best interest to end the relationship. This chapter refers readers to additional sources of assistance, including self-help groups, counseling, and books.

Although research suggests that improved communication can greatly increase a couple's satisfaction with their relationship, much work still needs to be done on the efficacy of specific techniques and their relationship to long-term outcome (Appendix 1 provides an overview of research on treatment outcomes). A broader view is necessary to evaluate current communicative approaches in relationships and to provide for improvement. We hope that this book will be an impetus for such work.

ANNOTATED BIBLIOGRAPHY

Getting Started

Lazarus, A. L. *Marital Myths.* San Luis Obispo, CA: Impact, 1985.

Written by one of the most influential counselors in the United States, this book for couples describes 24 mistaken beliefs that can ruin a relationship or make a bad relationship worse. The book is a useful starting point for couples who wish to take stock of their relationships.

Kanfer, F. H., and B. K. Schefft. *Guiding the Process of Therapeutic Change.* Champaign, IL: Research Press, 1986.

This book for the professional provides a useful overview of the helping process. The authors draw heavily on research concerning therapy motivation and change processes while maintaining a focus that is appropriate to professional practice. The book is strongly recommended as a starting point for anyone contemplating working with individuals or couples.

O'Leary, K. D., Ed. *Assessment of Marital Discord: An Integration for Research and Clinical Practice.* Hillsdale, NJ: Erlbaum, 1987.

This book for professionals deals with the assessment of couples on a variety of levels: behavioral, affective, cognitive, and communicative, to name a few. Historical and theoretical perspectives, methodological problems, and directions for research and practice in each area are discussed.

Gender and Relationships

Tannen, D. *You Just Don't Understand.* New York: Ballantine, 1990.

Maltz, D., and R. Borker. "A Cultural Approach to Male-Female Miscommunication." In J. J. Gumperz, Ed., *Language and Social Identity.* Cambridge, England: Cambridge University Press, 1982.

Both works review gender differences in communication. The Tannen book offers several intriguing ideas about the ways in which men's and women's worlds influence their communication and cause misunderstanding between the genders. Intended for a nonprofessional audience, the book has become a best-seller. The Maltz and Borker book also has a cultural perspective on male-female communication but is directed toward a scholarly audience.

Baucom, D. H., C. I. Notarius, C. K. Burnett, and P. Haefner. "Gender Differences and Sex-Role Identity in Marriage." In F. D. Fincham and T. N. Bradbury, Eds., *The Psychology of Marriage: Basic Issues and Applications.* New York: Guilford, 1990.

This is a scholarly review of research on behaviors that occur during conversations between husbands and wives in distressed and nondistressed marriages. It also discusses sex role identity and its association with behavior and marital quality.

Multicultural Relationships

Hall, E. T. *Beyond Culture.* New York: Anchor, 1976.

Written by an anthropologist, this book for both nonprofessionals and professionals is at the forefront of multicultural communication. Topics include the basis of culture, cultural differences, cultural influences, and nonverbal communication.

Pederson, P. *A Handbook for Developing Multicultural Awareness.* Alexandria, VA: American Association for Counseling and Development, 1988.

This book is intended as an aid for developing the counselor's cultural awareness in clinical practice.

Sue, D. W., and D. Sue. *Counseling the Culturally Different: Theory and Practice,* 2nd ed. New York: Wiley, 1990.

The first edition of this book emerged as the most frequently cited text on multicultural counseling. This edition discusses issues of interest to counselors working with culturally diverse populations in the United States. Specific emphasis is given to African Americans, Native Americans, Asian Americans, and Hispanic Americans.

Gay and Lesbian Relationships

Isensee, R. *Love Between Men: Enhancing Intimacy and Keeping Your Relationship Alive.* New York: Prentice-Hall, 1990.

This book explores the application of communication skills in gay male relationships. It also deals with issues of concern to many gay couples, such as being out, fidelity, and AIDS.

Kus, R. J., Ed. *Keys to Caring: Assisting Your Gay and Lesbian Clients.* Boston: Alyson, 1990.

Meant primarily for professional counselors, this book addresses many topics that concern gay and lesbian clients. Each chapter is devoted to a key topic, such as homophobia, homosexuality and the legal system, family relationships, and long-term gay and lesbian relationships.

Boston Lesbian Psychologies Collective, Eds. *Lesbian Psychologies.* Champaign, IL: University of Illinois Press, 1987.

As the title implies, this book covers many psychological topics from a lesbian perspective. Many though not all of the chapters have a feminist viewpoint.

Learning to Communicate Effectively

Lederer, W. J. *Creating a Good Relationship*. New York: Norton, 1984.

This book outlines a 5-week program to improve any type of relationship. It includes 33 assignments, described briefly and in simple terms. This is a useful resource for couples who do not want to do much reading but who are willing to engage in daily exercises to improve their relationships. The book is also a good resource for professionals.

Gottman, J. M., C. Notarius, J. Gonso, and H. Markman. *A Couple's Guide to Communication*. Champaign, IL: Research Press, 1976.

Although the research review in this book is now outdated, a substantial section directed at couples is still useful for the general audience. Some basic communication skills are taught in each chapter, and exercises are provided.

Jacobson, N. S., and G. Margolin. *Marital Therapy*. New York: Brunner/Mazel, 1979.

At one time the standard of the field, this book still provides an excellent introduction to a skills-oriented approach to marital therapy. A central section is a detailed communication skills manual for couples; however, the work is really a textbook for students and professionals.

Bornstein, P. H., and M. T. Bornstein. *Marital Therapy*. New York: Pergamon, 1986.

This is a brief and well-written guide for conducting couples therapy from a communication skills perspective. The model is behavioral but also includes cognitive and affective elements of communication. An extended case study is presented.

Baucom, D., and N. Epstein. *Cognitive-Behavioral Marital Therapy*. New York: Brunner/Mazel, 1990.

The three sections of this book cover basic research on marital dysfunction, assessment, and therapy. Each section includes chapters on cognition, affect, and behavior. The skills-oriented approach to marital therapy presented here is comprehensive, and it incorporates advances made in the field since the publication of Jacobson and Margolin's text.

Sex

The Joy of Sex series. New York: Simon & Schuster.

These books for couples use illustrations and text to convey information on sexual pleasure, sexual techniques, and sexual problems. *The Joy of Sex* (A. Comfort, Ed., 1972) is directed toward heterosexual couples. *The Joy of Gay Sex* (C. Silverstein and E. White, Eds., 1977) and *The Joy of Lesbian Sex* (E. Sisley and B. Harris, Eds., 1977) are for gay male and lesbian couples, as their titles imply.

Barbach, L. *For Each Other: Sharing Sexual Intimacy*. New York: Signet, 1984.

This well-written self-help book is for women who wish to increase their capacity for sexual pleasure. It deals with the psychological elements of sexual relationships and addresses specific problems such as inorgasmia, lack of sexual desire, and poor body image.

Hawton, K. *Sex Therapy: A Practical Guide.* Oxford, England: Oxford University Press, 1984.

This excellent introduction to sexual problems and their management is full of useful, practical information. It discusses sexual responses, sexual problems, and the assessment and treatment of sexual difficulties.

Heiman, J. R., and J. Verhulst. "Sexual Dysfunction and Marriage." In F. D. Fincham and T. N. Bradbury, Eds., *The Psychology of Marriage: Basic Issues and Applications.* New York: Guilford, 1990.

This scholarly review of the nature and prevalence of sexual problems in couples also deals with treatment approaches and their outcomes.

Spirituality

Clinebell, H. J., and C. H. Clinebell. *The Intimate Marriage.* New York: Harper & Row, 1970.

This book, directed at both couples and professionals, addresses many marital issues from a Christian/existential perspective. Chapter 9 is devoted to the spiritual dimension of marriage.

Dual-Career Couples

Rapoport, R., R. Rapoport, and J. Bumstead. *Working Couples.* New York: Harper & Row, 1978.

This edited volume brings together a series of readable essays, informed by research findings, on dual-career couples. Topics such as commuting, child care, and dual job searches are discussed.

Bielby, W. T., and D. D. Bielby. "Family Ties: Balancing Commitments to Work and Family in Dual Earner Households." *American Sociological Review, 54* (1989), 776–789.

Reviewing the relevant scholarly literature and analyzing data from a survey of over 1,000 employed spouses, the authors explore how dual-career couples commit to work and family role identities. Particular attention is devoted to gender differences in the balancing of commitments and the formation of identity.

Silberstein, L. *Dual-Career Marriage.* Hillsdale, NJ: Erlbaum, 1992.

This book by a clinical psychologist blends previous research findings with the results of a qualitative interview study of 20 upper middle class dual-career couples. The style is engaging, and the book is liberally sprinkled with quotations from the interviews. Both counselors and dual-career couples should find it interesting and useful.

Breakup or Divorce

For Adults

Gardner, R. A. *The Parent's Book About Divorce.* New York: Doubleday, 1977.

Written by a renowned child psychiatrist, this book for parents discusses a variety of issues that parents typically confront when contemplating or proceeding with a divorce.

The author provides in-depth coverage of children's reactions to divorce and suggests ways to maintain good relationships with children.

McKay, M., P. D. Rogers, J. Blades, and R. Gosse. *The Divorce Book*. Oakland, CA: New Harbinger, 1984.

Divided into four sections, this well-written book for adults provides detailed treatment of the effects of divorce, legal issues, children and divorce, and life after divorce.

For Young Children

Helmering, D. W. *I Have Two Families*. Nashville: Abingdon, 1981.

Written for the preschool or elementary school child, this book tells the story of Patty and Michael, two children whose parents are divorced. Although the children face the difficulties involved in having two homes, they also learn the joys of having two families.

Simon, N. *All Kinds of Families*. Chicago: Whitman, 1976.

Parents and preschool children can share this picture book, which emphasizes the importance of children in families and the supportive nature of the family.

For Older Children

Brown, L., and M. Brown. *A Dinosaur's Divorce*. Boston: The Atlantic Monthly Press, 1986.

This book for the elementary school child is possibly the most widely recommended reading for children experiencing a divorce, providing excellent treatment of the feelings and changes associated with divorce. The book is written in easy-to-understand language, has attractive illustrations, and includes a glossary of divorce-related words.

Gardner, R. A. *The Boys' and Girls' Book About Divorce*. New York: Science House, 1970.

The first work of its kind, this is an excellent resource for elementary school and middle school children who are experiencing changes associated with divorce. The book addresses such issues as blame, mixed feelings, relationships with parents, and step-relatives. An introduction for parents is included.

Rofes, E. E., Ed. *The Kids' Book of Divorce*. Lexington, MA: Lewis, 1981.

The authors are 20 children aged 11 to 14 who have experienced divorces in their families. The book, directed at older children and their parents, aims to help children and parents understand one another during the divorce process. It can provide a useful stimulus for discussion between parents and children.

For Adolescents

Boeckman, C. *Surviving Your Parents' Divorce*. New York: Franklin Watts, 1980.

Designed for the pre-teen child, this book offers advice for coping with parental divorce. Topics include custody, child support, visitation, guilt, loneliness, remarriage, and steprelatives.

Richards, A., and I. Willis. *How to Get It Together When Your Parents Are Coming Apart.* New York: David McKay, 1976.

This book, specifically for adolescents, provides good suggestions for helping them adjust to the changes typically associated with divorce. Changes that occur before, during, and after divorce are highlighted by true-life examples.

For Professionals

Emery, R. E. *Marriage, Divorce, and Children's Adjustment.* Newbury Park, CA: Sage, 1988.

This book is a scholarly overview of the research concerning children of divorce and accompanying family transitions. Research on the outcomes of therapeutic interventions in divorce is also surveyed, and legal policies are explained.

Furstenberg, F. F., and A. J. Cherlin. *Divided Families: What Happens to Children When Parents Part.* Cambridge, MA: Harvard University Press, 1991.

This book for professionals examines the central issues faced by divorcing families, identifies factors that promote positive adjustment in family members, and discusses how such factors might influence policy development.

Grych, J. H., & Fincham, F. D. (1992). "Interventions for Children of Divorce: Toward Greater Integration of Research and Action." *Psychological Bulletin,* Vol. 111, pp. 434–454, 1992.

Following a brief overview of the impact of divorce on children, this article examines three levels of intervention: interventions that focus on the child, on the family, and on environmental and institutional factors associated with divorce. Throughout, an attempt is made to integrate findings from basic and applied research.

Hodges, W. F. *Interventions for Children of Divorce.* New York: Wiley, 1991.

This useful volume provides an overview of the variety of interventions available for helping children from divorced families. It suggests how traditional, office-based forms of psychotherapy can be modified to help children adapt to divorce, and it discusses school-based interventions as well.

1 *A Research-Oriented Perspective for Professionals*

We have covered a great deal of ground in this book, being guided, wherever possible, by research findings. The purpose of this appendix is to outline broadly the empirical underpinnings of our approach. For those interested in more detailed examination of particular points, extensive literature reviews are cited.

We will address three major questions relevant to an understanding of the approach underlying our book. The first section deals with the question "Why is it necessary to pay attention to research?" and thus concerns our attempt to draw on research findings. The question addressed in the second section is "Why focus on communication when working with couples?" That section speaks to our decision to focus on communication as a means of enhancing relationships. The third section asks, "What have we learned from basic research on communication in couples?" and provides insights into the reasons for our extensive discussion of factors such as communication background (e.g., gender, cultural heritage), expectations, and feelings—factors not typically emphasized in communication training programs.

WHY PAY ATTENTION TO RESEARCH?

Most professionals who work with couples have at some time asked themselves, "Why should I pay attention to research when my primary goal is to counsel couples?" This is a reasonable and important question. It is particularly relevant in light of the demands made on practitioners to attend immediately to the pain and suffering of the couples who seek their help.

It is important, however, to acknowledge that good intentions alone do not prepare the practitioner to alleviate suffering. The effective helper also needs to know about effective intervention strategies and be able to translate that knowledge into action. Finally, even the best-intentioned professional can inadvertently harm the couple (Bergin, 1963; Gurman, Kniskern, & Pinsof, 1986).

Ethics

An initial answer to our question arises from our ethical responsibility to be fully informed professionals who strive to help couples by using the most effective interventions currently available. This sense of responsibility is in line with the ethical guidelines adopted by organizations of helping professionals.

Beach and O'Leary (1991) argue that ethical considerations dictate the application of a fundamental principle in working with clients: Professionals must select techniques that are "highest in efficacy and lowest in side effects" (p. 56). Nevertheless, we may still wonder why it is important to focus on empirical research. After all, we can draw on many useful sources of information about couples, including the artistic contributions of novelists, poets, playwrights, and filmmakers; books by professionals who work with couples; and the personal accounts of individual couples. Such insights are often far richer than anything current research can offer.

Anecdotal information is valuable for the new observations it offers (in a context of discovery), but we need a more systematic approach to check the validity of these observations (in a context of verification). Anecdotal accounts cannot provide the assurance that comes from a research-based practice for at least two reasons. First, different people viewing the same couple may see different and even contradictory behaviors because we all have biases and are selective in what we see or consider important. A lack of agreement can therefore arise about the behavior or phenomenon that is the basis of any insight. Second, even when there is agreement about the behavior observed, there are always many possible (and often contradictory) explanations for the behavior. Research helps us systematically test these explanations and choose among them.

The unfortunate rift that too often divides scientists and practitioners should not detract from the importance of subjecting to careful empirical scrutiny any insight or observation concerning relationships or interventions for couples. We must do this to determine how widely the insight or observation is applicable. For example, a case study may yield observations that are unique to the couple on whom it is based; in another instance, contradictory insights might emerge (e.g., "birds of a feather flock together" versus "opposites attract"). Also, observations may say more about the person making them than about the functioning of couples (e.g., the observer's selective memory or exposure to a very biased set of couples).

In view of the miscommunication that has characterized debates between scientists and practitioners, several observations about the relationship between science and practice are necessary. If the science-practice partnership is to be realized, we must view research broadly and be open to any method or approach as long as it entails systematic examination of empirical data and ongoing critical evaluation of beliefs. Also, though simply reading about research does not make one an effective helper, we must recognize that knowledge of research findings can combine with practical skills to maximize professional effectiveness. Finally, we must acknowledge the limitations of research; we will briefly highlight two of these limitations.

First, practitioners should not expect research to provide answers to all the difficult questions that they face; anyone who holds that expectation will surely be disappointed. Because the questions we ask as practitioners change as we learn more about intimate relationships (from research as well as from practice), research by definition can never answer all our questions. Still, this limitation is no reason to ignore research: It does provide direct answers to some questions, and it offers guidance on many others.

Second, just as knowledge of relationships changes, so do methods for approaching and conducting research on close relationships. For example, 25 years ago there were no methods for analyzing sequences of behavior in couple interactions. A 1960s practitioner who turned to the research literature to learn whether the reciprocation of negative behavior observed in a marital counseling session was idiosyncratic to the clients or characteristic of distressed couples in general would have been disappointed. In contrast, that practitioner's contemporary counterpart would quickly discover that the exchange of negative behaviors is one of the most thoroughly documented characteristics of distressed couples (see Weiss & Heyman, 1990a, 1990b). Similarly, the contemporary practitioner who favors a systems conception of relationships may be disappointed by the research literature because current research tools may not be fully adequate for testing the ideas that constitute that conception (though, as Bateson acknowledged in 1966, some ideas, such as his double bind hypothesis, are ultimately untestable). In sum, the answers gained from research are limited by the research tools available and may change radically as new research methods evolve.

Research, then, cannot address all our questions or offer absolute, immutable answers. In fact, being open to research findings entails a willingness to challenge and, if necessary, give up our most firmly held beliefs, including those based on previous research. This questioning attitude may be the most important contribution of research to clinical practice because people—including professional helpers—tend to look for evidence that confirms their beliefs and overlook disconfirming evidence (Cantor, 1982). For the practitioner who often must act in a decisive manner with couples, this can be disquieting. However, it is possible to act with certainty at any moment while maintaining a questioning attitude about one's beliefs over time.

Third-Party Reimbursement

A more pragmatic answer to our question about the importance of practice grounded in science involves the issue of third-party reimbursement. Many insurance companies do not reimburse couples for marital counseling. Those trying to change this circumstance are likely to succeed to the extent that they can document the efficacy of interventions designed to help couples. Only approaches of demonstrated efficacy are likely to be taken seriously by third-party payers.

The Alternative

Perhaps the best way to make a case for the research perspective is to consider the alternative of ignoring research. Given the wealth of information that surrounds us, it is not surprising that our species has developed heuristics or shortcuts for processing information (for examples of these heuristics, see Tversky & Kahneman, 1982; for their application to the clinical context, see Achenbach, 1985). Although these heuristics are often adaptive in everyday life, they result in numerous biases that are not appropriate in professional settings. For example, Chapman and Chapman (1967, 1982) have shown that practitioners ignore information on the frequency with which psychological test responses and symptoms actually co-occur, basing their judgments instead on prior beliefs about the association between test responses and symptoms—beliefs that are identical to those held by laypersons! Widespread agreement on erroneous clinical judgments does not make them correct or result in the rendering of any better services to clients.

Even if we apply no obvious cognitive biases in the processing of information, we may simply be mistaken in our beliefs. For example, not long ago professionals commonly believed that an important component of a satisfactory marriage was the quid pro quo (literally "something for something") or reciprocal exchange of behaviors between spouses (Lederer & Jackson, 1968). Not surprisingly, this belief resulted in the recommendation that counselors help couples increase the exchange of positive behaviors, using written contracts if necessary. However, subsequent research showed that reciprocal exchange of behavior characterized distressed couples and that when positive and negative behaviors were used in a statistical analysis to predict daily reports of marital satisfaction, negative behaviors (accounting for 65% of the variability) predicted marital satisfaction much more strongly than positive behaviors (which accounted for only 25% of the variability; see Bradbury & Fincham, 1987b). Accordingly, contemporary marital therapy programs focus on noncontingent exchanges and other facets of marital functioning.

The prospect of ignoring research is disquieting. How do we define various phenomena in relationships and in counseling (e.g., an effective intervention technique)? How do we determine whether the phenomena are reliable? How do we choose among various competing explanations for a phenomenon? Personal experience is undeniably important and takes us a long way, but it is not sufficient. In the absence of empirical scrutiny, even the most intuitively compelling insights can be quite misleading.

Summary

Although research falls short of satisfying all our needs as practitioners (and to some extent always will), it is our best tool for meeting our obligation to provide the most informed and effective services to couples. We do not mean to imply that there are no other valuable sources of information for guiding practice. Indeed, clinical observation is important not only for guiding practice but also for guiding research. However, we believe that insights gained from any source must be held tentatively and must be subjected to systematic empirical inquiry. (For further information on the relation between science and practice, see Andreozzi, 1985; Barlow, 1981; Kanfer, 1990.)

WHY FOCUS ON COMMUNICATION SKILLS?

The second broad question that we must answer in clarifying our approach is "Why focus on communication when working with couples?" By *communication* we mean the totality of behaviors that involve the transmission of information from one person to another. It includes both verbal (e.g., words, voice tone) and nonverbal (e.g., a glance, body posture) behavior. However, most communication programs emphasize changes in verbal behavior.

Our question—"Why focus on communication?"—has at least three different answers. The first is that communication is the foundation of social life; without it we could not relate to one another. In fact, it is impossible to conceive of an intimate relationship that does not include communication.

The second answer has to do with the reasons couples seek professional help: Communication is the relationship problem most frequently identified by couples (Broderick, 1981). Similarly, a random sample of marital therapists rated poor communication as the most common and damaging problem faced in their work with couples (Geiss & O'Leary, 1981). In fact, counseling professionals confront communication difficulties with remarkable frequency.

A third reason for the focus on communication is that communication programs are the most thoroughly studied form of intervention for couples (Beach & O'Leary, 1985). This is perhaps not surprising given the consensus among professionals of different theoretical orientations that communication is the most common problem area among couples. However, it also reflects the fact that the most frequently investigated "school" of therapy, behavioral marital therapy, strongly emphasizes communication skills. (For overviews of systems, psychoanalytic, and behavioral approaches to marital therapy, see Jacobson & Gurman, 1986.) Even when communication is not the focus of the intervention, communication training is often used in conjunction with other approaches (e.g., problem-solving training, contracting).

Although these reasons justify a focus on communication, the consistent demonstration that communication programs are effective in helping couples weighs most heavily in our choice. Before discussing the effectiveness of marital therapies, we will provide background on some issues that need to be addressed in outcome evaluation research. (Readers who are not interested in such detail should proceed to the section entitled "The Effectiveness of Interventions for Couples.")

Issues in Evaluating the Effectiveness of an Intervention

The criteria used to assess the effectiveness of an intervention are numerous. Some involve highly technical and seemingly esoteric points. Others elicit diverse reactions and are still the subject of debate. We are concerned with four salient issues: the need for a comparison group, the assignment of couples to treatment conditions, the assessment of outcome, and the need to ensure that treatment produces the desired outcome.

A more complete coverage of this topic can be found in papers devoted to conceptual issues (e.g., Baucom, 1983; Gurman et al., 1986) and methodological issues (e.g., O'Leary & Turkewitz, 1978b; Whisman, Jacobson, Fruzzetti, & Waltz, 1989) in research on marital treatment outcomes. Two lively debates on family therapy evaluation (Jacobson, 1985a, 1985c; Kniskern, 1985) and behavioral marital therapy (Bradbury & Fincham, 1987a; Gottman, 1985; Jacobson, 1985b, 1985d; Jacobson, Follette, & Elwood, 1984; Weiss & Frohman, 1985) are also informative.

Establishing a Comparison Group

Meaningful evaluation of an intervention requires a comparison or control group that does not receive the intervention. Without a control group, we cannot know whether the changes observed are related to the intervention (i.e., relationships might have improved simply with the passing of time). At the very least, an intervention should result in changes that are not observed in the control group. A slightly more stringent criterion compares the intervention group with a group that receives an equal *amount* of attention from the professional but receives no specific, focused intervention (often referred to as a "placebo" group). The group receiving the intervention should experience more dramatic changes than those observed in the placebo group. Many studies fail to include either kind of control group, and therefore their results are difficult to interpret.

One factor that accounts in part for this neglect of control groups is researchers' fascination with conducting "horse race" comparisons between different treatments. Instead of evaluating effectiveness per se, they focus on relative effectiveness. This practice has done little to advance understanding: Documented differences between treatments derived from different schools of therapy are rare. This is because multifaceted interventions typically share some features, and overall differences in their effects are likely to be negligible. Even when such differences are found, they are seldom replicated. Moreover, variability in treatment outcome is often determined as much by individual characteristics of therapists and clients as by treatment itself (Jacobson, 1985a); this fact suggests that treatment differences are likely to emerge only in interaction with such variables. For these reasons we concentrate on the absolute effectiveness of interventions and consider only in passing findings on comparative treatment outcomes. Two recent debates in the *Journal of Family Psychology* (Volume 4, Number 4, 1991) and the *Journal of Consulting and Clinical Psychology* (Volume 59, Number 1, 1991) provide useful and interesting resources for readers who wish to become familiar with issues in comparative outcome research.

Assigning Couples to Treatment Conditions

Couples must be randomly assigned to conditions. In the absence of random assignment, posttreatment differences between groups—concerning, for example, relationship satisfaction—may simply reflect differences that existed between the groups before treatment.

The existence of a comparison group and random assignment are crucial to the internal validity of treatment outcome research. One concern that can be raised is that random assignment to a rigidly structured treatment does not (and should not) occur in good clinical practice; instead, the treatment is tailored to the couple's needs. In contrast, the therapist in a treatment outcome study is constrained to follow a manual that standardizes treatment. It is widely assumed that this circumstance influences treatment efficacy and that outcome research is necessarily a conservative test of a treatment's impact (Kazdin & Wilson, 1978).

Jacobson (1985a) notes, however, that random assignment and rigid treatment regimes are not always necessary and that they indeed must be eliminated at a certain stage in treatment outcome research. (For a critique of these features of psychotherapy outcome research and proposed solutions, see Persons, 1991.) Once the efficacy of a treatment has been established (through use of comparison groups and random assignment), the treatment must be made more flexible so that its effectiveness can be evaluated under conditions that more closely mirror everyday clinical practice. Although such evaluations are rare, they are important: The effects of standardized versus flexible treatments are likely to be moderated by a number of factors, including the counselor's experience and the extent to which the relationship problem is typical rather than highly idiosyncratic.

In one such study, Jacobson et al. (1989) compared research-structured and clinically flexible versions of behavioral marital therapy that included communication training. In the flexible condition, therapists were free to tailor the treatment plan to the couple's needs on the basis of clinical judgment. The only requirement was that all treatment fall into one of the six categories of intervention (behavior exchange, companionship enhancement, communication training, problem-solving training, sexual enrichment, and generalization and maintenance) used in the structured intervention condition. After documenting that the treatments were delivered differently in the two treatment conditions, Jacobson et al. found no differences between the groups immediately following treatment with respect to marital satisfaction, reports of communication, and observed communication behaviors. However, 6 months later, the flexibly treated group showed better maintenance of treatment gains.

Another variant of research that comes close to testing the effectiveness of interventions in everyday clinical practice involves matching couples with treatment conditions. For example, a couple complaining of communication problems might receive a treatment tailored specifically to meet their needs (e.g., communication training) or a treatment not geared to those needs (e.g., emotionally focused marital therapy; Greenberg & Johnson, 1988). This kind of study lets us determine whether, as is widely believed, effectiveness is maximized when the treatment is matched to the couple's presenting difficulty. We will better understand treatment effectiveness as these approaches become more commonplace in outcome research on couples therapy.

Assessing the Outcomes

Several separate issues are involved in the assessment of outcomes. First, we must use reliable and valid measures. As simple as this requirement might sound, it is not always met in outcome studies and hence bears repetition.

Second, we must specify the level at which outcome is to be assessed. There are two potentially different levels of outcome: the outcome for individual partners and the outcome for the relationship. A treatment may increase the wife's satisfaction and decrease the husband's satisfaction (or vice versa), or both spouses may experience increased satisfaction. Most studies examine combined partner scores and hence do not address the outcome on the individual level.

Third, we must decide which areas of functioning should serve as criteria for assessing outcome. This means deciding what to assess and how it should be measured. Should improvement in the couple's presenting problem be the ultimate criterion for the success of the intervention? What if each partner's satisfaction with the relationship increases but the presenting problem remains unchanged? Should relationship stability serve as the criterion? If so, is treatment that is followed by dissolution of the relationship necessarily a failure?

The issues are complex, but it is safe to conclude that assessment using multiple outcome measures is more desirable than evaluation based on a single measure. The same principle can be applied to the "how" of assessment: It is more desirable to use multiple methods (e.g., self-report, behavioral observation) for assessing an outcome variable than to rely on a single method. In practice, most studies focus on self-reports of marital quality (based on either the Marital Adjustment or Dyadic Adjustment Scale; see chapter 4) in assessing treatment outcome.

Finally, in assessing outcome, we must consider the degree of impact a treatment must have before it is considered effective. Practitioners are justifiably frustrated by studies that simply report group means and examine whether differences in these means are statistically significant. Such practices do not answer important questions such as "What proportion of couples improved?" "What is the magnitude of the treatment effect?" and "Were the changes clinically relevant?"

The difficulty of answering these questions should not deter us from continuing to ask them. At present, there are no conventions (other than statistical significance) for assessing the proportion of couples who improved or for determining how much change constitutes improvement. One proposal has been to classify couples as improved if they show statistically reliable change and if this change places them outside the distribution of dysfunctional couples or within the distribution of functional couples (see Jacobson & Revenstorf, 1988). For an example of the way the use of different outcome criteria influences the results of studies, see Jacobson, Follette, Revenstorf et al. (1984).

Ensuring That the Treatment Produces the Outcome

If we are to infer that treatment is responsible for changes in a relationship, two requirements must be fulfilled. First, we must ensure that the treatment is implemented correctly (this is frequently referred to as "treatment integrity"). Ensuring treatment integrity entails selecting therapists competent in the delivery of the treatment approach in question, providing ongoing supervision during treatment, and rating treatment sessions for compliance with the treatment manual.

Second, we must examine whether the targets of the treatment (e.g., communication behaviors) actually changed as a result of the treatment. If the couples' satisfaction improves but there is no change in the targets of the intervention, the increase in satisfaction cannot be related to the treatment targets and most likely reflects changes in behaviors that are not targets of the intervention. Moreover, even if the targeted behaviors change and the relationship as a whole improves, we cannot necessarily conclude that change in the targets led to the overall improvement. To increase our confidence, we need to show that changes in the treatment targets correlate with changes in relationship satisfaction.

Summary

Four basic criteria that we need to use in evaluating research on the effectiveness of interventions are the presence of a comparison group, random assignment to treatments, assessment of outcomes, and assurance that the treatment is responsible for the outcome. These criteria have been more often breached than observed. Research that does not meet these minimal criteria is excluded from consideration as we continue to address our second larger question regarding the effectiveness of communication training: "Why focus on communication skills?"

The Effectiveness of Interventions for Couples

Before documenting the effectiveness of communication training interventions, we will broadly summarize what is known about the effectiveness of marital therapies and will provide a historical introduction to the treatment of couples.

Overview

Five broad generalizations can be made about marital and family therapy:

1. In about two-thirds of cases, most bona fide treatments produce beneficial outcomes that are superior to the results of no treatment.

2. The positive results that are typically obtained occur with relatively short courses of treatment (1 to 20 sessions).

3. The chances of positive outcome are greater when spouses are treated conjointly than when only one spouse is treated.

4. Marital and family therapy is probably as effective as—and may be more effective than—many commonly used (usually individual) treatments for problems relating to family or relationship conflict.

5. Therapists who provide little structure in early therapy sessions and then confront highly affective material promote more deterioration in relationships than therapists who engage in stimulating interaction and give support (Gurman et al., 1986).

There is often little or no research to document the effectiveness of most "schools" of couples therapy: When 15 approaches to marital and family therapy were cross-tabulated with 10 clinical disorders or problems, it was found that outcome studies had been conducted on only 35 of the 150 method-by-problem combinations

(Gurman et al., 1986). Our review focuses on the one method-by-problem combination (behavioral marital therapy by marital discord) that has received the most empirical attention.

Several excellent sources offer more detailed consideration of the treatment outcome research. Gurman et al. (1986) provide a comprehensive and detailed review of research on the process and outcome of marital and family therapy in the *Handbook of Psychotherapy and Behavior Change*. An updated review of this area will appear in that work's fourth edition, currently in preparation. A more focused overview of the status of marital therapy outcome research is offered by Beach and O'Leary (1985). Their relatively brief paper may be the best overall introduction to the subject. It should be read together with the update on outcome research included in Beach and Bauserman's (1990) work. Baucom and Hoffman (1986) provide another useful introduction to the area. In contrast to the authors of these narrative reviews, Hahlweg and Markman (1988) used an advanced quantitative approach called meta-analysis to review the effectiveness of behavioral marital therapy in 17 studies involving over 600 couples in Europe and North America. Finally, Piercy and Sprenkle (1990) provide a brief overview of trends in marital and family therapy research during the 1980s.

A Historical Perspective

Professional therapy aimed at helping couples is a relatively recent phenomenon. Throughout the first half of the century, the psychoanalytic perspective dominated the helping professions. In this perspective, unconscious and intrapsychic conflicts, rather than relationship interactions, were seen as the root of mental health problems. Accordingly, relationship problems were conceptualized as problems of the individuals in the relationship, and it was standard practice to treat each partner in individual therapy. From about 1930, this orthodox psychoanalytic practice began to be challenged by marital therapists who argued for the need to treat husband and wife in the same session (a radical idea at the time) and by therapists who sought to include family members in treatment for persons diagnosed as schizophrenic (for detailed histories, see Broderick & Schrader, 1981; Guerin, 1976). In the 1950s the family therapy movement was born, and our thinking about relationship problems changed dramatically. From this perspective it was argued that

> if individuals appear to differ from one another it is because the situations they are responding to are different . . . the difference between "normal" people and individuals with psychiatric problems would be a difference in the current situation (and treatment situation) in which the person is embedded. (Framo, 1972, pp. 14–15)

Despite its salutary impact on the conceptualizing of relationship problems, the systems approach advocated by family therapists was not examined empirically in great detail; yet, "despite this fact, the approach has flourished and has become the predominant mode of therapy with couples and families . . . family therapy has remained essentially unchanged in a quarter of a century, and hypotheses continue to be accepted by repetition" (Gottman, 1979, p. 256). Although this circumstance has since improved, there is still considerable need for systematic research on family therapy meeting the criteria outlined in the last section. (For reviews of family therapy research, see Bednar, Burlingame, & Masters, 1988; Hazelrigg, Cooper, & Bourdin, 1987.)

Systematic empirical investigation of interventions for couples began only in the 1970s following the application of learning principles to marital treatment (e.g., Liberman, 1970; Stuart, 1969). The expanding application of behavioral techniques to marital therapy was accompanied by attempts to carefully evaluate the effectiveness of interventions. To date, more outcome studies have been conducted on behavioral marital therapies than on any other form of therapy. In view of the fact that no controlled outcome study of behavioral marital therapy had been reported by 1976 (Jacobson & Martin, 1976), the progress since then in the documentation of the impact of behavioral marital therapy is quite remarkable.

From this brief historical sketch it is apparent that the evaluation of relationship interventions is in its infancy. However, even at this early stage we have learned a good deal about the effectiveness of the kind of communication training described in this book. It is to research on this subject that we now turn.

Communication Training

Various communication training programs have been tested, although most of those programs originate in either nonbehavioral approaches that stress listening skills (such as those emphasized in Rogerian client-centered therapy) or behavioral approaches that focus on the acquisition of communication skills needed for successful engagement in problem solving with a partner (Beach & O'Leary, 1985). In practice, the programs derived from different approaches overlap and target similar behaviors. Nonetheless, it is useful to distinguish between interventions that teach communication skills in the context of problem solving and those that address communication skills in a different context (e.g., improvement of emotional expressiveness).

The data suggest that outcome may vary when communication is learned in the context of problem solving versus other contexts. Interventions that do not focus on problem solving per se tend to be successful in teaching the specific communication skills that they emphasize but tend to have little effect on marital adjustment (Baucom & Epstein, 1990). In contrast, problem-oriented communication training appears to succeed in changing both communication skills and marital adjustment. This is why we made problem solving an important element in our chapters on communication skills. Some caution is necessary, however: Several of the investigative treatments that did not focus on problem-solving communication were delivered in a group format. In a direct comparison of group and one-couple treatment formats, Hahlweg, Schindler, Revenstorf, and Brengelmann (1984) found that the group format produced change only on an observational measure of communication behavior, whereas the couple format yielded changes on a number of measures.

Although communication training alone can be an effective intervention, most treatments have several components. Earlier we noted that, although communication training is a hallmark of behavioral marital therapy, it is often used in conjunction with other interventions. Indeed, most of our information about the sole use of communication training comes from component analyses of behavioral marital therapy. Because communication training is seldom used in isolation, the approach described in this book is not limited to traditional communication skills training; it includes supplementary techniques typically used in behavioral marital therapy (e.g., contracting) and procedures guided by findings of basic research on intrapersonal variables (e.g., thoughts and feelings) and individual difference variables (e.g., communication background) that have not gained much attention in the treatment literature. We will therefore briefly review the status of behavioral marital therapy and, in the next section, review findings from basic research.

In their quantitative review of the effectiveness of behavioral marital therapy, Hahlweg and Markman (1988) used the effect size method to integrate findings and document the magnitude of treatment effects. These effect sizes provide a measure that allows us to compare findings easily (the effect size is actually a z-score) when studies are grouped according to various criteria. Hahlweg and Markman found that the average number of outcome measures used in studies was 4.8 (a finding that shows sensitivity to the need for multidimensional assessment) and that the average of the 81 effect sizes obtained across studies was .95. This means that the average treated spouse was better off than 83% of the persons in the control group (this is comparable to what is found for individual psychotherapy, where the percentage is 80%; Smith, Glass, & Miller, 1980). To state it differently, the control couples' chance of improving was 28%, whereas the chance for treated couples was 72%. Thus, behavioral marital therapy increased a couple's chances for improvement by about 40%. These findings applied equally to studies conducted in Europe and in North America and to outcomes measured via self-reports and via observed behavior.

As is consistent with narrative reviews, the impact of behavioral marital therapy was diminished when improvement was defined in terms of posttreatment scores that fell into the range of satisfied couples' scores (Marital Adjustment Test > 100; Dyadic Adjustment Test > 97). The diminished effect size (.15) shows that substantial numbers of couples describe their relationships as unsatisfying after treatment despite the gains made. Jacobson, Follette, Revenstorf et al. (1984) reanalyzed the results of four studies and found that 35% to 40% of treated couples had marital satisfaction scores in the distressed range after treatment. Because most of the studies analyzed provided relatively few (10 to 14) treatment sessions, it is possible that greater gains result from longer treatment. Snyder and Wills (1989) recently offered treatment averaging 19 weeks and found that the reports of 55% of the couples fell in the nondistressed range after treatment.

It is important to place these findings in perspective. First, in Gurman et al.'s (1986) comprehensive review, behavioral marital therapy was rated as the only approach whose efficacy for treating marital discord had been firmly established. Second, we do not know how many couples who enter treatment lack the sincere desire to improve their relationships despite their requests for help. Most practitioners are familiar with clients who see therapy as a step toward the dissolution of a relationship. Nonetheless, there is considerable room for improving the effectiveness of the most thoroughly documented form of couples treatment.

A final consideration regarding the effectiveness of any intervention is whether treatment gains are maintained over time, a consideration that led us to address the issue of maintenance in chapter 9. As to behavioral marital therapy, Hahlweg and Markman's (1988) analysis included eight studies with follow-ups between 3 and 6 months posttreatment and five studies with 9- to 12-month follow-ups. Effect sizes did not change over these time periods. However, these stable effects reflect relatively short follow-up periods and couples who stayed together. In a 2-year follow-up study examining a behavior exchange treatment condition, a communication training condition, and a combined treatment condition, Jacobson, Schmaling, and Holtzworth-Munroe (1987) found deterioration rates across conditions of 25% to 66% at 2 years as well as deterioration in 27% to 42% of couples between first- and second-year follow-ups. As regards relationship dissolution, Snyder, Wills, and Grady-Fletcher (1991) found that

4 years following treatment, 38% of couples who had received behavioral marital therapy were divorced, as compared to 3% who had received insight-oriented marital therapy. Although this study has been challenged on several grounds (including the integrity of the behavioral marital therapy offered; see Jacobson, 1991), such findings nonetheless alert us to the importance of offering treatments that provide stable gains for couples. (For an interesting discussion of maintenance, see Jacobson, 1989.)

Closer examination of the Jacobson et al. (1987) study shows that deterioration differed considerably across treatment conditions, with the highest deterioration in the behavior exchange condition (80% at 6 months) and the lowest in the combined condition (25% at 2 years). Of the two-thirds of couples initially helped by treatment, about 70% maintained treatment gains for 2 years. The likelihood that a couple would benefit from treatment and maintain the gains for 2 years was therefore about 50%. Interestingly, the only factor predictive of relapse was stressful life events (even after maritally related stressors were statistically controlled); a variety of other factors—including whether the couple reported continued use of the skills learned in therapy, how satisfied they were with therapy, or how much they liked the therapist—did not predict relapse.

Finally, there is evidence that treatments tailored to a couple's needs improve maintenance. Jacobson et al. (1989) found that, although the results of flexibly administered and structured behavioral marital therapy did not differ immediately following treatment, couples who had received flexibly administered treatment maintained their gains better at the 6-month follow-up (33% deterioration versus 14%). As yet there are no data on such obvious factors that might maintain treatment gains, such as occasional booster sessions or participation in self-help groups. Available data, though quite limited, therefore suggest that maintenance of treatment gains is fostered by flexibly administered communication training that is part of a more comprehensive treatment package.

Such a comprehensive package should take account of each person's affect and cognition. There is some evidence that emotionally focused marital therapy (Greenberg & Johnson, 1988, and Johnson & Greenberg, 1985, provide a detailed overview that consists largely of a superbly written treatment manual) and insight-oriented therapy (Snyder & Wills, 1989; Snyder et al., 1991) are powerful interventions that may be superior to behavioral marital therapy (though superiority in each case is based on a single study and therefore awaits replication). Moreover, basic research shows that affect and cognition are reliably related to marital satisfaction. Not surprisingly, attention to affect and cognition is becoming part of behavioral marital therapy approaches (e.g., Baucom & Epstein, 1990; Margolin, 1987), rendering obsolete Hahlweg et al.'s (1984) observation that behavioral marital therapy may be "less well suited to deal with internal events affecting the emotional qualities of a relationship" (p. 21).

A substantial minority of couples do not benefit from professional help. Even some of those who benefit initially may relapse and ultimately separate. Clearly there is much room to improve the effectiveness of interventions for couples. Until this improvement occurs, the practitioner is likely to encounter clients for whom separation and divorce are the major issues in counseling. That is why we devoted chapter 11 to breakup and divorce.

The Effectiveness of Interventions for Divorce

In view of the attention given to this topic in chapter 11, we will briefly discuss research on divorce, including that which addresses interventions for children of divorce.

Relationship Partners

Our knowledge about helping people who experience relationship breakups comes almost exclusively from interventions targeted at either divorcing or already divorced individuals.

Although interventions for *divorcing* individuals include conciliation counseling (often court ordered), treatment in the context of general marital counseling, and divorce mediation, only for the last of these do we have sufficient high-quality data to draw any conclusions (for a review, see Sprenkle & Storm, 1983). Several studies show that mediation, compared to the traditional adversarial divorce process, leads to a higher rate of pretrial agreements, reductions in the amount of litigation following final court orders, and greater satisfaction with the divorce process (Emery & Wyer, 1987). Interestingly, husbands' and wives' beliefs that they "won what they wanted" are significantly positively correlated for couples who choose mediation and negatively correlated for couples who litigate (Emery, Matthews, & Wyer, 1991). However, mediation is not necessarily for everyone. It is clearly contraindicated where (a) abuse has occurred in the family, (b) there is a large power differential between partners, (c) one or both partners have not started "letting go" of the relationship, (d) the level of interpartner conflict is high, (e) many complex issues must be negotiated and resolved, (f) third parties are significantly involved in relationship disputes, or (g) attorneys do not support the mediation process. For a relatively brief but clinically rich example of mediation, see Emery, Shaw, and Jackson (1987).

For *divorced* individuals, two types of interventions exist. One type focuses on enhancing the individual's general adjustment; the other focuses on the parenting role and is designed to help divorced parents manage their children's behavior. Although several examples of such programs are available commercially, only three (Bloom, Hodges, Kern, & McFaddin, 1985; Stolberg & Garrison, 1985; Wolchick et al., 1990) have been empirically investigated (for a review, see Grych & Fincham, 1992). Until their effectiveness is replicated, they should be viewed—along with the literature documenting the impact of divorce on partners (for a review, see Kitson, Babri, Roach, & Placidi, 1989) —as useful sources of ideas about issues that may need to be addressed during divorce and as examples of possible ways to address these issues.

Children of Divorce

There is somewhat more literature on the impact of divorce on children (for reviews, see Amato & Keith, 1991a, 1991b; Demo & Acock, 1988; Grych & Fincham, 1992). Two important findings have recently emerged from this literature. First, a meta-analysis of 92 studies comparing children from divorced and nondivorced families showed that the median effect size across several areas of adjustment was very small (.14 of a standard deviation). This result suggests that looking for the overall effects of divorce per se is as fruitless as conducting comparative outcome studies. In both cases interaction effects are clearly more important. That is, the impact of divorce on children is likely to vary as a function of factors that accompany divorce, such as the degree of economic privation experienced by the child and the amount of interparental conflict to which he or she is exposed, both of which are reliably related to postdivorce adjustment.

Second, a recent longitudinal study using large samples in both England and the United States showed that, when predivorce levels of child functioning and of marital conflict were considered, the apparent effect of marital separation on behavior problems and achievement was substantially less (Cherlin et al., 1991). This finding underscores the critical role of marital conflict in understanding the effects of divorce on children.

In view of such findings we must recognize that parental separation, though undeniably a stressor for children, does not invariably lead to adjustment problems. Although children do tend to show some reduction in functioning after parental divorce, most return to predivorce levels of adjustment within 1 or 2 years of the divorce. Perhaps the truest statement that we can make about children's adjustment to divorce is that there is considerable individual variation. Because some children experience severe problems, we need to know about interventions for children of divorce.

A recent review of interventions specifically designed for children of divorce shows that existing programs are offered in group contexts and are as relevant to preventing adjustment problems as to remediating them (Grych & Fincham, 1992). One program, the Children of Divorce Intervention Project (Alpert-Gillis, Pedro-Carroll, & Cowen, 1989; Cowen, Hightower, Pedro-Carroll, & Work, 1989), clearly stands out as the intervention of choice. It consists of modules, each with associated exercises, that address children's understanding of feelings and family changes, coping skills (particularly social problem solving), parent-child relations, and children's perceptions of themselves and their families. This program is the most thoroughly documented intervention, has consistently produced positive outcomes, and has been used with multicultural and inner-city samples. Although most commonly implemented in school settings, it has recently been used in a mental health center in combination with an intervention for the children's parents (see Fernandes, Humphreys, & Fincham, 1991; Humphreys, Fernandes, & Fincham, 1992). However, this modification of the program has not yet been evaluated.

The existing programs are not suited for children who are experiencing serious problems associated with their parents' divorce. Moreover, there are no data on the maintenance of treatment gains obtained with interventions for children of divorce.

Summary

We have outlined some of the issues encountered in evaluating the efficacy of an intervention and summarized what we know about the efficacy of various interventions. There are many gaps in our knowledge, and, though outcome research answers some questions, it leaves many others unanswered. However, outcome research is not the only way data can contribute to practice. The practitioner can also look for guidance to basic research on marriage: Even though such research does not examine intervention per se, it sheds light on questions about intervention. Knowledge of the basic research literature and of the models used to understand couples functioning can help practitioners generate new approaches to intervention. Next to a well-documented treatment package, one of the best resources for effective practice is an empirically grounded approach to intervention. In addressing our final question, "What have we learned from basic research?" we hope to further explain why we chose the approach used in this book.

WHAT HAVE WE LEARNED FROM BASIC RESEARCH ON COMMUNICATION IN COUPLES?

Because the interdisciplinary literature on communication in couples is vast, we cannot give a complete answer to our question in just a few pages. We therefore limit ourselves to relevant research in psychology. The reason for this choice is that the marital research in psychology has, since its inception, focused on marital quality and marital stability. Although this focus limits psychologists' knowledge of general marital functioning, it makes the psychology literature somewhat more appealing to practitioners than marital literature in other disciplines. Even within this limited domain, however, we can only sample from the literature; wherever possible we cite review papers.

Relatively brief overviews of marital research in psychology are provided by Noller and Fitzpatrick (1990), Weiss and Heyman (1990a), and O'Leary and Smith (1991). A special issue of *Clinical Psychology Review* (Volume 13, Number 1, 1993) is devoted to marital conflict and addresses the subject from several different perspectives. Finally, a recent edited volume summarizing psychologists' contributions to an understanding of marriage includes review chapters on a number of topics (Fincham & Bradbury, 1990).

Systematic marital research began in psychology with the application of behavioral techniques to the treatment of couples. Not surprisingly, there was a strong reaction to the heavy reliance on self-report in previous research, and studies concentrated largely on documenting the behavior of distressed and nondistressed spouses (for more detailed histories, see Bradbury & Fincham, 1990b; Fincham & Bradbury, 1990; Jacob, 1987). This work resulted in a useful interplay between basic research and research on outcomes of behavioral marital therapy. In the remainder of this section we summarize what has been learned about marital behavior and consider research on intrapersonal variables that has broadened the scope of psychological inquiry into marriage.

Approaches to Behavior

Two approaches characterize the study of marital behavior. One uses the spouses as observers; the other uses trained coders to observe behavior. We will discuss each approach.

Spouses as Observers

Spouses have been employed as observers of behavior in two different ways (for reviews, see Bradbury & Fincham, 1987b; Christensen, 1987; Weiss & Heyman, 1990b). One strategy asks partners independently to complete a daily checklist of behaviors (e.g., communication behaviors, personal habits, instrumental behaviors, affectional behaviors) and to make a daily relationship satisfaction rating over a period of 1 to 3 weeks with the goal of identifying the daily behaviors that covary with day-to-day satisfaction. Research on this strategy has shown that:

1. Daily behaviors account for about 25% of the variance or variability in daily satisfaction ratings.

2. Negative behaviors (e.g., "Spouse was sarcastic toward me," "Spouse did not pay the bills on time") are better predictors of satisfaction than positive behaviors.

3. Distressed spouses differ reliably from nondistressed spouses in the daily frequency of negative behaviors and, less consistently, of positive behaviors.

4. Distressed spouses are more reactive to partner behavior (i.e., the relation between behavior and satisfaction is stronger for distressed than for nondistressed spouses).

5. Spouses do not agree on the occurrence of a behavior (average agreement across various behaviors is usually about 50%).

6. Training spouses to keep track of daily behaviors does not appreciably increase their agreement (average agreement is 61%).

An intriguing finding from two early studies (Howard & Dawes, 1976; Thornton, 1977) is that the *relative* frequency of positive and negative behaviors is critical for satisfaction. These studies showed that the difference between the frequencies of sexual intercourse and of marital arguments was strongly related to satisfaction. Although later research has not addressed this issue of relative frequency, that early finding is remarkably consistent with a major finding from studies using trained observers. In view of the documented lack of agreement between spouses on the occurrence of a behavior, it is not clear whether a spouse's reports of daily behavior reflect observation of behavior rather than beliefs. Nonetheless, results obtained with spouses as observers are consistent with those obtained when trained observers are used.

The second strategy using spouses as observers examines ongoing ratings of communications that occur during specific problem-solving interactions in the laboratory. In this approach, partners are seated on either side of a "talk table," and only one is allowed to speak at a time. For each speaking turn, the speaker rates the intended impact or intent of the message, and the listener rates the impact of the message. These studies directly address processes outlined in our communication model, described in chapter 4.

A central finding of research using this strategy is that discrepancy between intent and impact ratings distinguishes distressed from nondistressed couples. More specifically, both groups send messages with positive intent and thus do not differ on intent ratings, but only the messages of nondistressed spouses have positive impact. One clinical implication of this finding is that we should make distressed spouses aware of their tendency to perceive messages as more negative than they are intended to be and encourage them to engage in the kind of message clarification described in our chapters 6 through 8. A further, rather surprising result emerges from examination of the sequencing of communications: Neither distressed nor nondistressed spouses reciprocate positive behavior; this suggests that "perhaps it is precisely this *lack* of reciprocity in a context of high positive exchange that characterizes stable positive interaction in nondistressed couples" (Gottman, Notarius, Markman et al., 1976, p. 21). This finding challenges the widespread view that satisfied couples are characterized by the quid pro quo and suggests that they are better described as behaving according to a "bank account" principle: To the extent that they expect positive behaviors to be reciprocated, reciprocation occurs over the long term.

The talk table procedure has also been used to predict future satisfaction. Impact ratings made premaritally have been found to correlate with marital satisfaction 2.5 and 5.5 years later! Discrepancies in the intent and impact ratings of partners also predicted degree of satisfaction 5.5 years out (for a review, see Markman, 1984). Such findings emphasize the importance of communication skills not only for current relationship functioning but also as a marker for future problems when the relationship is satisfactory at present.

Attempts to compare spouses' ratings of communication behaviors to observers' coding of these behaviors have been rare. However, there is some evidence that the ratings of nondistressed spouses are closer to observers' ratings than are the ratings of distressed spouses (Gottman, 1979; Robinson & Price, 1980). This suggests strongly that distressed spouses have a private message system that the practitioner needs to understand in order to work effectively with couples. In sum, talk table studies have shown that "the power of variables obtained by the couples coding their own behavior to discriminate between distressed and nondistressed couples is somewhat greater than that obtained by observer-coding studies" (Gottman, Notarius, Markman et al., 1976, p. 22). Despite this early support for an examination of spouses' communication backgrounds and the thoughts and feelings that influence their communications, marital studies continued to focus almost exclusively on spouses' behavior, particularly behaviors coded by trained observers. Our approach, however, takes account of those earlier findings and strongly emphasizes spouses' communication backgrounds, thoughts, and feelings.

Trained Coders as Observers

Our knowledge of observed communicative behavior in couples comes largely from studies in which couples are asked to engage in problem-solving discussions during visits to the researcher's laboratory. These studies have yielded a number of important findings:

1. Distressed couples reliably display more negative behaviors than do nondistressed couples and, less reliably, fewer positive behaviors.

2. Distressed spouses are more likely to reciprocate negative partner behaviors than are satisfied spouses. In fact, negative reciprocity is considered the most important and reliable signature of a distressed marriage.

3. Nonverbal behavior accounts for more variation in marital satisfaction than verbal behavior and, unlike verbal behavior, does not change when spouses are asked to intentionally fake good and bad marriages. It is therefore more reliable than verbal behavior as an indicator of marital satisfaction.

4. Compared to those of nondistressed couples, the interactions of distressed couples show greater structure or patterning—that is, the sequences of behavior that occur during interactions are more predictable in distressed marriages and are often dominated by negative behavioral chains that are difficult for the couple to stop.

Although these four observations are the most salient, many others emerge across studies. (For a review of early work, see Schaap, 1984; later work is reviewed by Weiss & Heyman, 1990b.) Given the large body of research on observed marital behavior, it is easy to become entangled in myriad findings about very specific behaviors and find oneself unable to see the overall patterns. One way to summarize this extensive literature is with a simple ratio:

$$\text{for happy couples} \quad \frac{\text{agreements or positive behaviors}}{\text{disagreements or negative behaviors}} \quad > 1$$

$$\text{for unhappy couples} \quad \frac{\text{agreements or positive behaviors}}{\text{disagreements or negative behaviors}} \quad < 1$$

This may seem like common sense. However, it might not have turned out this way (e.g., distressed and nondistressed spouses might have differed only in their evaluations of behaviors and not in the actual behaviors exchanged).

Although we have learned a great deal about the behaviors that occur in conversations between spouses, three cautions are necessary. First, recent evidence suggests that the behaviors associated with marital satisfaction at a particular time may be quite different from those that predict future satisfaction. Although the available data on this topic remain controversial (for a useful overview of the issues, see Smith, Vivian, & O'Leary, 1991), longitudinal research has recently taken center stage (for a review, see Bradbury & Karney, 1993).

Second, there have been few attempts to ensure that laboratory-observed discussions capture events that occur in more natural settings. This is perhaps understandable given the enormous ethical and practical difficulties of doing observational research in the home. (For an intriguing example of such research where the observers actually moved in with the families, see Vetere & Gale, 1987.) This concern is mitigated somewhat by the fact that in problem-solving discussions held in the laboratory most couples readily become totally absorbed, often revealing the most intimate details of their lives. Moreover, a comparison of conversations in the home and in the laboratory revealed that, if anything, laboratory data tend to yield a more conservative test of differences between distressed and nondistressed spouses.

Third, very little is known about the ways in which differences in communication background—and individual differences more generally—influence communications between spouses. Gender differences in communication have been found from time to time and have led to the suggestion that the woman is the barometer of relationship satisfaction. The tendency for wives to engage topics that involve negative feelings and for husbands to avoid or withdraw from such topics has received theoretical attention (cf. the Communication Patterns Questionnaire in chapter 4 and Appendix 2). Some suggest that diffuse physiological arousal is more aversive for men than women and that men take longer to recover from such arousal; this would account for gender differences in overt behavior (Gottman & Levenson, 1988). However, gender differences in behavior have not been a topic of systematic inquiry until very recently (for a review, see Baucom, Notarius, Burnett, & Haefner, 1990).

Perhaps the most noteworthy feature of the literature on marital behavior is the consistency of results that has been obtained across methods. As noted in chapter 4, it is through behavior that spouses change their communication, and it is important that we have learned so much about spouses' behaviors. However, as is also apparent from our analysis of communication and from the talk table studies, attention to behavior alone yields an incomplete picture of communication in relationships. We must therefore consider research on variables from the private worlds of individuals, their feelings and thoughts, that can enhance our understanding of couples communication.

Intrapersonal Variables: Affect and Cognition

Systematic research in psychology on factors that cannot be observed directly in conversations began in the 1980s. As we might expect in a field dominated by a focus on observable behavior, both the methods used to investigate feelings and thoughts and the need to do so have been challenged.

Feelings

We previously noted the importance of observed nonverbal behavior for predicting current marital satisfaction. Because nonverbal behaviors are often viewed as indices of affect, one can justifiably argue that affect has always been a target of inquiry in psychological research on marriage. The 1980s, however, witnessed a more intense focus on affect along with the introduction of physiological and self-report methods to study it (cf. the Positive Feelings Questionnaire in chapter 4 and Appendix 2). The hallmark of reliable research findings, replication, has not yet been seen in this important area of inquiry, a circumstance that most likely reflects its recent origin and the technical sophistication needed to conduct the kind of research that has emerged. We therefore urge caution regarding the following summary of findings. At present, these observations appear to be true:

1. The extent to which spouses' physiological responses mirror each other ("physiological linkage") during a high-conflict discussion is strongly related to their current marital satisfaction, accounting for about 60% of the variance or variability in satisfaction.

2. Self-report of feeling adds further information to the prediction of marital satisfaction. Considered together, physiological responses and self-report strongly predict degree of marital satisfaction, accounting for 76% of the variance or variability in marital satisfaction. Compare this to the widely replicated finding that observed nonverbal behavior accounts for up to 30% of the variance in satisfaction.

3. Self-reported affect is significantly related to affect coded by observers. Also, when spouses report their affect after the discussion while viewing a videotape of the discussion, they show similar physiological responses to those that occurred during the original conversation.

4. Concerning the prediction of future marital satisfaction, physiological arousal just before and during a problem-solving discussion accounts for up to 85% of the variation in satisfaction 3 years later. For self-report measures, more reciprocity of the husband's negative affect by the wife and less reciprocity of negative affect by the husband predict declines in marital satisfaction. This finding suggests that husbands prefer to express negative affect and be left alone, whereas wives prefer to express that affect when some response is likely to follow. Physiological linkage did not predict later marital satisfaction.

5. Couples who show more negative affect than positive affect in their interactions are at greater risk for separation and divorce.

Although still preliminary, these findings are consistent with the patterns of affect and affective exchange obtained from observations of nonverbal behavior during interaction. The clinical implications of this research are intriguing. One is that spouses, especially husbands, may benefit from learning how to "self-soothe" when they become physiologically aroused so that they can continue interacting with their partners rather than withdrawing. As suggested in our communication chapters, spouses may need a time-out to soothe themselves, but they should return to the conversation once they have done so. A professional can help a couple identify events or situations that reliably produce physiological arousal so that the partners can either avoid such arousal or begin self-soothing early when the arousal is detected. A direct implication of our suggestion is that couples be allowed to experience intense emotion in counseling sessions. Interestingly, this implication runs counter to earlier wisdom in behaviorally oriented therapies, whereby counselors were taught to prevent escalating emotion in sessions by interrupting and teaching a communication skill such as nondefensive listening.

Affect is clearly central to understanding a relationship, and an exciting body of findings is emerging on this topic. Several sources are available for the interested reader. Weiss and Heyman (1990a, 1990b) provide a succinct summary of this literature. Bradbury and Fincham (1987b) also summarize the literature and consider its clinical implications. Gottman (in press) provides an overview of his research on this topic, reporting several preliminary findings and noting their clinical implications. Finally, armed with knowledge about research findings, the practitioner can consult Greenberg and Johnson (1988) for numerous procedures that have direct clinical implications.

For the practitioner interested in spouses' thoughts, perhaps the most intriguing implication of the research on affect is that it highlights the importance of cognition in understanding marriage. That is, the finding that physiological measures before and during interaction are related to satisfaction supports the idea that, when a couple interacts, their responses reflect expectations based on past interactions. (This is one reason we have devoted a whole chapter to expectations.) That is, previous experience has led distressed spouses to expect that future interactions will be similarly negative, and this learning history or set of expectations leads to a self-fulfilling prophecy. Thus, emotional factors underlying the maintenance of dissatisfaction may be understood in terms not only of a spouse's feelings but also of his or her thoughts. In any event, consideration of expectations comprises much of what occurs in good marital therapy (O'Leary & Turkewitz, 1978a), and this is another important reason for considering what has been learned about cognition in marriage.

Cognition

Research on cognition in marriage has focused exclusively on the content of thoughts (rather than on thought processes), and it closely parallels research on behavior in its emphasis on distinguishing distressed from nondistressed spouses. Most of the research concerns three types of thoughts. First, given the role accorded irrational beliefs in rational-emotive therapy, one line of research examines unrealistic relationship beliefs. The second and third kinds of thoughts that interest researchers deal with two questions presumed to arise regarding relationship conflict: "Why is the conflict occurring?" and "What can I do to resolve the conflict?" The first question concerns the attributions for the conflict; the second deals with efficacy expectations or the extent to which a spouse believes that he or she can perform the behaviors necessary to resolve the conflict. Within this limited coverage of partners' thoughts, a number of findings have emerged, many of which have been replicated by different researchers. Here are some of these findings:

1. Distressed spouses hold more unrealistic beliefs about their relationships than do nondistressed spouses. Moreover, unrealistic relationship beliefs combined with irrational beliefs about the self are more reliable than beliefs about the self alone in predicting expectations of marital therapy outcome, preference for maintaining rather than terminating the relationship, and marital satisfaction.

2. Unrealistic relationship beliefs are related to interactants' ratings of communication following a videotaped review of an interaction; they also correlate with trained observers' ratings.

3. Compared to nondistressed spouses, distressed spouses make less benign attributions for partner behavior and marital events. Attributions for negative events are likely to promote or maintain distress in that they involve unchanging and

globally influential characteristics of the partner (e.g., an undesirable personality trait such as selfishness). In addition, the partner is seen to be blameworthy and to act with negative intent and selfish motivation. This pattern of attributions is reversed for positive events, where nondistressed spouses tend to make relationship-enhancing attributions.

4. Attributions are related to the affect spouses display during interactions, especially the affects of anger and whining to rates of negative behavior, to the ineffectiveness of problem-solving behaviors observed during a problem-solving discussion, and to the reciprocation of negative partner behavior during such discussions. These relationships are stronger for distressed than for nondistressed spouses.

5. Stronger efficacy beliefs are related to higher levels of marital satisfaction, more frequent positive behavior during interactions, better problem-solving approaches exhibited during interactions, and higher observer ratings of spouses' satisfaction with a problem-solving discussion.

6. Attributions and efficacy expectations predict marital satisfaction 12 months out, though the consistency of this finding varies across studies.

Findings such as these are important for at least three reasons. First, they provide much needed empirical confirmation for long-standing clinical observations. For example, practitioners frequently encounter the spouse who sees his or her partner as the cause of relationship difficulties and holds the partner accountable for those difficulties. In fact, an effort to change such attributions is at the heart of many interventions that "reframe" the problem for the couple (cf. the Relationship Attribution Measure in chapter 4 and Appendix 2). The confirmation that distressed spouses make distinct attributions that are not shared by all couples adds considerable support to such clinical practices.

Second, the data on cognition provide a clue for understanding the signature of distressed relationships, the reciprocation of negative behavior. Distressed spouses may reciprocate negative partner behavior because of the way they interpret the behavior. To state it another way, attributions for the behavior may mediate responses to it. This suggests that it is not the behavior per se that is important but rather the attributions that confer meaning on it. There are limits to this notion: Some behaviors (e.g., hitting a spouse) are clearly undesirable and leave little room for interpretation.

This last observation suggests a third reason why research findings concerning cognition are important—namely, their clinical implications. One obvious implication is that careful assessment must determine whether a spouse's thoughts should be the target of intervention. Changing the way a spouse views and thinks about the other's behavior may be just as effective as changing that behavior. However, we must exercise considerable caution to ensure that interventions targeting one individual's cognitions do not either explicitly or implicitly maintain dysfunctional behavior in the partner. For example, attributing abusive behavior to the abuser's troubled childhood could make the spouse feel a greater need to accept the behavior and reduce the abuser's responsibility to change it. In such cases there is no substitute for focusing on the victim's welfare and making the abusive behavior an immediate target of intervention.

The findings regarding attribution also point to an interesting general precept for professional behavior: Given the potential impact of attributions, professionals should not allow themselves or their clients to be seen as the source of positive partner behavior. It is not uncommon for a spouse to complain that the change in the partner is superficial and temporary because it simply reflects compliance with an instruction from the counselor. Similarly, a spouse may complain that it is only his or her insistence that has brought about a desired behavior and that the partner will maintain the behavior only if the insistence is continued. Such considerations can also be illustrated with regard to the negotiation of agreements. Instead of having each spouse request specific changes from the other, the counselor can have each one suggest what she or he can do to satisfy the other's needs. In short, the practitioner should consider any procedures that remove external reasons for positive partner behaviors.

As with affect, research on cognition appears to be quite relevant for the practitioner. General summaries of the literature can be found in Baucom and Epstein (1990) and Fincham, Bradbury, and Scott (1990). A comprehensive review of research on attributions is provided by Bradbury and Fincham (1990a). The clinical implications of this research and of the cognitive perspective for intervention are explored by Baucom and Epstein (1990); Fincham, Bradbury, and Beach (1990); and Fincham and Bradbury (1991). Beach (Beach & Bauserman, 1990; Beach, 1991) provides a number of intriguing examples of the use of cognitive models to facilitate the therapy process and overcome client resistance. Such applications are important because the few cognitive interventions studied thus far in treatment outcome research have been quite unsophisticated. Not surprisingly, no evidence has yet emerged to show that adding a cognitive component to behavioral marital therapy increases its effectiveness.

CONCLUSION

In this appendix we have highlighted some of the empirical underpinnings of our approach for enhancing relationships. Rather than trying to provide an exhaustive coverage, we have attempted to offer an overview that can also serve as a point of departure for further exploration of the research literature on marriage. Although the practitioner need not become an expert on this literature, maximal professional effectiveness requires familiarity with research findings. Given the current state of our knowledge, there is clearly much to be learned. Scientists and practitioners must inform each other's efforts if we are to best serve the couples who turn to us for help.

2 *Technical Information on the Measures Used to Assess Relationships*

The following is psychometric information on the measures discussed in chapter 4.

Marital Satisfaction

The Marital Adjustment Test (MAT; Locke & Wallace, 1959) is a measure of marital satisfaction used widely in both basic research on marriage and therapy outcome studies. It has adequate reliability (split half = .90) and discriminates between nondistressed spouses and spouses who have documented marital problems (Locke & Wallace, 1959). Scores on this instrument also correlate with clinicians' judgments of marital discord (Crowther, 1985) and they are sensitive to changes in marital therapy (e.g., Baucom & Aiken, 1984; O'Leary & Arias, 1983). Factor analysis shows that the measure is unidimensional, reflecting global happiness (Kimmel & Van Der Veen, 1974).

Although more reliability and validity studies have been conducted on the MAT than on any other marital measure (Cohen, 1985), the Dyadic Adjustment Scale (DAS; Spanier, 1976) is often viewed as preferable to the MAT because it was designed as a multidimensional measure of marital adjustment (comprising subscales of dyadic satisfaction, dyadic cohesion, dyadic consensus, and affectional expression) and is more contemporary in its items and its conceptual foundation. However, the dimensions of the DAS may simply reflect the differing formats of the items used in each subscale (Norton, 1983); research has not always replicated its multidimensional structure (e.g., Sharpley & Cross, 1982). In any event, this 32-item measure includes 11 of the MAT items and correlates very highly with the MAT. The two measures do not appear to have different correlates. Scores from one measure can easily be compared to scores on the other through a simple transformation (Crane, Allgood, Larson, & Griffin, 1990). Sabatelli (1988) provides an excellent and easily understood evaluation of measures of marital satisfaction, including the MAT and the DAS. For a critique of the construct of marital satisfaction and its operationalization, see Fincham and Bradbury (1987a).

Communication Style

Clinical theories of marriage discuss the importance of communication styles in relation to marital satisfaction, yet little attention has been devoted to verbal report measures of the behavioral patterns accompanying these styles. Christensen and colleagues developed the Communication Patterns Questionnaire and three subscales—(a) Mutual Constructive Communication, (b) Demand-Withdraw Communication, and (c) Demand-Withdraw Role—to better assess interaction patterns and improve interpartner agreement (see Christensen, 1988). Ongoing research suggests that items and subscales of the Communication Patterns Questionnaire discriminate between spouses in happy and unhappy marriages (Noller & White, 1990). Of the subscales, the Mutual Constructive Communication scale was found to correlate best (r = .79) with relationship satisfaction as measured by the Dyadic Adjustment Scale (DAS). In particular, unhappy partners tend to avoid each other more often than happy partners do. Demand-Withdraw Communication was found to correlate negatively (r = − .55) with the DAS, whereas Demand-Withdraw Role was found to correlate negligibly (r = − .12) with the DAS (Christensen, 1988). Interpartner agreements for the subscales were found to be reliable (.80, .73, and .74, respectively). In addition, preliminary investigation of the Communication Patterns Questionnaire suggests that the measure may be sensitive to gender differences in communication style. In particular, Christensen and Heavey's (1990) study of the measure found that women tended to be as demanding as men when discussing a change they wanted, although men overall tended to be more withdrawn.

Areas of Difficulty

The Inventory of Relationship Problems is designed to help couples become more specific about areas of their relationships that are sources of difficulty. Although this questionnaire (along with its many variants) has been used in a number of studies, it has not been investigated as a psychometric instrument. Instead, researchers usually use it to identify topics for a problem-solving discussion that is the focus of study. In view of these considerations, we do not offer any psychometric information on this measure.

Thoughts

Beliefs

Although irrational beliefs individuals hold about themselves (see Ellis & Greiger, 1977) are relevant to relationship dysfunction, Epstein and his colleagues (e.g., Epstein & Eidelson, 1981; Eidelson & Epstein, 1982) reasoned that unrealistic beliefs specific to relationships would provide even more information about relationship distress. Accordingly, they constructed the Relationship Belief Inventory (RBI), based on the irrational beliefs emphasized in rational-emotive therapy and on clinical experience. They found that the internal consistency of the five beliefs was acceptable (coefficient alpha ranged from .72 to .81), and they demonstrated that relationship beliefs combined with irrational beliefs about the self were better than beliefs about the self alone in predicting expectations about therapy outcome, preference for maintaining rather than terminating the relationship, and marital satisfaction (Eidelson & Epstein, 1982).

Further research using the RBI has shown that (a) its inverse relation to marital satisfaction is highly reliable (e.g., Epstein, Pretzer, & Fleming, 1987; Fincham & Bradbury, 1989); (b) some beliefs correlate with interactants' ratings of communications following a videotaped review of an interaction (Gaelick, Bodenhausen, & Wyer, 1985); and (c) it is related in the expected manner to a number of correlates of marital distress (e.g., reports of communication behaviors, Epstein et al., 1987; marital attributions,

Fincham & Bradbury, 1987b). For further information on the clinical use of the RBI, see Baucom and Epstein (1990).

Attributions

Attributions are the cognitions most frequently studied in marital research; they are reliably related to marital satisfaction across a number of studies. The Relationship Attribution Measure (RAM; Fincham & Bradbury, 1992) is a short, simple measure of attributions that uses "hypothetical" partner behaviors as stimuli for attributions. The behaviors used as stimuli are in fact reported to occur in over 90% of marriages. This measure assesses two different types of attributions or explanations. *Causal attributions* concern who or what produced the event and can be evaluated on three dimensions: (a) where the cause resides (e.g., in one's partner, in oneself, in the relationship); (b) whether the cause is permanent (e.g., one's ability) or temporary (e.g., one's current mood); and (c) whether the cause is globally influential and affects other areas of the marriage. On the other hand, *responsibility attributions* deal with blame or fault and are related to judgments of the person's intentions and motivations. Thus, dimensions pertaining to blame, intent, and motivation are used to assess this type of attribution. Although in chapter 4 couples are instructed to compute only a single attribution score, an index of causal attribution (sum of the first three items following each behavior) and of responsibility attribution (sum of the last three items following each behavior) can be obtained.

Although distinguishing causal from responsibility attributions may seem unnecessarily complex, the need for two attribution indices emerged from a confirmatory factor analysis of responses to the RAM. The causal and responsibility indices yielded by the RAM show good internal consistency (coefficient alpha varies from .86 to .91) and high test-retest reliability over a 3-week period (correlations vary from .61 to .87).

The validity of the RAM was established in several ways. Responses on the measure were shown to correlate with attributions for behaviors that had recently occurred in the marriage and with attributions for marital difficulties. Confirming theoretical predictions, attributions correlated with specific affects—namely, with self-reported anger in response to the behaviors for which attributions were made and with anger and whining observed in a problem-solving discussion (see Fincham & Bradbury, 1992, for further details). As expected, RAM responses were related to marital satisfaction across several studies. For discussion of the role of attributions in therapy, consult Baucom and Epstein (1990) and Fincham, Bradbury, and Beach (1990).

Feelings

General Mood

Negative affect is conceptualized in the Positive and Negative Affect Schedule (PANAS; Watson, Clark, & Tellegen, 1988) as a "general dimension of subjective distress and unpleasurable engagement that subsumes a variety of aversive mood states, including anger, contempt, disgust, guilt, fear, and nervousness" (p. 1063). The measure does not, therefore, discriminate between negative affect states such as anxiety and depression that may be important clinically. Nonetheless, it is a very efficient, cost-effective assessment of negative affect. Users can vary the instructions to refer to different time frames (e.g., the past few days, the past year) without appreciably altering the measure's reliability (across various referents coefficient alpha varies from .84 to .87). The scales of the PANAS correlate with a variety of positive and negative mood scales concerning depression (correlation with the Beck Depression Inventory is .58), anxiety (correlation with the State-Trait Anxiety Inventory is .51), and mental health (correlation with the Hopkins Symptom Checklist is .74).

Feelings in the Relationship

The Positive Feelings Questionnaire (PFQ; O'Leary, Fincham, & Turkewitz, 1983), developed at the University Marital Therapy Clinic at the State University of New York at Stony Brook, assesses the overall level of positive affect that a person feels toward his or her partner. It has high internal consistency (coefficient alpha = .94) and high test-retest reliability over an interval of 1 to 3 weeks (.93). All items in the measure discriminate between happily married spouses and spouses seeking marital therapy; scores on the measure are sensitive to changes that occur during marital therapy (O'Leary & Arias, 1983).

References

Achenbach, T. (1985). *Assessment and taxonomy of child and adolescent psychopathology.* London: Sage.

Alpert-Gillis, L. J., Pedro-Carroll, J. L., & Cowen, E. L. (1989). The Children of Divorce Intervention Program: Development, implementation, and evaluation of a program for young urban children. *Journal of Consulting and Clinical Psychology, 57,* 583–589.

Amato, P. R., & Keith, B. (1991a). Consequences of parental divorce for the well-being of children: A meta-analysis. *Psychological Bulletin, 110,* 26–46.

Amato, P. R., & Keith, B. (1991b). Parental divorce and adult well-being: A meta-analysis. *Journal of Marriage and the Family, 53,* 43–58.

Andreozzi, L. L. (Ed.). (1985). *Integrating research and clinical practice.* Rockville, MD: Aspen Systems.

Barbach, L. (1984). *For each other: Sharing sexual intimacy.* New York: Signet.

Barlow, D.H. (1981). On the relation of clinical research to clinical practice: Current issues, new directions. *Journal of Consulting and Clinical Psychology, 49,* 147–155.

Bateson, G. (1966). Slippery theories. *International Journal of Psychiatry, 2,* 415–417.

Baucom, D. H. (1983). Conceptual and psychometric issues in evaluating the effectiveness of behavioral marital therapy. In J. P. Vincent (Ed.), *Advances in family intervention, assessment, and theory* (Vol. 3, pp. 73–88). Greenwich, CT: JAI.

Baucom, D. H., & Aiken, P. A. (1984). Sex role identity, marital satisfaction and response to behavioral marital therapy. *Journal of Consulting and Clinical Psychology, 52,* 438–444.

Baucom, D. H., & Epstein, N. (1990). *Cognitive-behavioral marital therapy.* New York: Brunner/Mazel.

Baucom, D. H., & Hoffman, J. A. (1986). The effectiveness of marital therapy: Current status and application to the clinical setting. In N. S. Jacobson & A. S. Gurman (Eds.), *Clinical handbook of marital therapy* (pp. 597–620). New York: Guilford.

Baucom, D. H., Notarius, C. I., Burnett, C. K., & Haefner, P. (1990). Gender differences and sex-role identity in marriage. In F. D. Fincham & T. N. Bradbury (Eds.), *The psychology of marriage: Basic issues and applications* (pp. 150–171). New York: Guilford.

Beach, S. R. H. (1991). Social cognition in the relationship repair process: Toward better outcome in marital therapy. In G. J. O. Fletcher & F. D. Fincham (Eds.), *Cognition in close relationships* (pp. 307–308). Hillsdale, NJ: Erlbaum.

Beach, S. R. H., & Bauserman, S. A. (1990). Enhancing the effectiveness of marital therapy. In F. D. Fincham & T. N. Bradbury (Eds.), *The psychology of marriage* (pp. 349–374). New York: Guilford.

Beach, S. R. H., & O'Leary, K. D. (1985). Current status of outcome research in marital therapy. In L. L'Abate (Ed.), *The handbook of family psychology and therapy* (pp. 1035–1072). Homewood, IL: Dorsey.

Beach, S. R. H., & O'Leary, K. D. (1991). Treatment of depressed–maritally discordant individuals: Is there a psychological treatment of choice? *The Clinical Psychologist, 44,* 55–62.

Bednar, R. L., Burlingame, G. M., & Masters, K. S. (1988). Systems of family treatment: Substance or semantics? *Annual Review of Psychology, 39,* 401–413.

Bergin, A. E. (1963). The effects of psychotherapy: Negative results revisited. *Journal of Counseling Psychology, 10,* 244–250.

Bloom, B. L., Hodges, W. F., Kern, M. S., & McFaddin, S. C. (1985). A preventive intervention program for the newly separated: Final evaluations. *American Journal of Orthopsychiatry, 55,* 9–26.

Booth, A., Johnson, D., & Edwards, J. N. (1983). Measuring marital instability. *Journal of Marriage and the Family, 45,* 387–393.

Bornstein, P. H., & Bornstein, M. T. (1986). *Marital therapy: A behavioral-communication approach.* New York: Pergamon.

Bradbury, T. N., & Fincham, F. D. (1987a). Assessing the effects of behavioral marital therapy: Assumptions and measurement strategies. *Clinical Psychology Review, 7,* 525–538.

Bradbury, T. N., & Fincham, F. D. (1987b). Assessment of affect. In K. D. O'Leary (Ed.), *Assessment of marital discord* (pp. 59–108). Hillsdale, NJ: Erlbaum.

Bradbury, T. N., & Fincham, F. D. (1990a). Attributions in marriage: Review and critique. *Psychological Bulletin, 107,* 3–33.

Bradbury, T. N., & Fincham, F. D. (1990b). Dimensions of marital and family interaction. In J. Touliatos, B. F. Perlmutter, & M. A. Straus (Eds.), *Handbook of family measurement techniques* (pp. 36–61). Newbury Park, CA: Sage.

Bradbury, T. N., & Karney, B. R. (1993). Longitudinal study of marital interaction and dysfunction: Review and analysis. *Clinical Psychology Review, 13,* 15–28.

Broderick, C. B., & Schrader, S. S. (1981). The history of professional marriage and family therapy. In A. S. Gurman & D. P. Kniskern (Eds.), *Handbook of family therapy* (pp. 5–35). New York: Brunner/Mazel.

Broderick, J. E. (1981). A method for derivation of areas of assessment in marital relationships. *The American Journal of Family Therapy, 9,* 25–34.

Brown, L., & Brown, M. (1986). *A dinosaur's divorce.* Boston: The Atlantic Monthly Press.

Cantor, N. (1982). "Everyday" versus normative models of clinical and social judgment. In G. Weary & H. Mirels (Eds.), *Integrations of clinical and social psychology* (pp. 27–47). New York: Oxford University Press.

Chapman, L., & Chapman, J. (1967). Genesis of popular but erroneous psychodiagnostic observations. *Journal of Abnormal Psychology, 72,* 193–204.

Chapman, L., & Chapman, J. (1982). Test results are what you think they are. In D. Kahneman, P. Slovic, & A. Tversky (Eds.), *Judgment under uncertainty: Heuristics and biases* (pp. 239–248). Cambridge, England: Cambridge University Press.

Cherlin, A. J., Furstenberg, F. F., Chase-Lansdale, P. L., Kiernan, K. E., Robins, P. K., Morrison, D. R., & Teitler, J. O. (1991). Longitudinal studies of effects of divorce on children in Great Britain and the United States. *Science, 252,* 1386–1389.

Christensen, A. (1987). Assessment of behavior. In K. D. O'Leary (Ed.), *Assessment of marital discord* (pp. 13–57). Hillsdale, NJ: Erlbaum.

Christensen, A. (1988). Dysfunctional interaction patterns in couples. In P. Noller & M. A. Fitzpatrick (Eds.), *Perspectives on marital interaction* (pp. 31–52). Philadelphia: Multilingual Matters.

Christensen, A., & Heavey, C. L. (1990). Gender and social structure in the demand/withdraw pattern of marital conflict. *Journal of Personality and Social Psychology, 59,* 73–81.

Christensen, A., & Sullaway, M. (1984). *Communication Patterns Questionnaire.* Unpublished manuscript, University of California, Los Angeles.

Cohen, P. (1985). Family measurement techniques: Locke Marital Adjustment Scale and the Dyadic Adjustment Scale. *American Journal of Family Therapy, 13,* 66–71.

Cowen, E. L., Hightower, A. D., Pedro-Carroll, J. L., & Work, W. C. (1989). School-based models for primary prevention programming with children. In R. Lorion (Ed.), *Prevention in human services* (Vol. 7, pp. 133–160). Binghamton, NY: Haworth.

Crane, D. R., Allgood, S. M., Larson, J. H., & Griffin, W. (1990). Assessing marital quality with distressed and nondistressed couples: A comparison and equivalency table for three frequently used measures. *Journal of Marriage and the Family, 52,* 87–93.

Crowther, J. H. (1985). The relationship between depression and marital adjustment: A descriptive study. *The Journal of Nervous and Mental Disease, 173,* 227–231.

Demo, D. H., & Acock, A. C. (1988). The impact of divorce on children. *Journal of Marriage and the Family, 50,* 619–648.

Duncan, G. J., & Hoffman, S. D. (1985). Economic consequences of marital instability. In M. David & T. Smeeding (Eds.), *Horizontal equity, uncertainty, and economic well-being* (pp. 427–470). University of Chicago Press.

Eidelson, R. J., & Epstein, N. (1982). Cognition and relationship maladjustment: Development of a measure of dysfunctional relationship beliefs. *Journal of Consulting and Clinical Psychology, 50,* 715–720.

Ellis, A., & Greiger, R. (1977). *Rational-emotive therapy: A handbook of theory and practice.* New York: Springer.

Emery, R. E., Matthews, S., & Wyer, M. M. (1991). Child custody mediation and litigation: Further evidence on the differing views of mothers and fathers. *Journal of Consulting and Clinical Psychology, 55,* 179–186.

Emery R. E., Shaw, D. S., & Jackson, J. A. (1987). A clinical description of a model of child custody mediation. In J. P. Vincent (Ed.), *Advances in family intervention, assessment, and theory* (Vol. 4, pp. 223–262). Greenwich, CT: JAI.

Emery, R. E., & Wyer, M. M. (1987). Divorce mediation. *American Psychologist, 42,* 472–480.

Epstein, N., & Eidelson, R. J. (1981). Unrealistic beliefs of clinical couples: Their relationship to expectations, goals, and satisfaction. *The American Journal of Family Therapy, 9,* 13–22.

Epstein, N., Pretzer, J. L., & Fleming, B. (1987). The role of cognitive appraisal in self-reports of marital communication. *Behavior Therapy, 18,* 51–69.

Fernandes, L. O. L., Humphreys, K., & Fincham, F. D. (1991). The whole is greater than the sum of its parts: Part I. A group intervention for children from divorced families. *The Family Psychologist, 7,* 26–28.

Fincham, F. D., & Bradbury, T. N. (1987a). The assessment of marital quality: A reevaluation. *Journal of Marriage and the Family, 49,* 797–809.

Fincham, F. D., & Bradbury, T. N. (1987b). The impact of attributions in marriage: A longitudinal analysis. *Journal of Personality and Social Psychology, 53,* 481–489.

Fincham, F. D., & Bradbury, T. N. (1989). The impact of attributions in marriage: An individual difference analysis. *Journal of Social and Personal Relationships, 6,* 69–85.

Fincham, F. D., & Bradbury, T. N. (Eds.). (1990). *The psychology of marriage: Basic issues and applications.* New York: Guilford.

Fincham, F. D., & Bradbury, T. N. (1991). Marital conflict: Towards a more complete integration of research and treatment. In J. P. Vincent (Ed.), *Advances in family intervention, assessment and theory* (pp. 1–24). London: Kingsley.

Fincham, F. D., & Bradbury, T. N. (1992). Assessing attributions in marriage: The Relationship Attribution Measure. *Journal of Personality and Social Psychology, 62,* 457–468.

Fincham, F. D., Bradbury, T. N., & Beach, S. R. (1990). To arrive where we began: A reappraisal of cognition in marriage and in marital therapy. *Journal of Family Psychology, 4,* 167–184.

Fincham, F. D., Bradbury, T. N., & Scott, C. K. (1990). Cognition in marriage. In F. D. Fincham & T. N. Bradbury (Eds.), *The psychology of marriage: Basic issues and applications* (pp. 118–149). New York: Guilford.

Framo, J. L. (1972). *Family interaction.* New York: Springer.

Gaelick, L., Bodenhausen, G. V., & Wyer, R. S. (1985). Emotional communication in close relationships. *Journal of Personality and Social Psychology, 49,* 1246–1265.

Gardner, R. A. (1977). *The parent's book about divorce.* New York: Doubleday.

Geiss, S. K., & O'Leary, K. D. (1981). Therapist ratings of frequency and severity of marital problems: Implications for research. *Journal of Marital and Family Therapy, 7,* 515–520.

Gottman, J. M. (1979). *Marital interaction: Experimental investigations.* New York: Academic.

Gottman, J. M. (1985). Observational measures of behavior therapy outcome: A reply to Jacobson. *Behavioral Assessment, 7,* 317–321.

Gottman, J. M. (in press). An agenda for marital therapy. In S. M. Johnson & L. S. Greenberg (Eds.), *Emotion in marriage and marital therapy.* New York: Brunner/Mazel.

Gottman, J. M., & Levenson, R. W. (1988). The social psychophysiology of marriage. In P. Noller & M. A. Fitzpatrick (Eds.), *Perspectives on marital interaction* (pp. 182–200). Philadelphia: Multilingual Matters.

Gottman, J. M., Notarius, C., Gonso, J., & Markman, H. (1976). *A couple's guide to communication.* Champaign, IL: Research Press.

Gottman, J. M., Notarius, C., Markman, H., Banks, S., Yoppi, B., & Rubin, M. E. (1976). Behavior exchange theory and marital decision making. *Journal of Personality and Social Psychology, 34,* 14–23.

Greenberg, L. S., & Johnson, S. M. (1988). *Emotionally focused therapy for couples.* New York: Guilford.

Grych, J. H., & Fincham, F. D. (1992). Interventions for children of divorce: Towards greater integration of research and action. *Psychological Bulletin, 111,* 434–454.

Guerin, P. J. (Ed.). (1976). *Family therapy: Theory and practice.* New York: Gardner.

Gurman, A. S., Kniskern, D. P., & Pinsof, W. M. (1986). Research on the process and outcome of marital and family therapy. In S. L. Garfield & A. E. Bergin (Eds.), *Handbook of psychotherapy and behavior change* (3rd ed., pp. 565–624). New York: Wiley.

Hahlweg, K., & Markman, H. J. (1988). Effectiveness of behavioral marital therapy: Empirical status of behavioral techniques in preventing and alleviating marital distress. *Journal of Consulting and Clinical Psychology, 56,* 440–447.

Hahlweg, K., Schindler, L., Revenstorf, D., & Brengelmann, J. C. (1984). The Munich marital therapy study. In K. Hahlweg & N. S. Jacobson (Eds.), *Marital interaction: Analysis and modification* (pp. 3–26). New York: Guilford.

Hall, E. T. (1976). *Beyond culture.* New York: Anchor.

Hazelrigg, M. D., Cooper, H. M., & Bourdin, C. M. (1987). Evaluating the effectiveness of family therapies: An integrative review and analysis. *Psychological Bulletin, 101,* 428–442.

Helmering, D. W. (1981). *I have two families.* Nashville: Abingdon.

Howard, J. W., & Dawes, R. M. (1976). Linear prediction of marital happiness. *Personality and Social Psychology Bulletin, 2,* 478–480.

Humphreys, K., Fernandes, L. O. L., & Fincham, F. D. (1992). The whole is greater than the sum of its parts: Part II. A group intervention for parents from divorced families. *The Family Psychologist, 8,* 19–20.

Isensee, R. (1990). *Love between men: Enhancing intimacy and keeping your relationship alive.* New York: Prentice-Hall.

Jacob, T. (1987). Family interaction and psychopathology: Historical overview. In T. Jacob (Ed.), *Family interaction and psychopathology* (pp. 3–22). New York: Plenum.

Jacobson, N. S. (1985a). Family therapy outcome research: Potential pitfalls and prospects. *Journal of Marital and Family Therapy, 11,* 149–158.

Jacobson, N. S. (1985b). The role of observation measures in marital therapy outcome research. *Behavioral Assessment, 7,* 287–308.

Jacobson, N. S. (1985c). Towards a nonsectarian blueprint for the empirical study of family therapies. *Journal of Marriage and Family Therapy, 11,* 163–165.

Jacobson, N. S. (1985d). Uses and abuses of observational measures. *Behavioral Assessment, 7,* 323–330.

Jacobson, N. S. (1989). The maintenance of treatment gains following social learning–based marital therapy. *Behavior Therapy, 20,* 325–336.

Jacobson, N. S. (1991). Behavioral vs. insight-oriented marital therapy: Labels can be misleading. *Journal of Consulting and Clinical Psychology, 59,* 142–145.

Jacobson, N. S., Follette, W. C., & Elwood, R. W. (1984). Outcome research on behavioral marital therapy: A methodological and conceptual reappraisal. In K. Hahlweg & N. S. Jacobson (Eds.), *Marital interaction: Analysis and modification* (pp. 113–129). New York: Guilford.

Jacobson, N. S., Follette, W. C., Revenstorf, D., Baucom, D. H., Hahlweg, K., & Margolin, G. (1984). Variability in outcome and clinical significance of behavioral marital therapy: A reanalysis of outcome data. *Journal of Consulting and Clinical Psychology, 52,* 497–504.

Jacobson, N. S., & Gurman, A. S. (Eds.). (1986). *Clinical handbook of marital therapy.* New York: Guilford.

Jacobson, N. S., & Margolin, G. (1979). *Marital therapy.* New York: Brunner/Mazel.

Jacobson, N. S., & Martin, B. (1976). Behavioral marriage therapy: Current status. *Psychological Bulletin, 83,* 540–556.

Jacobson, N. S., & Revenstorf, D. (1988). Statistics for assessing the clinical significance of psychotherapy techniques: Issues, problems, and new developments. *Behavioral Assessment, 10,* 133–145.

Jacobson, N. S., Schmaling, K. R., & Holtzworth-Munroe, A. (1987). Component analysis of behavioral marital therapy: 2-year follow-up and prediction of relapse. *Journal of Marital and Family Therapy, 13,* 187–195.

Jacobson, N. S., Schmaling, K. R., Holtzworth-Munroe, A., Katt, J. L., Wood, L. F., & Follette, V. M. (1989). Research-structured vs. clinically flexible versions of social learning–based marital therapy. *Behaviour Research and Therapy, 27,* 173–180.

Johnson, S. M., & Greenberg, L. S. (1985). Emotionally focused marital therapy: An outcome study. *Journal of Marital and Family Therapy, 11,* 313–317.

Kanfer, F. H. (1990). The scientist-practitioner connection: A bridge in need of constant attention. *Professional Psychology, 21,* 264–270.

Kanfer, F. H., & Schefft, B. K. (1988). *Guiding the process of therapeutic change.* Champaign, IL: Research Press.

Kazdin, A. E., & Wilson, G. T. (1978). *Evaluation of behavior therapy: Issues, evidence, and research strategies.* Cambridge, MA: Ballinger.

Kimmel, D., & Van Der Veen, F. (1974). Factors of marital adjustment in Locke's Marital Adjustment Test. *Journal of Marriage and the Family, 36,* 57–63.

Kitson, G. C., Babri, K. B., Roach, M. J., & Placidi, K. S. (1989). Adjustment to widowhood and divorce: A review. *Journal of Family Issues, 10,* 5–32.

Kniskern, D. P. (1985). Climbing out of the pit: Further guidelines for family therapy research. *Journal of Marital and Family Therapy, 11,* 159–162.

Lederer, W. J., & Jackson, D. D. (1968). *The mirages of marriage.* New York: Norton.

Liberman, R. P. (1970). Behavioral approaches to family and couple therapy. *American Journal of Orthopsychiatry, 40,* 106–118.

Locke, H. J., & Wallace, K. M. (1959). Short marital-adjustment and prediction tests: Their reliability and validity. *Marriage and Family Living, 21,* 251–255.

Margolin, G. (1987). Marital therapy: A cognitive-behavioral–affective approach. In N. S. Jacobson (Ed.), *Psychotherapists in clinical practice* (pp. 232–285). New York: Guilford.

Markman, H. J. (1984). The longitudinal study of couples' interactions: Implications for understanding and predicting the development of marital distress. In K. Hahlweg & N. S. Jacobson (Eds.), *Marital interaction: Analysis and modification* (pp. 253–281). New York: Guilford.

McKay, M., Rogers, P. D., Blades, J., & Gosse, R. (1984). *The divorce book.* Oakland, CA: New Harbinger.

National Center for Health Statistics (1991). *Vital and Health Statistics.* Hyattsville, MD: Author.

Nichols, M. (1987). Lesbian sexuality: Issues and developing theory. In Boston Lesbian Psychology Collective (Eds.), *Lesbian psychologies: Explorations and challenges* (pp. 97–125). Urbana, IL: University of Illinois Press.

Noller, P., & Fitzpatrick, M. A. (1990). Marital communication in the eighties. *Journal of Marriage and the Family, 52,* 823–843.

Noller, P., & White, A. (1990). The validity of the Communication Patterns Questionnaire. *Psychological Assessment, 2,* 478–482.

Norton, R. (1983). Measuring marital quality: A critical look at the dependent variable. *Journal of Marriage and the Family, 45,* 141–151.

O'Leary, K. D., & Arias, I. (1983). The influence of marital therapy on sexual satisfaction. *Journal of Sex and Marital Therapy, 9,* 171–181.

O'Leary, K. D., Fincham, F. D., & Turkewitz, H. (1983). Assessment of positive feelings toward spouse. *Journal of Consulting and Clinical Psychology, 51,* 949–951.

O'Leary, K. D., & Smith, D. (1991). Marital interactions. *Annual Review of Psychology, 42,* 191–212.

O'Leary, K. D., & Turkewitz, H. (1978a). Marital therapy from a behavioral perspective. In T. J. Paolino & B. S. McCrady (Eds.), *Marriage and marital therapy: Psychoanalytic, behavioral and systems theory perspectives* (pp. 240–297). New York: Brunner/Mazel.

O'Leary, K. D., & Turkewitz, H. (1978b). Methodological errors in marital and child treatment research. *Journal of Consulting and Clinical Psychology, 46,* 747–758.

Persons, J. B. (1991). Psychotherapy outcome studies do not accurately represent current models of psychotherapy: A proposed remedy. *American Psychologist, 46,* 99–106.

Piercy, F. P., & Sprenkle, D. H. (1990). Marriage and family therapy: A decade review. *Journal of Marriage and the Family, 52,* 1116–1126.

Richards, A., & Willis, I. (1976). *How to get it together when your parents are coming apart.* New York: David McKay.

Robinson, E. A., & Price, M. G. (1980). Pleasurable behavior in marital interaction: An observational study. *Journal of Consulting and Clinical Psychology, 48,* 117–118.

Sabatelli, R. M. (1988). Measurement issues in marital research. *Journal of Marriage and the Family, 50,* 891–916.

Schaap, C. (1984). A comparison of the interaction of distressed and nondistressed married couples in a laboratory situation: Literature survey, methodological issues, and an empirical investigation. In K. Hahlweg & N. S. Jacobson (Eds.), *Marital interaction: Analysis and modification* (pp. 133–158). New York: Guilford.

Sharpley, C. F., & Cross, D. G. (1982). A psychometric evaluation of the Spanier Dyadic Adjustment Scale. *Journal of Marriage and the Family, 34,* 739–741.

Smith, D. A., Vivian, D., & O'Leary, K. D. (1991). The misnomer proposition: A critical reappraisal of the longitudinal status of "negativity" in marital communication. *Behavioral Assessment, 13,* 7–24.

Smith, M. L., Glass, G. V., & Miller, T. I. (1980). *The benefits of psychotherapy.* Baltimore: John Hopkins University Press.

Snyder, D. K., & Wills, R. M. (1989). Behavioral versus insight-oriented marital therapy: Effects on individual and interspousal functioning. *Journal of Consulting and Clinical Psychology, 57,* 39–46.

Snyder, D. K., Wills, R. M., & Grady-Fletcher, A. (1991). Long-term effectiveness of behavioral versus insight-oriented marital therapy. *Journal of Consulting and Clinical Psychology, 59,* 138–141.

Spanier, G. B. (1976). Measuring dyadic adjustment: New scales for assessing the quality of marriage and similar dyads. *Journal of Marriage and the Family, 38,* 15–28.

Sprenkle, D. H., & Storm, C. L. (1983). Divorce therapy outcome research: A substantive and methodological review. *Journal of Marital and Family Therapy, 9,* 239–258.

Stolberg, A. L., & Garrison, K. M. (1985). Evaluating a primary prevention program for children of divorce: The Divorce Adjustment Project. *American Journal of Community Psychology, 13,* 111–124.

Stuart, R. B. (1969). Operant-interpersonal treatment for marital discord. *Journal of Consulting and Clinical Psychology, 33,* 675–682.

Sue, D. W., & Sue, D. (1990). *Counseling the culturally different: Theory and practice* (2nd ed.). New York: Wiley.

Thornton, B. (1977). Toward a linear prediction of marital happiness. *Personality and Social Psychology Bulletin, 3,* 674–676.

Tversky, A., & Kahneman, D. (1982). Judgment under uncertainty: Heuristics and biases. In D. Kahneman, P. Slovic, & A. Tversky (Eds.), *Judgment under uncertainty: Heuristics and biases* (pp. 2–22). Cambridge, England: Cambridge University Press.

Vetere, A., & Gale, A. (1987). *Ecological studies of family life.* New York: Wiley.

Watson, D., Clark, L. A., & Tellegen, A. (1988). Development and validation of brief measures of positive and negative affect: The PANAS Scales. *Journal of Personality and Social Psychology, 54,* 1063–1070.

Weiss, R. L., & Frohman, P. E. (1985). Behavioral observation as outcome measures: Not through a glass darkly. *Behavioral Assessment, 7,* 309–315.

Weiss, R. L. & Heyman, R. (1990a). Marital distress and therapy. In A. S. Bellack, M. Hersen, & A. E. Kazdin (Eds.), *International handbook of behavior modification* (2nd ed., pp. 475–503). New York: Plenum.

Weiss, R. L., & Heyman, R. (1990b). Observation of marital interaction. In F. D. Fincham & T. N. Bradbury (Eds.), *The psychology of marriage: Basic issues and applications* (pp. 87–117). New York: Guilford.

Whisman, M. A., Jacobson, N. S., Fruzzetti, A. E., & Waltz, J. A. (1989). Methodological issues in marital therapy. *Advances in Behavior Research and Therapy, 11,* 175–189.

Wolchik, S. A., Westover, S., West, S. G., Sandler, I. N., Martin, A., Lustig, J., & Tien, J. (1990, August). *Evaluating an empirically based parent training program for divorced families.* Paper presented at the meeting of the American Psychological Association, Boston.

Author Index

Subject Index

Note. Italicized page numbers refer to exercises in the text; "t" and "f" following page numbers indicate tables and figures, respectively.

About the Authors

A practicing clinical psychologist and professor at the University of Illinois at Urbana-Champaign, Frank D. Fincham is the author of numerous research articles on marriage and coeditor of *The Psychology of Marriage* and *Cognition in Close Relationships*. He also serves on the editorial boards of several journals in social and clinical psychology. A fellow of the American Psychological Association and American Psychological Society, he is the recipient of numerous professional awards, including a Rhodes Scholarship, an early career award from the British Psychological Society, and, most recently, the Berscheid-Hatfield Award from the International Network on Personal Relationships for "sustained, substantial, and distinguished contributions to the field of personal relationships."

Born and raised in Hawaii, Leyan O. L. Fernandes is currently a doctoral candidate at the University of Illinois at Urbana-Champaign. She received an A.B. from Cornell University and an A.M. in clinical psychology from the University of Illinois. Her clinical and research interests concern the psychophysiological processes associated with developmental psychopathology, especially communication dysfunction, emotion, and neuropsychological difficulties.

Keith Humphreys received a B.A. in psychology from Michigan State University in 1988 and a Ph.D. in community/clinical psychology from the University of Illinois in 1993. His research focuses on self-help programs and substance abuse treatment and has appeared in *Psychotherapy* and the *Journal of Consulting and Clinical Psychology*. He is a research scientist at the Center for Health Care Evaluation, a research group affiliated with the Department of Veterans Affairs and Stanford University School of Medicine.